# LABOR RELATIONS

## *A Diagnostic Approach*

**KENNETH A. KOVACH**

UNIVERSITY
PRESS OF
AMERICA

Lanham • New York • London

Copyright © 1992 by
**University Press of America®, Inc.**
4720 Boston Way
Lanham, Maryland 20706

3 Henrietta Street
London WC2E 8LU England

**Library of Congress Cataloging-in-Publication Data**

Kovach, Kenneth A.
Labor Relations : A Diagnostic Approach / Kenneth A. Kovach.
p.   cm.
1. Trade-unions—United States.
2. Industrial relations—United States.   I.  Title.
HD6508.K67    1992    331'.0973—dc20    91-37394 CIP

ISBN 0-8191-8171-4 ( alk. paper)

 The paper used in this publication meets the minimum requirements of
American National Standard for Information Sciences—Permanence
of Paper for Printed Library Materials, ANSI Z39.48–1984.

# Table of Contents

## (Readings)

## Public Employees

### (Cases)

# Do We Still Need Labor Unions?

### In light of recent history, the answer may surprise you.

It is common knowledge today that organized labor is losing strength in both numerical and political terms, as well as in the influence it exerts over the rest of the labor force. Numerically, labor unions have gone from 42% of the labor force in the 1950's to less than 20% today, with every indication that this downward trend will continue. Were it not for the large number of newly organized public employees, the outlook would be even more ominous for labor unions. And many labor students contend that because of the restrictions on unions in the public sector (many cannot discuss wages and are prohibited from striking), the value to labor as a whole of a certain number of public employees organizing is not nearly as great as a similar number of privately employed workers organizing. Thus, even the decreasing numbers may not tell the whole story of labor's deteriorating position.

### Losing Clout

Politically, it should be clear to even the most casual observer that unions are losing their clout. The day when the powerful labor boss could "deliver" the labor vote, and hence was admitted to the inner circles of politics and politicians, is gone. It is hard to imagine a modern-day John L. Lewis working closely with the President to draft key pieces of legislation, or inviting congressional leaders to his office to "discuss" their votes on upcoming issues, practices that were once a source of pride and status for powerful labor leaders. Labor's present political influence can best be gauged by their track record on such major issues as the Common Situs Picketing Bill, the original Humphrey-Hawkins Full Employment Bill and Labor Law Reform—all defeats.

While organized labor has long been considered the trend-setter for wages and terms of employment, even here we are witnessing the declining strength of unions. Except in a few big industries (steel, auto, etc.) where unions enjoy a virtual monopoly, the increasing number of nonunionized firms have reintroduced the cost of labor as a competitive factor in market strategies. More and more frequently, unions have had to consider the impact of their economic demands on the employers' ability to attract enough business to maintain employment levels. The construction industry is the most dramatic and widely known example of this phenomenon, but is is happening in an increasing number of less publicized instances. The "Southern strategy" of the auto employers, the move to the South of the big steel companies and the inability of the mining unions to organize new mines are all indicators that even in industries long considered union strongholds, this factor will become increasingly important in the future.

## A Look Backward

The question growing out of the above discussion is obvious: Do we still need labor organizations? Is it now possible that they have outlived their usefulness?

To answer questions such as these, it is important to take a brief look at labor history, that reaffirms one of the more important lessons to be learned from history in general: if people are pushed hard enough and subjected to adverse enough conditions, they will take actions they would never have dreamed of—had things been more equitable. It is only within the context of the time that today's labor student can understand why otherwise normal individuals would sit in unheated Michigan and Ohio automobile plants in the middle of winter for 44 days, or why they would barricade themselves in steel mills and vow to fight to the death unless working conditions were improved. Read about what workers did to organize the first textile unions, the first mining unions, the first railroad unions, and then ask yourself if you would be willing or able to endure what they did. I contend that you would probably be willing if you were subjected to the treatment that those individuals were.

My purpose here is not to discuss the historical plight of the American worker, yet it is crucial to my main point to understand what this plight was. For the first 150 years of this country's independence, the American worker was free politically, but a virtual slave industrially. A look backward at management practices such as company-owned housing, water supplies, stores, etc., with their inflated prices, the payment of workers in company scrip, the unsafe and unhealthy working conditions, the unbelievably long work week, the ridiculously low wages which made it impossible for most families to live on the earnings of a single breadwinner, the completely arbitrary employment and personnel practices, and the company police forces, to mention only a few—in fact the complete lack of consideration of the worker as a human being—puts the remarkable growth of labor unions in the early 1900's in a different light. Certainly at this point in U.S. history, workers were ready to support any type of organization that promised them relief from their miserable industrial existence. Thus, labor unions filled a real need: they brought humanitarianism to the work place and a degree of dignity to the American worker.

Yet, ironically enough, because of their success, unions have eradicated most of the conditions that led to their foundation. Thus, an often heard argument today is that while unions were necessary once, they are no longer necessary now. Proponents of this argument contend that the American worker today enjoys a higher standard of living than ever before, that we now have laws such as the Fair Labor Standards Act, the National Labor Relations Act, the Occupational Safety and Health Act, etc., which set a floor for wages, working conditions and general treatment of employees below which no employer is entitled to go.

### The Deterrent Effect

While there is much support for this point of view, the author must take exception to it. Law and subsequent conditions of employment may have changed, but basic human nature has not. While it may be a pessimistic assessment of mankind, and one with which the reader will likely disagree, I firmly believe that a high percentage of humanity will still take advantage of their fellows if the price is right. Through the ages, history has repeatedly proven this to be a truism and anyone who does not realize it is either uninformed, extremely idealistic or naive. While the laws provide deterrents to employee abuse in the form of minimum acceptable standards, it would certainly be unacceptable to the majority of our working population to exist at those minimum standards. For many, even a small retreat backward, be it in terms of compensation, working conditions or safety standards, would be completely unacceptable. Yet if the law were the only minimum, the only deterrent, there would be plenty of room for retreat in the standards enjoyed in the work place by the majority of the American labor force.

The biggest single deterrent, besides the law, to the reduction of standards in the work place is the combined action of the workers—call it a "union" or any other name you wish. This action does not even have to come to pass to serve its purpose, for in many instances, the mere possibility of such action is sufficient. (There can be no doubt that the level of benefits received by many nonunion workers is in part buttressed by their employers' desire to reward them at such a level that they remain unorganized.)

Thus, while unions may have outlived their usefulness in terms of their original objectives, they are still needed because of what I have been referring to as their "deterrent" effect. If they are in fact the instrument prohibiting exploitation of the worker, not in the traditional browbeaten sense, but in today's more humanistic, less extreme context, then they are in fact needed. The irony is that even those individuals in the blue-collar sector who would suffer first and most if unions disappeared tomorrow, don't realize the vital role labor organizations play in today's economy. It is not necessary for them to be as strong as they once were, for the problems they are trying to correct are not as severe and the government has taken over part of their original role through various pieces of legislation. Yet it is still vital that they continue to exist, not only for those who benefit directly from them, but also for those who believe in the need to maintain the dignity of the worker. Unions find themselves in the same peculiar position as the military, in that what they cause to happen may not be nearly as important as what they cause **not** to happen. This fact alone, in my opinion, continues to make unions what they've always been—an absolute necessity to the well-being of the workplace.

# Organized Labor's Deteriorating Condition

Any serious student of organized labor is aware that the American labor movement has experienced—and will continue to experience—hard times. Its membership is declining, the industries upon which its strength was built are in serious trouble and unfavorable demographic, economic and political trends have seriously weakened the once unparalleled influence of organized labor. Many who work in the field view this as a favorable trend, destined to mitigate problems from high inflation and unemployment to an unfavorable balance of payments, while others see it as a threat to the "checks and balances" necessary for reasonable labor management relations. Regardless of one's perspective, there can be no doubt that the deteriorating position of organized labor and its resultant effects in other sectors of the economy is one of the major socio-economic trends in the U.S. over the past fifteen years.

The author proposes to examine this phenomenon by dissecting the problem itself and discussing its various components; exploring the major factors contributing to the problem; looking at the response to the problem by management, the government and independent consultants, and finally; assessing labor's potential for rectifying the situation.

## The Problem

There are three equally important components of labor's present unenviable condition: one numerical, one political and one jurisdictional. Numerically, the picture could not be worse for labor organizations. Despite growth in the labor force over the last fifteen years, unions now have fewer dues-paying members than they did in 1980. In the last seven years alone, total membership has dropped from twenty million to barely over eighteen million and there is every indication that this trend will continue. Obviously, with the increasing number of jobs and the decreasing number of union members, the percentages present an even more ominous picture.

Organized labor's percentage share of the labor market has dropped from 42 in 1954, to 28 in 1965, to 18.8 today.[1] This numerical decrease (which translates into dues, which translates into economic clout) is the independent variable that drives all the other dependent variables discussed in this section. Organized labor has long dismissed this trend as attributable to demographic factors, but the validity of this claim is undermined when one considers the magnitude of the numbers. Any institution that loses ten percent of its membership while the universe from which it can draw increases twenty-five percent, is in serious trouble. The numbers, as they say, speak for themselves.

Politically, the loss of influence by organized labor is obvious. Every American who follows the news is aware that labor poured more than ten million dollars and deployed thousands upon thousands of volunteers to support the Democratic congressional candidates in the latest election. Their politically stated goal was to deliver sixty-five percent of the union households for Democrats while holding Republicans to thirty-five percent. Exit polls showed that nearly one-half the labor household vote went for Republicans.[2] Yet, one must look beyond this well-publicized failure to understand the severity of the political component of labor's deteriorating condition. The failure to wrestle a new Labor Law Reform Bill out of Congressional committee, the revision of the Davis-Bacon Act, the lifting of import quotas on Japanese automobiles despite labor opposition, the fact that two more states have Right-To-Work Laws than was the case in 1985, and the high probability that the Administration's sub-minimum wage for teenagers will weather the AFL-CIO's attack, all speak loudly and clearly to labor's political condition. Regardless of what advances it achieves at the bargaining table (an area to be discussed later), unless labor reverses its political direction, it may well "win a few battles but lose the war."

Jurisdictionally, the overwhelming percentage of organizing successes has appeared in the public sector. Over twenty percent of total union membership is now in this area. In the federal sector, sixty-one percent of the workforce is now represented, while in the non-federal public sector, thirty percent are represented. Even in these sectors, however, the growth is slowing markedly since the big increase in the late sixties to mid-seventies. More important is the fact that these new public members are being recruited to replace (not in addition to) private sector members. With many in the public sector being prohibited from negotiating over wages and technology, from striking and from covering their union with a security clause, one must question whether public sector employees give labor organizations as much clout as an equal number of their private sector counterparts would. Thus, the numbers may tell only part of the story regarding labor's deteriorating position. The jurisdictions covered by the numbers may provide additional insight.

### The Factors

The five major factors contributing to the present condition of organized labor are the outcome of certification and decertification elections, the shift from blue- to white-collar jobs in the economy, the increasing number and percentage of women in the workforce, the biological and philosophical generation gap between union leaders and members, and the Bush Administration and the National Labor Relations Board.

Regarding union elections, even among the decreasing number of workers receptive enough to listen to labor's message, the numbers bode ill. Over six hundred bargaining units decertified their unions in each of the last three years. Unions won less than one-half of the certification elections in each year since 1981 and have lost three-quarters of the increasing number of decertification elections during the same time period. When studied longitudinally, one sees that these trends are, in fact, accelerating and I have every expectation that they will continue into the foreseeable future.

Another contributing factor is the shift we have seen in this country away from blue-collar manufacturing jobs to white-collar, service-oriented jobs. While the blue-collar manufacturing worker has traditionally been the cornerstone of the movement, there was only a .4 percent growth in such jobs from 1984 to 1990 and no growth since then. The blue-collar base of organized labor has been dependent upon industries that are shrinking, automating, closing, moving, or going international. The millions of new jobs created have been almost exclusively in the white-collar service-oriented sector, where union organizing success has been mediocre at best. While efforts to organize this sector have increased drastically in the last decade, the successes have not been of such a magnitude to offset the losses in the blue-collar sector. Thus, labor, while it is making progress in the white-collar area, is not advancing rapidly enough to keep pace with the industrial shift from blue- to white-collar work.

Additionally, the increasing number and percentage of females in the workforce is a factor that should not be underestimated when diagnosing labor's present condition. Since 1988, the percentage of women unionized has fluctuated between thirteen and sixteen, compared with twenty-eight percent for men. As women, who are organized at approximately one-half of the rate of men, constitute an increasing percentage of the labor force, unions have increased their efforts to organize this "pink collar" sector. Effort should not be confused with results, however, for, as stated above, the percentage of women organized has not increased noticeably over the last few years.

I believe the big problem in this area has been unimaginative union leadership. Fortunately for organized labor, groups such as the Coalition of Labor Union Women, The National Education Association and the Service Employees Union, with their female leadership and large female membership, are working hard from within the system to educate the traditional white male hierarchy to the importance of organizing drives aimed at women and to the issues essential to such drives (pay equity, health and safety issues, equitable job classifications, etc.). Despite the best efforts of such groups, however, it does not appear to me that women will become full-fledged members of the labor community in the near future, since they are concentrated in occupations where unions are not well entrenched: administrative, service, part-time, and high-technology industries with many small and union-resistant companies. For these reasons, the increasing number and percentage of females in the workforce is a contributing factor to organized labor's deteriorating position.

The biological and philosophical generation gap between union leaders and members must also be recognized as a factor. The union workforce, in addition to becoming smaller, is becoming younger and better educated. Many old-line union leaders have failed to recognize the fact that this change makes it impossible to conduct business as they did twenty years ago. The civil rights and antiwar activists of the 1960's have become disenchanted with their ossified and lethargic leaders and they see the traditional union structure as incapable of responding to their needs and desires, because of the type of individuals who hold key hierarchical positions. Additionally, young workers, unlike their parents, take a living wage as a given, not a benefit to be earned. They see work as more than just a financial necessity and the relative generosity of state and supplemental unemployment benefits exacerbates this feeling. The post-war baby boomers are—and will continue to be—labor's dominant age group in the 1990's. The fact that they are confounding labor's establishment with values and needs different from their parents is even more threatening than the normal young-versus-old split. Their increasingly middle-class outlook, made possible by the struggles of the two preceding generations of union members, makes them less likely to devote themselves to the labor struggle. Their present is no longer measured by fears of the past, but by hopes for the future.[3] The changes within this generation gap are critical, because it is in the industries with the most union growth potential that the problem is most acute. Better educated workers in the high-technology industries may well come to regard the unions as bureaucratic entities, as much a damper on their aspirations as any unenlightened corporation. One of the most serious threats to future union growth may come from this generational schism.

The final contributing factor to labor's condition is the Reagan and Bush Administrations and the National Labor Relations Board. President Reagan's campaign promise to "get regulators off the backs of business" has had a direct effect on unions: the way labor laws have been interpreted and enforced has changed drastically since 1981. Labor leaders have been unable to protect their members from what they perceive to be (and what under previous administrations would have been) violations of the National Labor Relations Act, the Railway Labor Act, the Labor Management Relations Act, and the Labor Management Reporting and Disclosure Act.

The reasons for this are twofold. First, the number of enforcement personnel budgets of the agencies administering these acts have been cut drastically. This creates a backlog that discourages the filing of charges and it means that, among those filed, a smaller percentage can actually be heard and, if need be, prosecuted. Second, Reagan appointees to political positions within the regulatory agencies have shown no reluctance to reverse previous and, in many cases, long-standing decisions.

In no agency has this been more evident or important than in the National Labor Relations Board. To mention just one of many important examples to illustrate this point, the Board reversed a pre-Reagan appointee decision and ruled, in Milwaukee Spring Division II,[4] that an employer may relocate operations from a union to a nonunion facility during the term of a labor agreement, nonunion even if the move is solely designed to escape the higher labor costs of the unionized plant, so long as such relocation is not specifically forbidden in the existing labor agreements.[5] Decisions such as this have become commonplace under the Reagan and Bush Administrations and, while differences of opinion arise concerning their propriety, there can be no argument that they weaken the position of organized labor and, in turn, make unions less attractive to potential members. While this factor is not as readily apparent and visible as those mentioned previously, it is equally important.

### The Responses

Responses to the situation discussed in the first section of this chapter have come from three main sources: management, local governments, and independent consultants. Management's most direct response has been to relocate to the southeast and southwest. In the last twenty years, the number of manufacturing jobs grew by forty-five percent in the southeast and sixty-seven percent in the southwest. It is crucial for the reader to realize that the **jobs** moved first, then the well-documented population shift was pulled along. It is somewhat of a "chicken and egg" phenomenon, but large numbers of individuals cannot relocate unless there are jobs available at the new location. Certainly their very presence will create some new jobs, particularly in the service sector, but with the sophisticated logistics system in this country today, it is not as imperative as it used to be that most jobs be performed within the immediate, geographic market they serve. Hence, in the classic economic "push/ pull" situation, the jobs pushed first and the population was then 'pulled'.

As a result, for the first time since reconstruction, the northeast and midwest (once our industrial heartlands and solid union strongholds) no longer hold the majority of the American population. A response favored by other companies has been to transfer jobs overseas or to subcontract work to countries with lower wage scales. The average consumer would be hard-pressed to notice the difference in quality between the work of a unionized American seamstress and a Taiwanese seamstress, yet a company will surely notice the ten-to-one wage differential. The result is that management shifts union jobs not only to the American south, but to foreign countries as well.

A final management response has been to seek "give-backs" at the bargaining table. Many times unions are faced with the alternatives of either granting these concessions or losing some or all of their jobs. Major contracts settled during 1990 produced wage increases of 2.8 percent over the life of the contract, versus 6.6 percent increases three years ago. In fact, nonunion wage increases have been exceeding those of union workers during recent times.[6]

Local government has been another respondent to unions' deteriorating condition. While management's response is to relocate, many local governments have begun to compete to be the beneficiaries of this relocation. In an attempt to retain or attract private capital, state and local governments have begun to give present or prospective industrial citizens tax and labor law relief. The creation of a "pro-business climate" is one of the major marketing points local jurisdictions are using to attract industry. Conversely, jurisdictions presently housing these industries have been forced to grant similar relief in an attempt to hold onto what they have. One need only look at the tax base and resultant city services and physical plants in industrial centers across different geographic regions, to realize the magnitude and implications of this particular response.

Finally, a new breed of independent consultant has surfaced as a response to labor's plight. Use of these "union avoidance" consultants has become fashionable, widespread and effective. Such consultants as Stephen Cabot, Anthony McKeown, Alfred DeMaria, and Scott Myers are making fortunes teaching management how to keep a company union-free. Their success is based on their ability to convince employers that treating employees properly makes good economic sense. Stephen Cabot states that employers should blame themselves if their workers unionize, because it may well be an indication that they have not been fair, even-handed, or open-minded.[7] Success rates approaching 90 percent in keeping unions out are an indication of the effectiveness of such consultants. In addition to the success rate, the high fees paid to such people are easily justified when one stops to consider the economic advantage to a large company of remaining union-free. Rational economic thought connects the economic benefits to the company, to the high fees they are willing to pay for this service, to the high number of individuals attracted to this line of work. Hence, the final response is simply the end result of economic evolution.

## Conclusion

The logical question to be addressed in light of all the above is "What Can Labor Do Now?". Given the magnitude and diversity of the factors contributing to the problem, there are no simple answers. Addressing one or two particular aspects of the problem at a time will not be enough.

First, there must be a philosophical rapprochement between organized labor's leadership and the work force of the 1990's. These leaders must recognize that the nature of American business has changed and that things will never be as they were when they were young workers. The reality of a better educated, high-technology or white-collar, service-oriented workforce must be dealt with. Extensive use of simple attitude surveys among present and potential union members would go a long way toward making decision-makers within the unions aware that the use of self-reference criteria is no longer appropriate. Unlike thirty years ago when today's decision-makers were in their positions, today's workers and potential union members have a middle-class outlook that gives rise to different objectives, images and behavior than their unionized parents.

Until today's union leader realizes this and reacts accordingly, little will be done to improve the unions' position. Attitude surveys are a quick, inexpensive way to find out about respondents' desires, attitudes, etc., so that the labor organization can bring itself and its actions in line with those of the individuals it is trying to attract. I believe that such surveys will show that today's worker expects more than wages from the job, regards demands for wage increases beyond a certain point as job-threatening and sees incessant union bickering over trivial work rules as needless and unproductive. Health and safety, job enlargement and enrichment, quality of work life, and pay equity may well emerge as issues labor should be addressing more vigorously at the bargaining table. Progress in these areas may well be the key to enrolling the new, better-educated and female members the unions need so desperately to attract while increases may frequently only exacerbate the existing problem.

Additionally, more emphasis must be placed on retraining programs for workers displaced by automation and less on the lock-step protectionist policies of the past. For example, labor spends money to lobby for import quotas on automobiles. If one-half that money were spent on retraining existing workers for the new jobs in that industry, the union, the industry and the entire economy would be that much improved.

Another tactic labor should try is to play economic hardball through the use of the billions of dollars in union pension funds. Shifting, or threatening to shift, these monies to "encourage" companies or local governments to modify their thinking and actions in the area of labor relations holds tremendous potential. The dollar value of corporate stock and local government securities held by union pension funds makes this, like the use of attitude surveys, a direct and immediate response by labor to its present situation.

While attitude surveys, retraining programs and pension funds all offer hope for the unions, I must close on a pessimistic note. These and many other policies that could be recommended must still be implemented through those at the top of the hierarchy. In a recent survey of seventy-nine top labor officials[8], several agreed that arrogance, inability to prepare successors, dogmatism, adherence to outdated ideas, and shortsightedness are problems with the leadership of organized labor today. The movement has lost its role as a cause for many leaders and is now simply a job. Many are more interested in holding union office for money and power, than they are in effecting significant change.

If this is truly the attitude of many union leaders, and I feel it is, then to expect them to distribute attitude surveys and respond accordingly, shift bargaining emphasis toward retraining and enrichment, and use the pension funds as indicated, is to expect too much. I have proposed what I feel are the best and most immediate solutions, but one must be realistic enough to realize that human beings must be willing and able to implement them. Given the current composition of labor leaders and their attitudes toward their jobs, I cannot attach a high degree of probability to trying these ideas on a large scale; and given the magnitude of the problem, piecemeal implementation by individual leaders will not suffice.

Thus, the human factor becomes the overriding one in this situation and causes the author to be pessimistic about any reversal in the condition of organized labor in the foreseeable future. Those species and institutions that do not adapt over time become, at worst, extinct or, at best, lose their position of dominance. Organized labor has not adequately adapted to economic, environmental or sociological changes. As a result, it has lost much of the strength it enjoyed thirty or forty years ago. The real problem for labor today is not that this has occurred, for these things go in cycles, but that there is no effective, coordinated attempt being made by the leadership to reverse the situation. The most alarming question for a labor leader today should be: "Given present trends and your inability to combat them, what in the world will you look like in ten or fifteen years?".

## Footnotes

[1]David S. Broder, "A 'New Day' For Unions," *Washington Post*, March 10, 1990, p. E-1.

[2]Mark Erlick, "Hammer Out A Warning," *The Progressive*, October 1984, p. 18.

[3]Gus Tyler, *The Political Imperative: The Corporate Character of Unions* MacMillan Publishing Company, 1968, p. 290.

[4]1983–84 CCH NLRB ¶16,029, 268 NLRB No. 87 (1984).

[5]Arthur F. Silbergeld, "How Recent NLRB Decisions Have Tilted Toward Management on Critical Issues," *Management Review*, July 1984, pp. 14–15.

[6]Carey W. English, "Why Unions Are Running Scared," *U.S. News and World Report*, September 10, 1990, p. 62.

[7]Carey W. English, "Business is Booming for 'Union Busters'," *U.S. News and World Report*, May 16, 1983, pp. 61–64.

[8]Harry Graham and Brian Heshizer, "Are Unions Facing a Crisis? Labor Officials Are Divided," *Monthly Labor Review*, August 1984, pp. 24–25.

# Why Motivation Theories
# Don't Work

Despite voluminous writing on the subject, today's manager is no closer to understanding employee "motivation" than counterparts of 50 years ago. If anything, employee motivation is more of a problem now than it was in the early 1900's. This is not to say that the work of behavioral scientists has been counter-productive, for, in fact, their efforts have given today's manager a better insight into motivation. Rather, it is to suggest that the advances made in understanding what motivates workers have not kept pace with the more rapid changes in employee attitudes and motivations.

Employee attitudes should provide insights into motivation, but by the time data on these are studied and the results disseminated, it is already too late. Rapidly changing technology, crumbling traditions, media influence, and other factors have all conspired against the manager to change the workers' attitudes, desires and motivations. These changes take place so rapidly that most theories of motivation are outdated by the time they are implemented.

## Reliance on Self-Reference

But that's not the full problem. Another difficulty encountered when dealing with employee motivation is that the theories for improving performance are just that—theories—until implementing. Unlike physical science theories that can be tested before implemented, social science theories can only be tested by implementation on human subjects. Managers, like all humans, have the tendency to shy away from applying unfamiliar theories that are not in accordance with their own preconceived notions. They are, like all of us, subject to what I call "self-reference criteria," practicing only those suggested behavioral patterns that are most closely aligned with their own thinking.

Managers may offer rewards to or exhibit encouraging behaviors toward workers that would motivate themselves, but this may not necessarily be what will motivate the employees. Managers forget that, by virtue of being a supervisor, they receive different levels of monetary—and different types of psychological—rewards, often resulting in a different lifestyle than those people below.

It has been my experience that, while many practitioners feel that self-reference used to be a problem, they do not view it as a major obstacle today. This change in thinking can be attributed to the fact that the earnings gap between nonsupervisory employees and first-line supervisors has been drastically narrowed by labor organizations, thus creating a wage-earning middle-class that holds similar values and is similarly motivated. The logical conclusion of this line of reasoning is that self-reference is not a problem, since both levels hold the same values and respond to the same motivators.

I could not disagree more with this. While this argument has surface validity, the underlying evidence argues against it.

### The Case Against Self-Reference

Numerous surveys have been conducted since World War II to determine what employees want from their jobs, that is, what can be offered to motivate them. A study representative of these was completed in 1946 by the Labor Relations Institute of New York and reported in *Foreman Facts*. Subjects were first-line supervisors and the employees who worked directly for them. After the employees had ranked ten items in order of importance to them, their supervisors were asked to rank the same items as they thought their employees would. The results are shown in Figure 1.

**Figure 1**
**What People Want From Their Work**
**(1946)**

| Employee Ranking | | Supervisor Ranking |
|---|---|---|
| 1 | Full appreciation of work done | 8 |
| 2 | Feeling of being in on things | 9 |
| 3 | Sympathetic help with personal problems | 10 |
| 4 | Job security | 2 |
| 5 | Good wages | 1 |
| 6 | Interesting work | 5 |
| 7 | Promotion and growth in the organization | 3 |
| 8 | Personal loyalty to employees | 6 |
| 9 | Good working conditions | 4 |
| 10 | Tactful discipline | 7 |

The absolute ranking of the items is not the most important issue. Rather, the significance of the survey findings lies in the wide variance between what the employees considered to be important in their jobs, and what their supervisors thought was important to the same employees. And, clearly, this variance is evidence of the use of self-reference by the supervisors. Since these results are representative of the many surveys during the immediate postwar era, their use of self-reference must certainly have been a problem.

However, the more relevant question today is, does this gap still exist between workers' wants and their supervisors' perceptions of these wants? If it does, then self-reference is still a major stumbling block in motivating employee performance.

To answer this question, the 1946 questionnaire was administered to a group of over 200 employees and their immediate supervisors, to see if the results bore any resemblance to those of 45 years ago. The findings are shown in Figure 2.

**Figure 2**
**What People Want from Their Work**
**(Present)**

| Employee Ranking | | Supervisor Ranking |
|---|---|---|
| 1 | Interesting work | 5 |
| 2 | Full appreciation of work done | 8 |
| 3 | Feeling of being in on things | 10 |
| 4 | Job security | 2 |
| 5 | Good wages | 1 |
| 6 | Promotion and growth in the organization | 3 |
| 7 | Good working conditions | 4 |
| 8 | Personal loyalty to employees | 7 |
| 9 | Sympathetic help with personal problems | 9 |
| 10 | Tactful discipline | 6 |

While a comparison of the results shows an improvement in the sum of the differences between the two groups (from 42 in 1946, to 34 in the recent study), seven of the eight improvement points are attributable to the change in the ranking of "sympathetic help with personal problems." With the exception of this one factor, the gap between supervisors and their employees has not narrowed since 1946.

Perhaps the most revealing comparisons come from two sets of items — "security"/"wages" and "appreciation"/"being in on things." In 1946, "wages and "security" were ranked as having middle importance by employees and as having top importance to employees by supervisors, while "appreciation of work" and "feeling in on things" were of top importance for employees, yet perceived by supervisors as being of least importance to employees. The same discrepancy was uncovered by the present survey. There has been no improvement since at least 1946. Hence, any argument that self-reference is not still a major problem, is not supported by the evidence.

### Getting The Information Needed

A major goal for today's manager to improve worker performance is to find out what it is that employees want from their work—in other words, what will motivate them. As shown by Figure 2, any reliance on personal judgment about what will motivate employees, will likely only aggravate the situation.

The use of attitude surveys is the cheapest, most direct approach to gathering the information needed. Such surveys can employ ranking, the Likert scale or some other technique to easily quantify, tabulate, and understand the results. With very little time and monetary investment, an organization, and particularly its supervisors, are likely to get very insightful results that can go a long way toward motivating employees.

A word of additional advice is necessary here. We must learn from our earlier mistakes and make sure that the results are transmitted to those supervisors who *most directly interact* with the employees involved. Many times, the results were made available only to managers at levels *above* those having direct, daily employee contact. As a result, the individuals who could best use the findings were never made aware of them, or, at best, received a biased verbal summary (remember our human tendency to emphasize personal points of agreement during verbal recall).

Allowing for the cost and length of time needed to administer the instrument, a good rule of thumb is to conduct the attitude survey approximately once a year. Such frequency is necessary to avoid the problem discussed at the beginning of this article, that of attempting to motivate employees using outdated, and often inaccurate, information.

It is also important to analyze the responses collectively and in subsets, based on organizational and earning levels, if there is a variance within the respondent group. According to Abraham Maslow's theory, we are motivated by our desire to fulfill certain hierarchical needs. Once one level of need is fulfilled, there is a desire to satisfy the next higher level. Individuals at different organizational levels, receiving different levels of earning, may well be at different levels of need in Maslow's hierarchy. Hence, what motivates individuals at one level in the organization very likely will not be the same, as what motivates those at another level, thus necessitating differentiation by level of need when analyzing attitudes for motivational purposes.

### Different Strokes for Different Folks

The results shown in Figure 2 indicate that nonsupervisory employees in this country have progressed beyond the basic needs that can be satisfied by economic rewards. Yet it is important to remember that these results are averages for all the employees sampled, and are only intended to show discrepancies between the two groups. They do not mean that all employees regard money as having middle, relative importance, or that all employees view interesting work and appreciation of work as what they want most from their jobs.

Within a given organization, and certainly among different individuals, results will vary. This is why it is so important that each organization conduct a customized attitude survey. Reward systems can then be established and ensuing (hopefully, improved) performance measured. The direct return—by implementing worker-selected motivators derived from investing in a tailor-made attitude survey—to a company revealed in increased employee output, performance and morale. If, for instance interesting work is the major motivator of the particular respondents, then perhaps job enlargement or enrichment can be tried on a limited basis. Conversely, if higher wages are what motivates other employees, then the introduction of an incentive pay system might be an appropriate move.

Robert Townsend, past president of Avis Rent-a-Car, put it this way in his book, *Up the Organization*:

> Get to know your people—what they do well, what they enjoy doing, what their weaknesses and strengths are, and what they want and need from their job. And then try to create an organization around your people, not jam your people into those organization-chart rectangles.

As a manager, you need to remember that you cannot motivate people. That door is locked from the inside. What you can do, however, is to create a climate in which most of your employees will find it personally rewarding to motivate themselves and, in the process, contribute to the company's attainment of its objectives. If you can achieve this attitude among a reasonable number of your subordinates, many of your other problems as a supervisor will take care of themselves.

# Management By Whom?
## — Trends In Participative Management

A subject of increasing controversy in the field of management is the application of participative techniques to nonmanagerial personnel. Such techniques have been widely used—and even more widely debated. The debate involves the philosophical question of whether it is proper for workers to be included in such traditional management areas as planning, operational decision making and performance evaluation. It also involves questions of capability and motivation, which challenge the potential effectiveness of whatever participative strategies are utilized. While the philosophical question broadly embraces virtually all such strategies, the question of effectiveness more pragmatically addresses the results to be obtained by using worker participation in structuring jobs, defining management-labor relationships and managing the firm itself.

Of the two issues, pragmatic effectiveness is of more importance. A negative finding for effectiveness would surely render the philosophical question moot.

A wide variety of participative techniques have been used in many different job environments, but the range of such techniques is basically limited to those that are relatively traditional in concept, representing a "bottom-up" approach, and a group of more recently developed techniques that involves "top-down" participation.

The bottom-up approaches embody the goal of providing the worker with managerial values through participation in operational decisions, communications or benefits. These programs include such well understood and popular techniques as job enlargement, job enrichment, Management By Objectives, team building, and profit sharing.

The top-down approach envisages the worker or groups of workers in an executive role, participating directly in decision making, e.g., long-range planning. This participation includes the worker in actions and responsibilities traditionally reserved for the board of directors or the chief executive officer. The European experience in this area involves participation mandated by law, with detailed and explicit procedures developed over a long period of time. The American experience, on the other hand, is based on localized programs, usually initiated by management.

By examining the current status of bottom-up and top-down approaches to worker participation in the management of an organization, it is possible to draw some conclusions concerning the future application of these approaches in the United States.

### Bottom-Up Approaches

Job enlargement, one bottom-up approach, is the process of providing more variety in the number of tasks contained in a given job. Moving from the specific, individual job description to an enlarged responsibility for a wider scope of activities is the primary objective of the job enlargement process. For example, a machine operator's job may be narrowly defined to machine a specific material. Alternatively, the job may be enlarged or broadened by also requiring the person to obtain materials, maintain the tools and equipment and inspect the work. This method of involving workers in a greater variety of activities is viewed by many theorists as the most basic participative strategy.

Walker and Guest, in their landmark study in the 1950's, found that worker participation in a wider range of physical activities reduced fatigue and boredom, thereby increasing expected productivity. Job enlargement, however, did not represent an attempt on their part to increase significantly workers' sense of personal achievement or share of responsibility for results.

Strategies for enhancing the employee's personal identification with a job are called job enrichment. This approach, successfully adopted by the Texas Instrument Corporation and other firms, attempts to build employee motivation by loading a person's job with components of responsibility and autonomy, so that the individual then identifies with important managerial goals. There is considerable evidence that job enrichment can exert a positive influence on workers' attitudes and productivity. Nevertheless, the potential for generalizing this approach is controversial, since some critics claim that reported results are unrepresentative. Mitchell Fein, in summarizing prevalent reservations about the validity of the many enthusiastic reports of job enrichment successes, named the following shortcomings of research in this area:

- Selective reporting of results, distorting any evaluation of the effectiveness of the programs;
- Too few empirical studies, representing a limited range of working environments;
- Biased results, reflecting the views of managers who initiated the programs of job enrichment, not the views of workers or unions.

The last point suggests that part of the difficulty in implementing job enrichment is that it is management-imposed, rather than a product of workers' or unions' initiative.

Management By Objectives (MBO) is a strategy for involving lower-level managers and rank-and-file workers in the planning and evaluation process that directs employee efforts toward organizational objectives. The technique was first proposed by Peter Drucker in the 1950's. Since then, it has been elaborated and systematized for use in virtually every organization and has enjoyed widespread popularity. MBO has been used extensively in industry during the last decade, but observers have noted mixed results. While some firms have embraced MBO enthusiastically, others have found it more difficult to apply than anticipated. In particular, the benefits of joint manager-subordinate goal-setting and review have been questioned. While MBO has become a popular managerial tool, in government as well as business, there have been questions about its efficacy in motivating public-sector employees.

Team building is a concept that assumes that group participation in work activities will develop positive job attitudes and motivate individual members of work groups. Much attention in training managers has been devoted to this method. Like MBO, team building approaches are oriented to managerial recognition of the value of contributions by subordinates. Despite a great deal of managerial enthusiasm for this method, it remains to be seen whether subordinates will prove to be as enthusiastic as their superiors, i.e., those individuals who initiate group decision making and problem solving and normally retain final authority.

Profit sharing approaches to employee participation vary considerably, but they do share a common assumption—a belief that workers will be motivated to excel in their jobs, when their compensation depends on the organization's profits. There have been some notable successes in this area, such as the Lincoln Electric plan. Many other attempts at profit-sharing have been disappointing or, at best, have yielded mixed results.

In my opinion, this grab bag of approaches makes it difficult to praise or blame any of the participative strategies outlined above, even in those situations where there are clear-cut results shown to be beneficial or harmful to employee morale or productivity. This is not to say, however, that other individuals have found it similarly difficult to pass judgment on the value of these participative techniques. Labor leaders in particular, as we shall now see, have consistently been very outspoken in their criticism of them.

## The Union Perspective

Generally, organized labor has looked with skepticism on the traditional approaches to participative management discussed above. Most of these techniques are viewed as the theoretical constructs of academics who lack practical experience in day-to-day contact with nonsupervisory employees. One objection is the implicit assumption made in participative plans (e.g., job enlargement, job enrichment, MBO etc.) that the job can become a major part of the individual's life—that it can be made challenging enough to produce an attitude change toward a position. In certain situations, this is true. It is in those instances that the traditional participative programs work best.

When the skills and intellect of the individuals performing the job are at a level high enough, allowing them to incorporate significant enlargement or enrichment features into their present job description, such programs are successful. If the job is at a high enough level in the organization to include meaningful and challenging objectives, or if the responsibility that increases from job enrichment is not simply a facade, then the program has a chance of leading to a desirable employee attitude change. But in lower-level jobs, where employees' possession of intellectual abilities and skills is demonstrably poor, participative programs have had little success. Among urban blue-collar workers, for example, the track record of participative management programs has been nothing short of disastrous. So, in the area where changes envisioned by the introduction of such programs are most urgently needed—at the lowest levels where major motivation and identification problems arise and the potential for increased productivity is greatest—participative management programs have realized the least success.

The sector of the labor force where these programs are least successful is precisely that sector where unions have their strongest representation; it is not surprising, therefore, that unions generally look with disfavor on such programs. Labor organizations question the practicality of these programs, but it is not simply because they see them blurring the traditional "us and them" labor-management relationship (as many have charged). Rather, it is because the very people who comprise these labor organizations are the ones holding the lower-level jobs where the programs have realized the least success.

Is there a cause and effect relationship between the variables involved: is it union opposition that causes these programs to fail at lower organizational levels, or do the programs fail for other reasons? To answer that question, it is necessary to examine employee attitudes.

Since the days of Frederick Taylor and Scientific Management, it has been an article of faith among the managements of manufacturing concerns that, for production efficiency, jobs need to be broken down into small increments, with a specific task assigned to each worker. This, in turn, has created hundreds of thousands of repetitive, unchallenging jobs. Naturally, these are the jobs where the identification, motivation and increased productivity expected to be gained through participative management are most needed, but they are also the types of jobs that (if held by an individual for a number of years) can cause an employee to adopt a very negative mental attitude to the work. This mental attitude is manifested in attempts, usually through a union, to get more time away from the job. More holidays, vacations, sick leave, etc., are demanded, since the worker now seeks satisfaction not at the job, but away from it. This same attitude can also result in demands for more monetary compensation to tolerate the same job. If a worker likes the job, a given rate of pay may be enough to keep him or her on it; if the person hates the job, he or she will invariably insist on more reward for the same level of performance. After years of conditioning in this approach to their employment, is it any wonder that many of these employees who belong to unions by virtue of their position, are not wholeheartedly embracing participative management?

The situation is made even worse by the changing educational, financial and social levels of the typical union member. The blue-collar sector of the labor movement is becoming better-educated and better-paid, while a larger percentage of overall union membership is white-collar and professional. The better educated and financially secure employees become, the more they resist superficial attempts at participation. Even profit-sharing plans will suffer, in terms of the attitude changes they seek to foster: as employees become better-educated, they begin to expect more than a paycheck from the job.

These forces indicate the need to introduce employer practices reflecting genuine participation by employees in the operation of the enterprise. Instead of techniques that emphasize employee input at the lowest organizational levels, "top-down" plans would give employees a collective voice in operating decisions traditionally made by upper-level management. The introduction of such plans is crucial to improve not only the mental health and attitude of the individual employee, but also the performance of the firm and, if implemented on a wide enough scale, the economy as a whole. While not seen as a cure-all in and of itself, I see the emergence of a top-down approach to management as a beacon of hope on an economically bleak horizon.

## Top-Down Participative Management

The insistence on input from the workforce regarding control and direction of the firm, is based primarily on an increasing recognition of "property rights" in a job. These "property rights" were even recognized in a recent decision in a U.S. District Court in Cleveland. Judge Thomas D. Lambros issued an injunction prohibiting the shutdown of the Youngstown plant by U.S. Steel. The injunction was based, in part, on the judge's conclusion that "a property right has arisen from the lengthy, long-established relationship among U.S. Steel, the steel industry as an institution, the community in Youngstown, and the people in Mahoning County and Mahoning Valley, in having given and devoted their lives to this industry."

"Top-down management" is usually defined as management that makes decisions, sets the rules, enforces standards, and generally exercises all the traditional powers of the owner/entrepreneur. "Top-down participation," on the other hand, implies sharing by the employee/worker in this process. Major decisions concerning the direction of the firm, products and markets, plans and policies, and conditions of work and employment are set by, or with major input from, the worker/employee. The philosophy of a property right in the job underlies the concept of top-down participation and may explain in part the resistance of management to worker participation in the direction of the firm.

Two methods of top-down participation by employees have received widespread attention in the past few years. Both methods place the employee in a position to influence the direction and operation of the firm, through membership on the policy-making boards of the organization.

In West Germany, *Mitbestimmung* (codetermination, an equal say in management) is required by law. In this mandated system, one-third of the supervisory board (comparable to a board of directors in U.S. corporations) is drawn from the workfers. The board is responsible for the overall operation of the firm, including the development of plans and policies, the allocation of funds, and decisions on issues such as products, marketing areas, etc. It also appoints a management board to conduct the day-to-day business of the firm.

Work councils, comparable in a very broad sense to union locals in the United States, must be formed in any West German firm employing more than five workers. Blue- and white-collar workers are represented proportional to their numbers in the company. The works council does not bargain for wages and working conditions are normally negotiated on a regional or national basis, but it has a right to codetermination in deciding such issues as job evaluation, piece rates and wage structures; working hours, overtime arrangements, breaks and holiday schedules; staffing policies, including guidelines for recruiting, assigning and dismissing workers; social plans—i.e., measures to mitigate the effects of layoffs on workers facing reduction; training, occupational safety and welfare schemes; allocation of company housing, and; workers' conduct on the shop floor.

Hiring, discharge, work allocation, promotion, and demotion decisions require the consent of the council. Unilateral action by the employer in these areas is not allowed.

In the actual conduct of the business of the firm, the powers of the works council are more limited. In firms with more than 100 employees, the works council appoints an economic committee. The committee has the right to obtain information on such major issues as manufacturing methods, automation, production programs, and the financial condition of the firm. Analysis of this information is the responsibility of the economic committee. The consent of the works council is required for major actions such as plant closings and staff cuts.

In an article in the *Harvard Business Review*, Ted Mills said he saw little potential for European-style industrial democracy systems in the United States. I reached the same conclusion from research reported in the Winter 1980 issue of *MSU Business Topics*. Renato Mazzolini found a clear trend in European countries toward formal participation, as exemplified by the West German Model, and away from the noninstitutional confrontation. However, he noted in *Sloan Management Review* that:

> The introduction of participative systems in countries where antago-nism is the dominant mode may change little of substance. Both workers and employers may be severely disappointed.

Karl Frieden discussed two specific cases of codetermination in *Workplace Democracy and Productivity* in the United States. In 1982, a Kaiser Steel contin-uous-weld mill with 80 employees established a labor-management committee in a last-ditch attempt to prevent a shutdown. The committee was formed at the request of the union, a request reluctantly agreed to by management. In three months' time, production increased 32 percent, and the mill was saved. Some workers were displaced, but they were either given other jobs or took early retirement. Although many beneficial effects were noted, management was apparently embarrassed by the success of the experiment. Information required by the committee was restricted and the committee lapsed into disuse.

In the second case, a subsidiary of Youngstown Sheet and Tube Company formed a labor-management committee in 1984. The potential for improve-ment was not as great as had been the case in the Kaiser plant, but the commit-tee was credited with a 5.5 percent increase in production during the three years it functioned. Production delays fell from 10 percent to 3 percent and absenteeism fell from approximately 15 percent to 7 percent. The committee was phased out, ostensibly due to high turnover among committee members. Frieden stated that "the primary reason, however, was that increasing tensions within the steel industry made cooperative efforts between labor and manage-ment extremely difficult at the plant."

A review of our country's labor history reinforces the idea of the voluntary basis of our labor/management relations and reduces the likelihood for adop-tion of the European method of codetermination. Systems like codetermina-tion are the result of national law (unlike the normal give-and-take between American management and labor), confirming that European industrial democracy was fought for and gained within the political arena. Codetermination's political origins in West Germany have resulted in hundreds of pages of manifold, complex legislation, bearing little relation to laws in this country. In my opinion, American workers and their representatives have both the expectation and the desire for two things that codetermination restricts: the freedom to create/operate systems independent of governmental influence and the freedom to contest any ensuing labor/management system.

In contrast to the mandated or contractual presence of the worker on worker/management committees, there are situations where the American worker actually can own all or part of the firm and have management rights by virtue of ownership. The Employee Stock Option Plan (ESOP) and its management arm, the Employee Stock Option Trust (ESOT), are employment benefit plans in which a company (usually a small, closely-held corporation) sells its stock to its employees. These plans work in conjunction with, or as replacements for, the normal retirement plans. San Francisco attorney Louis Kelso, who is credited with the concept, claimed it can

> . . . redistribute wealth within the framework of our capitalist system; assist in capital formation; motivate workers; promote economic growth; reduce welfare costs, and, accomplish a number of other ends that others consider desirable.

Writing in *The Academy of Management Review*, Timothy Jochim hypothesized that an employee-owned firm (either completely employee-owned, or partially through an ESOP) "should have (a) increased profitability, (b) a better growth record, (c) increased productivity, (d) more employment stability, (e) fewer work stoppages, and (f) lower turnover of workers." He examined reports on 10 employee-owned firms and found (using both the firms' history of before-and-after ESOP and comparative approaches) that seven of the firms were successes, in that they confirmed one or more of his hypotheses. Two firms experienced insignificant change in the indicators. In the tenth firm, the plan failed and the company was sold.

Jochim seven important factors within successful firms. These included a small-to-medium size with a skilled and highly interactive work force, a receptive attitude to good labor/management relations, a generally democratic management style, a stagnant or slowly-growing economy, project or job-shop production, a flat management hierarchy, and—where a union existed—a cooperative relationship with union leadership.

A study of 68 representative firms utilizing ESOP supports Jochim's findings. In the 30 firms for which profit data were available, the largest single correlate of profitability (among the characteristics of ownership measured) was worker ownership. The data indicate that employee ownership was associated with improvements in productivity and profits, along with improvements in worker and management satisfaction.

Democracy in the workplace seems justified on the basis of these results.

## Summary

Ted Mills wrote that "what has happened in America has been open, growing, groping—a process without discrete boundaries or manuals or formulas." He quoted John Dewey's definition of political democracy, American-style, as:

> . . . faith in human nature, faith in human intelligence, and the power of pooled and collective experience. It's not a belief that these things are complete but that if given a show, they will grow and generate the knowledge and wisdom needed to guide collective action.

This faith in the average person's innate common sense and ability to make optional decisions bodes ill for a national application of codetermination as practiced in West Germany. At the same time, the principles of codetermination are part of labor/management relationships in the American future. Employee ownership of the firm and the concomitant responsibilities will occur. Neither codetermination nor ownership, however, will be mandated. The American system will retain the process characteristics outlined by Mills. Boundaries, systems and rules will be developed in individualistic, *ad hoc* ways. Both management and unions will resist the intrusion of the legislative process into labor/management relations.

# Blacks in the U.S. Labor Movement

## Membership and power have increased,
## but more progress is predicted

Between 1965 and 1968, the cause of black labor was aided by the civil rights movement. Organizations like the Southern Christian Leadership Conference (SCLC), the National Association for the Advancement of Colored People (NAACP) and the Negro American Labor Council (NALC) were key actors in this movement.

The NALC changed its leadership in 1966, and with it came a change in policy. The new policy "stressed that black masses had to assume a greater leadership role in the alliance than in the past," in the words of leader Cleveland Robinson. The idea was to avoid the highest levels of union administration, while enrolling and organizing as many black workers as possible. These members then could bring pressure to bear, to have their demands met. In a sense, this was a social class movement, as much as a labor one.

Martin Luther King, Jr., must be mentioned here, not specifically as a labor leader, but as the figurehead for a racial upsurge. More than any other black leader, he helped blacks realize that by bringing organized pressure to bear on the establishment (unions), they could achieve equality.

The greatest victories for King, the NAACP, and the NALC were the Memphis, Tennessee, sanitation workers' strike and the Charleston, South Carolina, hospital workers' strike. Both were real tests of Cleveland Robinson's policy of organizing black service workers to reach parity with whites. In both cases, the grievances were black pay rates approximately equal to half the pay of whites on the same jobs, poor working conditions and biased behavior on the part of "lily-white" administrations. Neither group was organized when it struck and each probably would have failed, had it not been for the support of the SCLC and the black social and labor movement. Several important unions also backed the strikers: United Auto Workers, United Steel Workers and United Rubber Workers, as well as some AFL-CIO locals in the Memphis and Charleston areas. It is significant that these strikes were bitterly opposed by the power structure in the communities and were not readily supported by local white workers. Despite this opposition in both cases, the black workers were able to align themselves with social movements and use labor support to win outstanding victories.

Between 1966 and the escalation of the Vietnam war, many more blacks found employment in industry, especially young blacks, and joined the unions. Concurrently, the achievements of blacks in the civil rights movement gave them the impetus to try for total equality with white labor. Wayman Benson, then head of the Chicago Transit Workers, recognized that inequality and stated, "This is nothing different than the old plantation system. Here you have a union with about 65–70 percent blacks and the leadership is virtually all white. How long do you think we can stand for this?" In a 1968 speech to the NALC Convention, Cleveland Robinson complimented the same growing black union membership, but similarly criticized their unequal representation in local, international and executive councils. Using the word "power" in his speech, the idea of "black power" was immediately adopted by both friend and foe of the black labor movement.

As a result of this frustration, many black extra-union organizations were formed to put pressure on the unions. These groups were concentrated in the northern industrial cities, specifically Pittsburgh, Detroit and Chicago. These organizations (the Ad Hoc Committee to the USW and the Chicago Transit Workers of Local 241 Amalgamated Transit Union, to name two) did not want to disband and form black unions, for they realized they would be cutting their own throats. What they wanted was an active role in union policy formation.

The younger black unionists were more militant than the older leaders in their dealings with management. They criticized older blacks for not attacking union bias and for not forcing union management to allow blacks a greater role in union leadership.

> It was not long before these young black workers were challenging conditions that other auto workers have learned to live with or had concluded, after many years of fruitless efforts, were impossible to change . . . Before the auto corporations realized it, they were confronted with a new, and in some ways more basic opposition.[1]

It is interesting that the UAW, probably one of the most egalitarian unions of its time, had such problems. One group, the Dodge Revolutionary Union Movement (DRUM), was highly critical of both the union and Walter Reuther, its President. How many people joined the movement is difficult to ascertain, but the numbers are not important: union leadership and older black caucuses felt compelled to accommodate this angry, primarily young, militant movement. The revolutionaries were helped in their cause by the Ad Hoc Committee of Concerned Negro Workers, which said the younger people wanted the UAW to pay more attention to the needs of blacks, and not attack groups such as DRUM.

Some of the revolutionary movements even courted white employees. They argued that management and union leadership had also treated whites arbitrarily and unfairly. These groups did not advocate dissolving the unions, because they realized the unions were their lifeblood, too. They just requested equal treatment, both in working conditions and union representation.

## Federal Contract Compliance Required By Unions

The Office of Federal Contract Compliance (OFCC) was established in 1965 to ensure that, under any federal contract, minorities would not be discriminated against. At first this seemed a logical way to alleviate racial discrimination. However, the general nature of this office's responsibilities has caused it to become a "toothless lion."

One major reason for OFCC ineffectiveness is that much of its responsibility has been waived for a hometown policy:

> But instead of enforcing the law, instead of obtaining compliance with federal guidelines in the construction industry, the U.S. Department of Labor, at the insistence of the politically powerful building trades unions, is promoting and funding so-called "home-town" solutions. These local plans . . . do not establish contractual duties and obligations, they do not state time limitations, they do not contain legal sanctions, these are not guarantees of anything, nothing is spelled out. In short, the "home-town" solutions are a fraud.[2]

The hometown plans have often been used to circumvent the Philadelphia Plan, which stemmed from *Ethridge vs. Rhodes* in a district court in Ohio. In that case, the idea of hiring tables was developed, establishing "the legal principle that government agencies must require a contractual commitment from building contractors to employ a specific number of black workers in each craft, at each stage of construction."[3] Many black leaders believe that hometown solutions merely perpetuate the *status quo* in whatever trades and areas are affected. The Federal Contract Compliance doctrine is little more than a law on paper. The NAACP felt the "Cancellation of a single contract would have provided real evidence of intent to use enforcement powers embodied in the executive orders . . . This failure destroyed not only the real power of governmental authority in this field but the symbolic power as well."[4]

Most of the states have fair employment practice agencies with extensive powers. However, most have declined to use effectively. A large part of the problem is that they do not approach employment bias as a broad pattern deserving class action. Instead they settle each individual complaint, as if it were separate and distinct from all others.

The best argument in the OFCC's favor is this: at least the government is making an attempt to solve a problem, (that white labor refuses to solve) that black labor cannot solve—without help. Some successful steps have been taken under the compliance doctrine: on January 15, 1973 Labor Secretary James D. Hodgson ordered the Bethlehem Steel Corporation to open previously-restricted job classifications with Executive Order 11246, which requires government contractors to follow nondiscriminatory employment practices and to take affirmative action to ensure that job applicants and employees are not discriminated against on the basis of race, color, religion, sex, or natural origin.

### Seniority

The concept of seniority has evolved with the trade union movement. Unions have pushed for it as a defense against arbitrary dismissals by management. In many cases, it has forced management to change its old policy of displacing experienced workers with new employees at lower wages. The need for protection in this area has made the seniority system a vital part of the trade union movement.

Seniority gives an order of priority for promotion and layoff, based partly on length of service. In 1944, it was declared illegal (*Steel vs. Louisville + N. Ry.*) to restrict blacks to lower-paying jobs through the seniority system, whether by written rule or by common practice. Unions and companies were required to treat all employees fairly and not to discriminate on the basis of race. Under President Kennedy's Executive Order 10925, discrimination by government contractors was outlawed.

These systems contribute to the strength of organized labor as a whole, yet often discriminate against blacks. There is approximately a 20 percent difference in job tenure between white and black men,[5] which means that blacks suffer disproportionately from layoffs made according to seniority. The phrase "last hired, first fired" applies well. All seniority systems function on this principle. The more discriminatory seniority systems, however, ensure that the minorities are the last hired. A recession becomes a depression for black workers, who have unemployment rates much higher than do whites. In August 1985, the official unemployment rate for blacks and other minorities was 10.2 percent, compared to an overall rate of 6.8 percent. This 10.2 percent did not include the people who had given up looking for jobs.

In unfair seniority systems, the employer often discriminates by hiring minorities into subordinate positions, and then limits their prospects to a specific group of jobs through the operations of the seniority system. Damage remedy, a method to repay those who have been discriminated against, can lower the conflict between white and black workers and reduce the tensions between the civil rights and labor movements at the institutional and political levels. It could involve an equal opportunity fund—provided by the employer—to aid those who have been victims of seniority discrimination. These funds would be similar in function to automation funds.

There are many ways in which seniority systems discriminate. First, blacks may be hired into jobs from which there is no advancement. Second, blacks lag behind white workers in promotions. Third, when blacks are hired into all-black units (in janitors' or laborers' jobs, for example), they have no realistic chance to transfer without losing benefits. Fourth, in cases of plant seniority where whites and blacks are considered separate groups and are under separate collective bargaining contracts, blacks lose seniority when they transfer to the predominantly white union.

Many contradictory rulings have been made on seniority systems. Some courts have voided the seniority system and have encouraged other approaches they consider less discriminatory, including work-sharing and voluntary retirement. Many appeals courts reversed these decisions, upholding decisions against existing seniority systems only when the company previously had been ordered by the court to end its discriminatory employment practices. In cases such as these, sometimes the courts ordered reinstatement of the dismissed employees and then reduced workloads for others, as a way of preventing loss of jobs. Such measures could lead to imposed affirmative action programs. In general, the courts do not seem to be heading in any single direction.

### Apprenticeship Programs

The U.S. Department of Labor has sponsored an Outreach Program where blacks can obtain apprenticeships for skilled jobs in the building trades. Descriptions of the mostly union-controlled main programs follow.

The interest of the Joint Apprenticeship Program is placement of blacks in skilled jobs, not the setting of precedents. This program is concerned with the building trades and was instituted because a very high percentage of blacks in these trades worked as unskilled laborers. The Workers' Defense League, with the support of the A. Philip Randolph Educational Fund (AFL-CIO-sponsored), thought they deserved a higher proportion of skilled jobs. Thus, the apprenticeship program was instituted with an on-the-job training grant from the Department of Labor and grants from the Ford Foundation.

The Philadelphia Plan provides "clear but flexible" guidelines for employing a certain number of minority workers in the skilled jobs of the building industry. Labor unions claim it is a discriminatory quota system. The program proposed to raise, over a four-year period, black membership in six unions from 2 percent to 20 percent. The unions were those of the electricians, elevator constructors, iron workers, plumbers, steam fitters, and sheet metal workers. The effort was unsuccessful because (1) it applied to only six unions, (2) it applied only to federally-assisted projects costing more than $500,000, and (3) the labor movement did not cooperate.

The Chicago Plan resulted from street demonstrations by blacks. It has managed to get the full backing of the trade unions and is, therefore, more effective than its predecessor. It creates a pool of skilled labor, which the Philadelphia Plan never did. Also, it was negotiated at the local level, rather than the Federal and, therefore, stands a better chance for survival. Its strength is that it was derived from negotiations between blacks and the building trades, rather than being federally imposed.

The Pittsburgh Plan came along a few months after the Chicago Plan and is modeled on it. In this program, four major groups use apprenticeship training programs: manufacturing, construction, utilities, and trades and services. Where there is a union shop, management and labor decide the terms of apprenticeship through joint apprenticeship committees. Where there is no union shop, management sets up the program. Apprentice pay usually begins at half that of journeymen.

Even with the Outreach Programs, blacks and other minorities were still limited in certain ways. Since building is a seasonal industry and one of the most vulnerable to fluctuations in the economy, craft union members have tried to tighten the labor supply by limiting the number of apprentices. The main problem lies not in apprenticeship, however, but in getting black workers with journeyman licenses into the trade unions and the union-controlled jobs, since these unions resist change in hiring practices.

The basic, and largely unrealized, flaw of the Outreach Programs is that, even if full racial integration is achieved in the apprenticeship programs, no great integration of the craft unions will result, because more whites become journeymen without the apprenticeship programs. More than 70 percent of the whites learn directly on the job—they learn by doing. It is very discriminatory for 100 percent of blacks to be required to go through apprenticeship programs when less than 30 percent of employees hired in the building trades have undergone apprenticeship.[6]

### Coalition of Black Trade Unionists

The Coalition of Black Trade Unionists (CBTU) was organized in September, 1972 at a Chicago meeting attended by more than a thousand union officials, along with rank and file members from thirty-seven international unions. It was decided that the CBTU

. . . will work within the framework of the trade union movement. It will attempt to maximize the strength and influence of black workers in organized labor . . . as black trade unionists, it is our challenge to make the labor movement more relevant to the needs and aspirations of black and poor workers. The CBTU will insist that black union officials become full partners in the leadership and decision-making of the American labor movement.[7]

The president of the CBTU is William Lucy, also the secretary-treasurer of the American Federation of State, County, and Municipal Employees, an organization affiliated with the AFL-CIO. In addition to annual conventions, there are frequent meetings of the executive council. They deal with the same issues, but the council meets on a continuous basis and, thus, is able to cover more ground and remain current. Most issues raised are of national interest, such as consumer protection and revenue sharing. Some problems involving localities, e.g., the desegregation of certain school systems and certain affirmative action programs, are also of interest and receive attention.

Some CBTU goals are: (1) to work for the election of a Congress that will fight for programs needed by blacks and other minorities; (2) to offset the impact of an ailing economy on the black worker and the black community; and (3) to continue to increase its organizing efforts—the most important issue now. The coalition believes that the labor movement, since it includes more blacks than any other organization in the nation, is the only one with enough power to help the black worker. William Lucy notes, however, that neither the unions nor the Congress has been very helpful to black workers. He believes that neither completely understands ". . . not only the need but the opportunity to do something substantial."[8] The CBTU is vital and fairly influential now, but when it makes these groups better understand the importance of the black workers' needs, it will become a much stronger force.

### The Outlook

As the U.S. labor movement has progressed, would it be accurate to say that the black worker has been an integral part? Based on the preceding pages, the answer would have to be "no". Black laborers have been maligned by white workers to maintain their supposed superiority. Black laborers have been excluded—both formally and informally—from union membership. Their own unions were kept out of full federation membership until the mid-1950's and left to be the whipping boys of locals. At best, they were affiliated with the AFL, CIO, or AFL-CIO as unions in name only, and were almost powerless.

For many years, black labor has tried to use formal union machinery to advance its own interests within the labor movement. That approach has left blacks sadly behind. When there is only one black on a lily-white executive council (Philip Randolph was for many years the only black on the AFL-CIO Council), no practical policy decisions can be created to favor blacks. The seniority and apprenticeship arrangements of unions have made it extremely hard to get adequate advancement for blacks in unions. Labor leadership has had the historical power to enforce unions' anti-racist policies, yet has preferred to "sit on its hands" and let problems be solved at the local level. Such a do-nothing policy has led to no measurable change.

The greatest changes in black labor have come with the combination of black agitation (black power) from militant young blacks and external pressure brought to bear on the unions by civil rights groups and the federal government. The NAACP, Southern Christian Leadership Conference, and the Urban League have combined with various labor groups, primarily the NALC, to pressure local organizations with staged demonstrations. On the national level, they have brought test cases before the Supreme Court to lay a foundation for blacks to become more active in the labor force. These groups also helped to raise the total consciousness of blacks, to the point where they began demanding parity with white workers—not begging for it. It is the former, not the latter, type of action that brings results.

The federal government has tried to provide access to jobs and union membership through affirmative action policies and federal contract compliance. Affirmative action is slow, because complaints discrimination must be settled in the courts. Federal contract compliance has relied heavily on hometown solutions, suffering the same fate as early union locals dealing with blacks—accomplishing almost nothing.

Blacks have formed their own congregations of black business people and contractors to generate black union membership and advancement. Significant among these are the National Afro-American Builders Conference and the Coalition of Black Trade Unionists.

The black labor movement has been referred to by leader Philip Foner as a "sleeping giant who is awakening." Blacks' percentage of the total labor force is slowly increasing and they are finally becoming aware of the benefits that organized labor can and should assure them. Blacks are no longer going to settle for the "last hired, first fired" doctrine. They are now found in large numbers in several major unions—the United Auto Workers, the United Steel Workers, and the Teamsters—and will not take a backseat in deciding their futures. However, for their own sakes, they must use the tools that social movements and government legislation have created. If used effectively—not against unionism but in support of union organization of blacks—then most certainly the giant will finally awaken.

### Footnotes

[1]Philip S. Foner, *Organized Labor and the Black Worker* (New York: Atheneum, 1972), p. 412.

[2]Herbert Hill, "Racism and Organized Labor," *Ebony Handbook* (Chicago: Johnson Publishing Co., 1974), p. 275.

[3]*Ibid.*, p. 274.

[4]National Association for the Advancement of Colored People, *1968 Annual Report*, p. 110.

[5]Coalition of Black Trade Unionists, "The Seniority System and Affirmative Action," September 1976, mimeographed, p. 2.

[6]Thomas R. Brooks, *Black Builders: A Job Program That Works* (New York: League for Industrial Democracy, 1970), p. 53.

[7]William Lucy, "The Black Partners," *Nation*, September 7, 1974, p. 31.

[8]*Ibid.*, p. 33.

## Women in the Labor Force:
## A Socio–Economic Analysis

The numerical growth of women in the work force and their entry into traditionally male-dominated occupations has revolutionized our work attitudes. The Equal Pay Act of 1963, Title VII of the Civil Rights Act of 1964 and the Equal Rights Amendment proposed by Congress in 1972, have provided a legal framework to encourage and accomplish equality in hiring and pay. The women's liberation movement has altered how many Americans look at social, sexual and job equality, and the emergence of groups like the Coalition of Labor Union Women and the newly established Women's Department at the United Auto Workers clearly demonstrate attention to job equality issues and the recognition of women's participation within organized labor.

Changing employment trends reflecting a higher percentage of white-collar and service industry jobs in our economy and a lower percentage of manufacturing and blue-collar jobs, will affect employment opportunities for women, since they traditionally have been concentrated in low-skilled, low-paying retail trade and service industries with only minimal representation in the professional and technical job classifications.

Progress has been achieved in hiring practices, pay equality and recognition of women's skills, yet there are other facts that present a contrasting story. While nearly 40 percent of the civilian work force is composed of women, fewer than 2 percent of the 40 million working women have entered skilled crafts and trades, one reason the earnings gap between male and female workers is widening. In California there were only 147 female apprentices in 1985, among a total of 38,708 in State programs.[1] Despite the fact that more women are earning college degrees, large numbers of college-educated women, lacking professional preparation and experience, are relegated to office work and retail trade positions, e.g., department store clerks. About one in six working woman is in a profession, but normally in lower-paying subcategories like nursing and public school teaching. Only one in 20 is an executive or holds a middle-management position in private business. The ratio of male-to-female corporate executives stands at a "blatantly sexist" 600-to-1.[2]

The concentration of women in lower-skilled, lower-paid occupations is not merely a sign-of-the-times. The reasons for the massing of women in particular industries—and their exclusion from the skilled trades, blue-collar, and professional/technical vocations—is traceable to a socio-economic fiber that is pervasive at all levels of government and industry. Although only theories may be advanced for causes, and empirical documentation cited for evidence, I will present several aspects that have resulted in the concentration of women in lower-skilled and lower-paid occupations and industries. This overview will analyze several areas relating to women as workers. The areas include how women tend to define a career, why pay differences persist despite the protection of new laws, and why they belong to labor unions traditionally representing a majority of skilled-trade, blue-collar industries.

## Women and Careers: Changes in Attitudes and Expectations

The most recent statistics reveal that more than half of the 7.2 million female heads-of-household are in the labor force.[3] Although families headed by women constitute a small portion of America's population, they are, nonetheless, significant because of their growth in the last 25 years. Between 1945 and 1985, families headed by women doubled in number and now represent one out of six American families.[4]

The manner in which the latter view themselves has been changing as dramatically as their representation in recent years. Expectations regarding marriage and childbearing are most evident. Traditionally, childbearing has brought with it not merely a temporary absence from paid employment, but a complete withdrawal from the workforce for a period of years (the time being extended by the birth of each successive child). Of crucial importance to a woman's career development is the fact that this withdrawal generally occurs during those years in which job advancement would be most rapid. Thus, women lose the opportunity to establish their career, or to gain seniority or experience prior to withdrawal. Whereas, 18-to-24-year old wives in 1950 often expected to have four or more children, in 1982 the commonly expected number was two. From 1965 to 1983, the average number of children per husband-wife family dropped from 2.44 to 1.98.

Acceptance of childless marriages is increasingly widespread. The popularity of birth control and the enjoyment of paid employment have increased women's independence, and decreased family size.

Mature women are in the work force far more frequently than they expected to be in their earlier years. A 1968 longitudinal study of 18-to-24-year old women between the 1968–1983 period, indicated that about two-fifths altered their plans before age 35. And, overwhelmingly, they moved in the direction of labor force entry. Occupational aspirations of this same group of women are indicative of an increasing commitment to careers. About three-fourths of the white, and two-thirds of the black women, indicated preferences for white-collar occupations, with half of the white-collar aspirants looking forward to work in professional, technical or managerial jobs.

Some of the strongest evidence of the commitment of women to enter the labor market has emerged from the survey of women, aged 30 to 44. Among women in this age group, 60 percent of the white and 67 percent of the black workers reported that they would continue to work, even if they could live comfortably without their earnings. The findings are reinforced by the fact that the same women displayed considerable attachment to their current jobs.[5]

While that report deals primarily with married working women, it is inappropriate to exclude two additional categories while analyzing of changing attitudes and expectations. These are single women and "working-class" women (as opposed to professional or technical), who may be either married or single.

The single woman is likely to be younger, less educated and have less work experience than the average working wife. Consequently, her expectations will differ. Her social attitudes are more likely to be strongly influenced by economic necessity. For her, husband-finding may be secondary to job-finding. The following is an example of what she may term "economic necessity":

> When I was a young girl, I imagined I'd grow up to marry a doctor and walk down Michigan Avenue in fancy clothes and smoke imported cigarettes. Now I'm single and a clerk on Michigan Avenue, and I have problems affording a polyester suit.

> This Chicago woman reflects the hope and anxiety of a growing army of 8.6 million single women in the U.S. Often by choice, but sometimes not, they are carving lives for themselves outside traditional mating patterns . . . Few seem greatly concerned about discrimination and sexual harassment—minor problems, many say, in comparison with dull jobs and career doubts.[6]

In addition to wives seeking professional and technical careers and single women working retail trade clerks, a large number of working-class women contribute substantially to the labor force. They are likely to be factory and service workers, employed in textile plants, furniture factories, food processing plants, or countless other industries where they fill working-class occupations. The needs of working-class women and their reasons for employment are primarily, as are those of single women, based upon compelling economic necessity. They work to maintain their standard of living and to provide the opportunity for their family to survive the impact of inflation and/or unemployment of the husband, who is also likely to be employed in a manual or semi-skilled job. The working-class woman may not have a working husband, or even a husband at all—the number of female heads of households, although not classified by the Department of Labor, is probably higher for working-class female employees than their professional counterparts.

The growth of families headed by women has doubled in 25 years, while families headed by men has grown at a 70 percent rate over the same period. Unfortunately, the incidence of poverty among families headed by women is substantial, and, hence, is likely to affect the attitudes and expectations of working-class women. The accelerated growth of these families has been a serious social problem, because 1 out of 3, compared to 1 out of 18 families headed by men, is living at or below what is generally defined as the poverty level.

In 1984, for non-farm families headed by women, the poverty cutoff was $7,014 for a four-person family (6% higher than in 1983, due to inflation), $5,822 for a three-person family, and $5,167 for a two-person family. By these standards, about 2.8 million families headed by women were living in poverty. Typical traits of these families included having a family head who was likely to have graduated from high school, had little or no work experience during the previous year, worked in a low-paying occupation. A disproportionate share of all children under 18 in families headed by women, lived in poor families.[7]

A study performed by Dr. Burleigh B. Gardner, Chairman of the Board of Social Research, Inc., Chicago, Illinois, analyzed working women's attitudes developing from the impact of job and pay equality, and the women's liberation movement.

> Women—many blue-collar workers themselves—are getting, often unconsciously, a new image of themselves and new goals. Formerly the working-class women accepted with little question the idea that women must be subservient to their husbands and, in the working world, must accept lower pay and fewer opportunities than men. And she firmly reared her daughter to likewise accept this woman's role.

> Today, the working class woman is rejecting such limitations. She feels women should have free choice of careers or homemaking or of both, and should have equality with men in pay, in choice of jobs, and in opportunities—and not be restrained just because they are women. When she hears these demands made in the name of women's lib, she heartily concurs. This represents one of the most significant changes in attitude we have witnessed in more than a quarter century of probing the attitudes of working class women.[8]

### The "Why" of Income Differential and Hiring Discrimination

A summary of vital economic statistics shows a widening of the earnings gap, continued concentration of women in low-paid, low-skilled industries, and a high poverty rate for female heads. The news is not encouraging for women, especially during a time when major social and legal changes could have broken the economic bonds restricting them. The reasons for this continuing and pervasive inequality are an unfortunate commentary on the ability of our nation to recognize and solve a serious economic and social plight; they are complex, certainly not obvious, and probably interrelated with strong institutional forces which, at best, are slowly reacting to public attention.

The "whys" of our social dilemma over inequality in the work force have been carefully studied for clues regarding its nature and persistence. The following theory strongly suggests that three social and economic forces contribute to the dilemma.

Economists have exhibited increased interest in the relative economic statuses of the sexes. A number of facets of this problem have been examined, but one of the thorniest questions has been the role of sexual differentials. Although literature on this subject can be traced back more than half a century, it has been only in the last few years that there has been the ... theory, statistical techniques, and data necessary to begin answering the question in a meaningful quantitative fashion. To date, however, little progress has been made in sorting out the complex set of sociological and economic factors behind male-female income differences. The conclusions reached by various researchers sometimes have differed strikingly—a rather distressing situation given that this has become an important issue of social policy ... The debate about these causes involves essentially three broad questions ...

1. What part does occupational distribution play in explaining the observed sex differential in income?
2. How much of the sex differential is attributable to differences in male and female productivity?
3. How much of the observed sex differential is attributed to discrimination?[9]

An analysis of occupational distribution and median salary by sex shows that women are paid substantially less, regardless of the industry and occupations:[10]

| Major Occupation Groups | Median Salary Men | Women | Women's Median Expressed as a Percent of Men's |
|---|---|---|---|
| Professional, technical | $13,945 | $9,095 | 65.2 |
| Managers, administrators | 14,737 | 7,998 | 54.3 |
| Sales workers | 12,031 | 4,674 | 38.8 |
| Clerical workers | 10,619 | 6,458 | 60.8 |
| Craft & kindred | 11,308 | 6,315 | 55.8 |
| Operatives | 9,481 | 5,420 | 57.2 |
| Service workers, nonhousehold | 8,112 | 4,745 | 58.5 |
| Private household | _ | 2,243 | — |
| Nonfarm labor | 8,037 | 5,286 | 65.8 |

It is clear from these statistics that a substantial income differential by sex exists, despite the occupational group. The data by occupation must be combined with a distribution of females by occupations, to see exactly how serious the weighted differential is. For example, a closer examination of the professional and technical group reveals that women are heavily concentrated in such lower-paid subcategories as nursing and elementary school teaching. In general, the more one dissects the figures, the more obvious it becomes that differences in occupational distribution are an important factor underlying the observed sex differential in median incomes. A much larger percentage of female workers is concentrated in the lower-paid occupations, than is the case with male workers. Fifty-three percent (53%) of women are found in two relatively low-wage occupations: clerical workers and service workers. In contrast, only 14 percent of men fall in these categories. Thus, not only do women seem to find their way in disproportionate numbers into the lower-paid occupations, the lower-paid occupations tend to be those traditionally regarded as "women's work."[11]

A more recent analysis of trends by occupational groups brings into perspective the relationship between lower pay and low-paying occupations; the statistics are important because they include married or formerly married women and account for the largest share of the increase in payroll employment of women.

From January 1974 to January 1983, the number of women on payrolls in nonagricultural industries expanded from 19.1 to 27.9 million. Most of the 8.8 million labor force entrants or re-entrants found jobs in the four major industry divisions that were the fastest growing:

| Division | Increase In Women Workers |
|---|---|
| Services | 2,500,000 |
| Government | 2,400,000 |
| Wholesale, retail trade | 1,900,000 |
| Manufacturing | 1,100,000 |

In the late 1970's, the service industry maintained its position as a principle employer of women, and by 1983 employed more women, 6.8 million, than any other industry. In 1983, the trade industry was the second largest employer of women, 6.3 million, most of whom held jobs in retail stores. Women were only one-fourth, or 900,000, of the employees in wholesale trade, but nearly half, or 5,400, in retail trade. Within retail trade, women made up two-thirds of the employees in department stores, clothing and accessory shops, and drug stores, and over half in restaurants and other eating and drinking establishments.

Services provided by government agencies were responsible for the soaring employment of women on government payrolls, especially at the state and local levels. In January 1983, the state and local education industry accounted for nearly 60 percent of the 6.1 million women on government payrolls.

The industry division encompassing finance, insurance and real estate became predominantly female during the 1970's, and by January 1983, women accounted for 52 percent of the employees.[12]

What the occupational distribution clearly shows is that the concentration of women in the labor force is greatest in the major occupational groups that have the highest median income differential. The service industry, the major occupational group employing more women than any other group, has a median income for women that is only 58.5 percent of the male median income, or $4,745 for women, versus $8,112 for men. The trade industry, which constitutes the second largest employer of women, has an even greater income differential. The median income of women is a meager 38.8 percent of the same figure for men, or just $4,674 versus $12,031. The differential among clerical workers is a substantial $6,458 for women and $10,619 for men, or 60.8 percent.

The third question—how much of the observed sex differential is attributable to discrimination—is somewhat more difficult to evaluate. Pinpointing reasons for employer discrimination in hiring and pay practices is virtually an impossible task. Although it is highly unlikely that an employer would admit that hiring and pay discrimination occurs, certain non-institutional myths and inherent assumptions about women workers probably contribute, partially to discrimination. The biggest of these assumptions is that women are paid less, because of differences in important nonsexual characteristics that separate male and female workers, including absenteeism and turnover, age and job experience, and length of the work week. The first of these appears to be the most widely held, i.e., female workers tend to be less productive and more costly because they have higher rates of absenteeism and turnover.

Government research indicates that age, occupation and salary may be more important determinants of absenteeism than sex. In 1987, men between the ages of 25 and 45 lost 4.4 days per year due to illness, while women in the same age bracket lost 5.6 — a difference of only 1.2 days per year. In the 45-and-over age bracket, female employees lost fewer working days due to illness than men, making the overall averages 5.3 days per year for men, and 5.4 per year for women. To be sure, illness does not account for all employee absenteeism. In particular, because of the different family roles typically assigned to men and women, women are probably more likely to take days off to care for sick children or to meet other household responsibilities. However, Labor Department data show that, during an average week in 1987, 1.4 percent of women and 1.2 percent of men did not report to work for reasons other than illness or vacation, certainly a small difference.

The problem — or presumed problem — of employee turnover may have its greatest impact on female occupational distributions, but it might also affect relative pay. Employers, believing there is greater risk in investing in training for women, might attempt to recoup their expected loss by paying them less. If the sex differential in turnover rates is an important factor in explaining the sex differential in pay, it is a testimonial to the power of myth over economic fact, for the existing data show the differences in turnover to be small. Labor Department figures reveal that voluntary "quit" rates for the sexes are not very different — 2.2 per hundred male employees per month and 2.6 per hundred female employees in 1982.[13] Furthermore, it has been asserted that about one-half of this quit rate differential is attributable to the greater concentration of women in occupations where quit rates for both men and women are above average. Employers may mentally magnify the quit rate differential, perhaps to show greater sensitivity for a woman quitting to have a baby, than a man quitting to take a better job. Whatever the psychological cause, there seems little factual basis for the popular view of the size of the quit rate differential. Unfortunately, employers may act on their mistaken impressions and practice "statistical discrimination."

A discussion of the impact of on-the-job experience upon hiring and pay differentials is difficult, because training experience data is not readily available. Job training programs that attract employees are well publicized, because they provide an opportunity to learn a skill and gain employment. But data on male/female job experiences rarely provide insight into training, and one might conclude, therefore, that job experience and age are factors that employers may subconsciously lump together during selection and salary decisions. Since women are more likely to have fewer years of job experience at any given age than their male counterparts, a lack of female job experience probably contributes to the pay differential. Women, at least in past years, have tended to enter and leave the labor force at early ages, and then reenter at later ages. Women who have never married tend to have an age-earnings profile much like that of men, but for married women with spouses present, the differences between male and female average hourly earnings increases with age. It seems likely that, as women interrupt their careers to raise children, differences in work experience will give rise to a significant sex differential in earnings.

Income differences, and the accompanying pay discrimination, are also partially explained by the weekly overtime pay data. In 1981, women employed full-time on nonfarm and salary jobs worked an average of 39.9 hours per week—considerably less than the 43.6 hours averaged by similarly employed men. Only 15 percent of women with full-time jobs worked overtime in May 1981, compared with 30 percent of men. These disparities are in large part attributed to the relatively greater concentration of men in the blue-collar occupations. The Council of Economic Advisers recently estimated that the length of the work week differential accounted for about 6 percentage points of the 1982 sex differential in median income—a smaller share than in 1949, but still very significant.[14]

The analysis of changing attitudes and expectations of wage-earning women clearly shows that women now expect more, and statistically—because of the widening earnings gap and concentration in low-pay, low-skill areas—deserve more. Even a comparison of male and female employment by occupation shows that women are paid less for the same work.

An analysis of absenteeism and turnover, together with age and experience, dispels the commonly held view that women are paid less because they are absent more. Even though women are likely to have less job experience—although job training records are not readily available—at a given age because of absences from the workforce, the pay differential can hardly be justified within low-skilled occupations e.g., retail trade and the services industry, where experience does not necessarily equate to performance.

The final area of concern is the woman worker as a member of a labor union.

## Women in Labor Unions

In 1982, 4.5 million women belonged to labor unions, accounting for 21.7 percent of all union members. They accounted for more than half of the membership gain between 1980 and 1982 of unions affiliated with the AFL-CIO, and at least six large AFL-CIO unions now have more women than men as members.[15]

Although they comprise an increasingly larger percentage of the work force, nearly 80 percent of working women do not have the protection of a union contract. Women are concentrated in two of the largest unorganized sectors of the economy, the clerical and service sector and—the fastest-growing sector—banking, insurance, and finance. As a result of the large percentage of unorganized women, they generally lag behind male workers with respect to wages and working conditions, often suffering the additional burden of hiring and pay discrimination. The absence of union representation denies women the strong deterrent against low wages and job discrimination supposedly provided by a union working agreement.

In June 1976 at the Teamsters' General Election Convention in Las Vegas, Nevada, the following resolution was introduced by Local 743, Chicago, Illinois, on behalf of Teamster women to recognize the need for

> . . . equal opportunity on the job . . . to deal with the employers' tools of discrimination (i.e., wage differentials based on sex, dual seniority, etc.) . . . greater participation of women members at every level of the International Brotherhood of Teamsters.

> . . . acknowledgement and appreciation of the valuable contributions of Teamster women over the years.[16]

At the United Auto Workers' Convention in June 1975, President Leonard Woodcock of the UAW issued a proclamation on International Women's Year in support of their goals:

> Promotion of equality between men and women, support for the integration of women in the total economic, social and cultural development effort; recognition (and encouragement) of the role of women in the development of international cooperation.[17]

As is the case across the labor force, the earnings gap between men and women union members varies according to the industries in which they are employed. In 1980, the earnings gap between men and women was narrower among union members who were white-collar and service workers, but wider among union members who were blue-collar workers. Within any given industry, men are more likely than women to be union members. This holds equally for white-collar and blue-collar workers, and where adequate data are available for service workers as well. Both men and women were more likely to be labor union members if employed in industries predominantly composed of male workers, an industry is more likely to be unionized if most of its workers are men. In these industries, with increasing percentages of women covered by a labor contract, problems such as wage discrimination based on sex disappear.

Within the labor movement, some joining of forces between women union members and the women's liberation movement outside of organized labor has come about in common support of protective legislation such as the ERA. But the goals of the two groups are dissimilar and may roughly be summarized as economic opportunity for the women's liberation movement, versus economic necessity for the working women. The middle-income woman's interest in work as a career, or as a device for self-actualization, is something only remotely related to the blue-collar worker's interest in improvement of the quality of her work life. Women in the middle-income group, who largely compose the liberation movement, have choices which working women do not have: to work or not to work, the kind of work, part-time or full-time work, to further her education and thus upgrade her occupational level, etc. Most women in blue-collar jobs have few choices, they work because they must do so. To them, many of the issues so important to the women's liberation movement seem removed and even frivolous, compared to their own bread and butter issues.[18]

## Additional Considerations

While the rights of working women are to a certain degree protected by union membership, the EEOC has filed many discrimination suits against both corporations and unions to afford them additional protection. A classic example is the landmark case of *Patterson v. The American Tobacco Company*, an EEOC action to end hiring discrimination. A federal district court required the company to appoint a woman or a "minority individual" to the next vacant supervisory level position at one of its facilities. Unlike previous rulings where a company was given a number of years to comply, American was ordered to name a minority member to the very next management post to become available, and to continue to fill supervisory jobs with females and blacks, until the percentage of those minorities approximated that in the Company's local area (Richmond, VA).[19] Rulings such as this, while they may be branded as "reverse discrimination by some, are essential, if parity is to be reached in the foreseeable future.

Women have also experienced job discrimination because of health hazards. Working women have traditionally been relegated to "women's jobs" because they were the "weaker sex." But what about standards of safety and health as women increasingly penetrate what have traditionally been called "men's jobs?" As women, with the force of law behind them, move into "men's jobs," they share men's exposure to the full range of safety and health hazards. And again the question comes up: do men and women react differently to job stress and environmental factors like toxic substances?

Because of lack of information, many of the stereotypes about women workers rest on shaky foundations. Dr. David Wegman of the Harvard School of Public Health suggests that common beliefs—women are too weak to do heavy work, women cannot tolerate temperature extremes as well as men, women are more susceptible to toxic substances—are mostly well-cultivated myths. Studies show that, on the average, women's absolute strength is about two-thirds that of men . . . other studies reveal more differences in strength between working and nonworking women than between working women and working men. And although the temperature regulation mechanism apparently is different in the two sexes, women can regulate their body temperatures equally as well as men. Therefore, Wegman urges employers to set criteria on work strength and hire regardless of sex.[20]

The contribution of working women to national productivity cannot be overestimated—forty percent of the work force are women, and increasingly, women are heads of families and work out of economic need, and not for discretionary income. Women comprise approximately 22 percent of the membership of labor unions, even though their representation in the work force is concentrated in the service, retail trade and banking/finance industries where the percentage of organized workers is low, compared to the blue-collar sector. And most unfortunately, the income gap between men and women is widening, despite protective laws.

The future is brighter, however, as the country shifts from a predominantly production-oriented economy toward a service economy. White-collar jobs will grow faster than blue-collar jobs, and women should find the trends more favorable than what they have been forced to accept in the last several decades. It is well to keep in mind, however, that socio-economic change of this magnitude is by necessity, gradual. From an historical perspective, it is obvious that the majority of employers have not been, and to a certain degree are still not, receptive to the emerging role of women in the labor force. Sad commentary on our society though it may be, forceful employment legislation has thus far been the only effective technique for initiating changing the traditional "women's role". In my opinion, it is this vehicle that must continue to be used, if the progress made to date is to be continued. Additionally, efforts on the part of individuals or groups for more favorable legislation should not be directed, as so often in the past, at specific instances of injustice. While favorable settlements in these areas may prove a valuable point, the time and effort would ultimately be better spent, directed at the passage of basic pieces of legislation, such as the Equal Pay Act, Title VII of the Civil Rights Act and the Equal Rights Amendment. Once more legislation of this nature is activated, the specific battles and cases can be fought. Now, however, specifics should be of secondary importance. Favorable conceptual legislation is the hope of the future for women in the labor force.

### Footnotes

[1]"Women's Rights—Why the Struggle Still Goes On," *U.S. News and World Report*, May 27, 1984, p. 40.

[2]"The American Women," *U.S. News and World Report*, December 8, 1984, p. 58.

[3]U.S. Department of Labor, Women's Bureau, *1985 Handbook on Women Workers*, p.  .

[4]"Women Who Head Families: A Socio-economic Analysis," *Monthly Labor Review*, June 1985, p. 5.

[5]"The Changing Economic Role of Women," Manpower Report of the President, 1985, pp. 64–65.

[6]*U.S. News and World Report*, December 8, 1984, p. 54.

[7]*Monthly Labor Review*, June 1985, p. 3.

[8]"Women's Rights, Why the Struggle Goes On," *U.S. News and World Report*, May 27, 1984, p. 41.

[9]"The Incomes of Men and Women: Why Do They Differ?" *Monthly Labor Review*, April 1983, p. 3

[10]"The Earnings Gap," *U.S. Department of Labor, Women's Bureau*, March 1985.

[11]*Monthly Labor Review*, April 1983, p. 5.

[12]"Where Women Work—An Analysis By Industry and Occupation," *Monthly Labor Review*, May 1984, p. 5.

[13]*Monthly Labor Review*, April 1983, pp. 3–4.

[14]*Ibid.*, p. 6.

[15]"Women in Unions," *U.S. News and World Report*, March 17, 1985, p. 70.

[16]*Proceedings*, 21st Convention, International Brotherhood of Teamsters, Las Vegas, Nevada, 1976.

[17]*Cable*: UAW Detroit (Solidarity House) "UAW Proclamation on International Women's Year," May 1975, p. 5.

[18]"Working Women and Their Membership in Labor Unions," *Monthly Labor Review*, May 1985, p. 32.

[19]"Women Executives Are Different," *Dun's Review*, January 1985, pp. 47–48.

[20]"Women Workers and Job Health Hazards," *Job Safety and Health Magazine*, April 1985, p. 2.

# Subconscious Stereotyping In
# Business Decisions

By educating individuals about the legal aspects of employment discrimination, university courses, employer-sponsored training programs, various "human relations" seminars, and other sources are serving a valuable purpose—but they are addressing only half the problem. An individual may be extremely knowledgeable regarding the legal side of discrimination and yet, without consciously being aware of it, still discriminate in decisions involving such matters as selection, placement, promotion, training, and compensation. Based on the evidence of my numerous consulting experiences, I am convinced that this continues today, even among the most "enlightened" individuals, and this implicit discrimination is most likely to be based on race or sex. In the following study sex is the key variable.

## The "Who" and The "How"

To test my contention, a sample of 512 graduating college seniors, 271 males and 241 females, were surveyed. All subjects were taking a Personnel Management course that devoted considerable time to equal employment and fair employment practices. Thus, they had all been recently schooled in the legal aspects of employment discrimination and, I feel, were more sensitized to this issue, than might otherwise have been the case. Any implicit discrimination found in decisions made by this group might, therefore, underestimate the extent of the problem in the general business community.

Before being given the survey, the subjects were told that they would be evaluated on the quality of their responses to the various situations presented, and that the evaluation would be a factor in the grade awarded in the course (Personnel Management). In this way, I hoped that commitment to the exercise would be increased, with fewer subjects simply going through the motions. Subjects were told to respond to the situations, as if they were the personnel manager of a large business organization. They were then given eight incidents, each necessitating a typical personnel decision (e.g., hiring, firing), with forced-choice responses.[1] Each incident was presented in two forms, one with a female as the individual primarily involved in the incident (female version), and one with a male primarily involved (male version).

Of the 271 males in the subject group, 135 were given the male version of each incident and 136 were given the female version. Of the 241 female subjects, 120 were given the male version of each incident and 121, the female.[2] No subject was given both versions of any one incident, because I felt this

(a) would not be realistic—having two identical applicants differing only by sex, and (b) would make fairly obvious the intent of the study, thus distorting findings, since few people would respond in an overtly discriminately manner; it is, after all, the subconscious discrimination that I was interested in.

### Responses to Eight Incidents

The first three incidents involved a conflict between responsibilities on the job and at home. It is my belief that when these conflicts arise, most individuals expect the male to place job responsibilities first, and the female to give first priority to the home.

## Incident 1

Jack and Judy Garrison have been married three years. Jack is an aspiring business executive and Judy is a successful free-lance writer. This is part of a conversation they had after coming home from a cocktail party at the home of an executive in Jack's division.

Judy: Oh, boy, what a bunch of creeps. Do we have to go to these parties, honey?

Jack: Judy, you know we have to. These things mean a lot to me. Tonight I had a chance to talk to Mr. Wilson. On the job, it would take a week to get an appointment with him. I was able to get across two good ideas I had about our new sales campaign, and I think he was listening.

Judy: Is Wilson that fat slob who works in marketing, the one with the dull wife? I spent ten minutes with her and I nearly died! She's too much. Jack, the people there tonight were so dull I could have cried. Why did I major in English Lit. anyway? I prefer to talk to people who know what is going on in the world, not a bunch of half-wits whose main interests are their new cars and spoiled kids. I tried to talk to one guy about Virginia Woolf and he didn't even know who she was. These people are incredible. Do we have to go to another cocktail party again next week? I'd like to see "Look Back In Anger" instead. I've got the tickets. One of my wifely duties is to give you culture. What an uncouth bunch in the business world.

Jack: One of my husbandly ambitions is to get ahead in the business world. You know that these parties are required for bright junior executives coming up in the organization. And I'm a bright junior executive. If we don't go, who knows which of the other junior execs will get to Wilson with their good ideas?

Judy:  Can't you relax and work a 40–hour week? That's what they pay you for.

Jack:  I guess I'm too ambitious to relax.

Judy:  I'd still like to go to the play. At least we could think about real problems.

Jack:  And I'd be a mediocre, lower-management nobody for the rest of my career.

Judy:  I want you to be a success, Jack. But the idea of spending more evenings talking to idiots is too much!

The "female version" had Judy as the aspiring executive and Jack as the reluctant spouse, with all other details being identical. Subjects were then asked to choose one of three responses.

### Incident 1

|    |                                                                  | Female Version | Male Version |
|----|------------------------------------------------------------------|----------------|--------------|
| a. | The spouse should go to parties and stop making such an issue of it. | 30%            | 72%          |
| b. | The junior executive should attend the parties alone.            | 42%            | 18%          |
| c. | The junior executive should stop attending the parties.          | 28%            | 11%          |

It is obvious from these results that the subjects expected the female to suppress her personal desires and support the male in his work role to a much greater extent than the male in a similar situation. Such expectations make it easier for a male to succeed in balancing career and home demands than a female—that is, the male will have more assistance and less resistance in doing so.

The second incident looked at these competing demands from another angle.

### Incident 2

Ruth Brown, an accountant in the main office, has requested one month's leave beginning next week. She has already taken her vacation this year. She wants the leave to take care of her three young children. The day care arrangements the Brown's had made for the period covered by her request suddenly fell through, and they have been unable to make other arrangements satisfying their high standards. Ruth's husband is principal of the junior high school and he cannot possibly get off during the next month.

The problem is that Ruth is the only person experienced in handing the "cost" section in the accounting department. We would either have to transfer an accountant with the same experience from the Richardson Division or else train a replacement for only one month's work. I have urged Ruth to reconsider this request, but she insists on going ahead with it.

I have also checked with the legal department, and we do not have to hold the position open for Ruth if she insists on taking the whole month off.

I would appreciate it if you could give me your decision on this as soon as possible.

The male version was identical except it involved Ralph Brown, whose wife was a principal. Subjects were then asked if this was an appropriate leave request, and whether they would grant leave with pay, or without pay.

## Incident 2

|  |  | Yes—<br>Female<br>Version | Yes—<br>Male<br>Version |
|---|---|---|---|
| a. | Is this an appropriate leave request? | 51% | 31% |
| b. | Would you grant leave with pay? | 72% | 56% |
| c. | Would you grant leave without pay? | 11% | 3% |

In this case, the results indicated that sex stereotyping benefits females. A leave request for child care was considered acceptable by more than one-half of the subjects when it was made by a female, but by less than one-third of the subjects when it is made by a male. As in the first incident, the evidence suggested that when a job/home conflict arises, the male is expected to accommodate his work schedule, while it is more acceptable for the female to miss work and devote her energies to the home.

Such stereotyping creates increasing problems for both husbands and wives, as more and more wives pursue careers. Women will find it hard to advance, as long as most employers believe that their first allegiance is, or should be, to the home and not the job; at the same time, males are going to find themselves more often in situations where their absence from work is necessary because of a working spouse, yet where their employers view the reason for such absence as unacceptable.

### Incident 3[3]

Situation three presented a direct career conflict between husband and wife:

> As you know, Ronald Cooper is a computer operator in my section. He has played a key role in computerizing our inventory system. Recently Ronald's wife was offered a very attractive managerial position with a large retail organization on the West Coast. They are seriously considering the move. I told Ronald that he has a very bright future with our organization and it would be a shame for him to pull out just as we are expanding our operations. I sure would hate to lose him now. What do you think we should do about the situation?

The alternate form had Rhonda as the computer operator, and her husband offered the job on the West Coast. Subjects were asked to choose from among four alternative responses.

### Incident 3[3]

|     |                                                                                    | Female Version | Male Version |
| --- | ---------------------------------------------------------------------------------- | -------------- | ------------ |
| a.  | Try to convince the operator that too much has been invested in his (or her) career to leave now. | 41%            | 88%          |
| b.  | Don't try to influence the operator.                                               | 64%            | 19%          |
| c.  | Offer the operator a sizable raise as an incentive to stay.                        | 22%            | 28%          |
| d.  | Try to find an attractive position for the employee's spouse in the organization.  | 8%             | 8%           |

It is obvious from the response pattern that the subjects viewed male employees as more valuable to retain than female employees, even when the qualifications of each were the same.

When looking at responses to the first three situations, one gains some insight into why absenteeism and turnover rates are higher for females than males, even when they are at the same organization and compensation level. If employers do not make as much effort to retain females as they do males, and if, as seen in Incident 2, females are more readily granted unscheduled absences, is it any wonder that the government reports slightly higher absenteeism and turnover rates for females than for males?[4]

The fourth and fifth situations dealt with an employee's unacceptable conduct, the question being what disciplinary action, if any, should be taken.

**Incident 4**

I have a problem and I don't see how to solve it. It concerns one of the design engineers, Jill Diller, who has worked for me for the past 15 months. Jill persists in arriving late every morning. She is always 10 minutes late, more usually 15 minutes to a half hour. I am at my wit's end. I have tried everything I can think of—private discussions, written reprimands, threats, sarcasm, and more. She is still late every morning.

When Jill walks into the office, the work stops and everyone watches. Some of the designers are even joking that Jill's coming in late has something to do with her recent engagement. I don't like to get too tough with a creative girl like Jill, but her behavior is bound to hurt morale in the department.

The male version involved Jack Diller. Subjects were asked to select from among three courses of action.

**Incident 4**

|  |  | Female Version | Male Version |
|---|---|---|---|
| a. | Suspend for one week for continued tardiness. | 72% | 64% |
| b. | Threaten to fire and follow through if necessary. | 51% | 42% |
| c. | Don't make an issue of tardiness. | 8% | 11% |

In the case of both the female and male employee, the subjects considered the situation serious enough to warrant the more severe actions. Yet they were slightly more inclined to take such action when the employee involved was a female. This may be connected to the value the subjects attached to employees of different sexes, as exhibited by the responses to Incident 3. Both the willingness to risk losing an employee through more severe disciplinary actions and the lesser effort made to retain female employees, seem to me to provide insight into the value the subjects placed on employees of different sexes. The response patterns indicated that, when all else is equal, males were viewed as more valued employees—more effort was put into retaining them and severe discipline was less likely to be used for fear of losing them.

**Incident 5**

Situation five involved unacceptable personal, rather than work, conduct:
I would like to get your advice on a matter of great sensitivity involving one of the junior executives in our organization. It has been brought to

my attention by an unimpeachable source that Bill Holman, assistant comptroller in my division, is having an affair with a prominent young socialite. I understand it has reached the point where any day now Bill's wife will publicly denounce the socialite as a homewrecker. I have been reluctant to bring this up, but I know Bill's marital problems will hurt his work. I would appreciate any advice you could give me on this.

The female version involved Renee Holman having an affair with a young playboy. Subjects were asked to select from among three responses:

### Incident 5

|  |  | Female Version | Male Version |
|---|---|---|---|
| a. | Do nothing unless the junior executive raises the issue. | 50% | 52% |
| b. | Advise junior executive to see a marriage counselor. | 40% | 56% |
| c. | Confront employee and threaten termination unless affair stops. | 3% | 4% |

The only real difference between male and female respondents in this situation seemed to be in response (b); subjects were more likely to request that a male employee see a marriage counselor than a female. I would speculate that the almost identical results to response (a) may have to do with the equal number of male and female subjects given each version. It may be that members of one sex (regardless of which one) are less likely to approach members of the opposite sex on issues such as this. For response (a) then, it is not a question of the sex of the participant but of the sex of the subject relative to the participant. Response (b) indicates that the subjects were more willing to correct the unacceptable behavior of male employees than female, even when this behavior was of a personal, rather than a work nature. When the unacceptable behavior was personal (Incident 5) rather than work-related (Incident 4), the subjects were willing to expend more effort on male than on female employees.

### Incident 6

This situation is becoming all too common today: by playing a numbers game the organization has hired enough females to comply with the law, but through subtle forms of unintentional sex discrimination, does not allow them to develop as managers to the same extent that equally qualified males do. Then the females' comparative lack of advancement in the organization is used as evidence that they are not as well suited for the work. This failure to advance can also lead to higher rates of absenteeism and turnover, and so perpetuates the cycle. The difficulty here is that the decisions as to who advances may be made on the grounds of legitimate individual qualifications, and may not be discriminatory at all. The discrimination occurred earlier, however, when females, because of employers' subconscious discrimination, were not given the same opportunities to develop as males. Incident 6 addresses this type of situation.

> I am pleased that we have the opportunity to send a representative to the Dunbar conference on production supervision. I know from personal experience that it is a high-quality conference, and it has developed such a favorable reputation in this area, that it is considered an important form of recognition for those who are selected to attend.
>
> I have reviewed our supervisory staff quite carefully and have narrowed the choice down to two people, both of whom I feel are qualified to attend. Unfortunately, we can send only one person, and I will leave the final selection up to you, depending on what you feel we want to emphasize. The two candidates are Susan Adams and John Elms.
>
> Susan Adams is supervisor of knitting unit A. She is 25, married, and has no children. She has been employed by our company for three years. She is a college graduate with a general business degree, and we consider her to have good potential for higher-level positions.
>
> John Elms is supervisor of knitting unit B. He is 43, married, and has two teen-aged children. He has been employed by our company for 20 years. He is a high school graduate. He has been a steady, conscientious employee, advancing gradually from a helper's job to his present position, which may be as high as he will be able to go, judging from our assessment of the information in his file. Selection for this conference would mean a lot to John.

In the alternate form, the two names were reversed. Subjects were asked to select one of the two for to the conference. When all responses were considered collectively, without differentiation by sex of individual involved, the following results emerged.

**Incident 6**

| | |
|---|---|
| Send 25-year-old | 31% |
| Send 43-year-old | 69% |

Hence, regardless of sex, the majority of subjects felt that the older employee should be sent. When the results were sorted by the sex of the individual, however, the following occurred:

| | |
|---|---|
| Send 25-year-old-female | 23% |
| Send 25-year-old-male | 39% |

These results indicated that the subjects, when selecting younger workers with career potential to participate in a developmental conference, were more likely to expend company resources if the employee were a male, even when all other qualifications are equal.

## Incident 7

This situation dealt with a selection/promotion decision for a position requiring extensive traveling:

Pursuant to our recent discussion with you about the need to recruit a purchasing manager for the new operation, we have developed a set of brief job specifications and have located some candidates who may be suitable for the opening. Will you please review the attached resumes and give us your evaluation?

Job requirements for purchasing manager:

The major responsibilities of the new purchasing manager will be to purchase fabrics, materials, and clothing accessories (buttons, belts, buckles, zippers, etc.) for the production of finished goods.

For the most part, the purchasing manager will have to travel around the country visiting wholesalers and attending conventions and showings. The person hired for this position should have a knowledge of the quality of raw materials and have the ability to establish a "fair" price for goods purchased in large quantities. The person selected for this position will have to travel at least 20 days each month.

## RESUME

Name: Mr. Carl Wood

Position Applied For: Purchasing Manager

Place of Birth: Cleveland, Ohio

Marital Status:     Married; four children,
ages 11, 8, 7, and 4

Education: B.S. Business Administration,
Ohio State University.

Relevant Work Experience:   One year as purchasing trainee,
Campbell Textiles, Inc.
Ten years' experience in various
retail clothing stores, in sales,
buying and general management.

Interviewer's Remarks:   Good personal appearance; seems earnest
and convincing. Good recommendations
from previous employers.

The female version had Mrs. Karen Wood as the candidate. Subjects were asked to answer three questions.

### Incident 7

| | | Yes—<br>Female<br>Version | Yes—<br>Male<br>Version |
|---|---|---|---|
| a. | Would you select this candidate? | 23% | 33% |
| b. | Is the candidate favorably suited for the job? | 33% | 38% |
| c. | Does the candidate have the potential to remain on the job? | 30% | 35% |

Subjects apparently felt that employees with this set of characteristics, regardless of sex, were not suited for the position in question. I think the presence of four young children was the deciding variable for the subjects. Yet in all three areas of inquiry, males were selected more often or rated more favorably than females. This response pattern seems to me to indicate that the subjects were exhibiting the same values evidenced in the responses to Incident 2; that is, the first allegiance of males belongs to the job and that of females, to the home and/or family. This type of subconscious sex stereotyping makes it more acceptable for a male to be selected for a job involving extensive travel than a female—even when both have the same employment qualifications and the same situation at home.

### Incident 8

The final incident addressed the job vs. work dilemma even more directly:

We are at the point where we must make a decision on the promotion of Cathy Adams of our Personnel staff. Cathy is one of the most competent employees in the corporate personnel office, and I am convinced that she is capable of handling even more responsibility as Bennett Division Personnel Director. However, I am not altogether certain that she is willing to subordinate time with her family to time on the job, to the extent that may be required with Bennett. I have had the opportunity to explore with her the general problem of family versus job, and she strongly believes that she would rarely stay late at the office or participate in weekend meetings.

She believes that her first duty is to her family, and that she should manage her time accordingly. This viewpoint has not affected her performance in the past, but it could be a problem in the more demanding position as head of personnel with the Bennett Division.

The male version involved Gerald Adams. Subjects were given three possible courses of action.

**Incident 8**

|  |  | Female Version | Male Version |
|---|---|---|---|
| a. | Do not promote. | 34% | 10% |
| b. | Persuade the candidate to make a stronger job commitment prior to promotion. | 29% | 32% |
| c. | Base the promotion on past experience. | 40% | 58% |

The responses to (a) and (c) indicated that identical family demands and/or commitments did not disqualify males to the same extent they disqualified females. Not only were females expected to yield to family demands in the work vs. home dilemma (as shown in the previous situations), but even if they set priorities identical to those of their male counterparts, the males were still given more consideration for the job. The effects of this type of sex stereotyping will be difficult, at best, to overcome.

The conclusions to be drawn from this study are obvious. If the subjects used here are any indication, there is a good deal of unintentional, subconscious sex stereotyping taking place in the business sector of our society. I feel quite strongly that, if anything, these responses underestimate the extent of the problem. The subjects were younger than most people in business, were college-educated and were undergoing a learning experience (the personnel course) that sensitized them to the area of employment discrimination. It is reasonable to expect that responses from such a group would be different from those of a more general sample.

While we as a society can legislate against overt discrimination, equally important and necessary are efforts to eliminate the type of subconscious stereotyping evidenced in the present study. Even if all members of the business community fully comply with the written laws regarding equal/fair employment, the barriers erected by the underlying, unfair attitudes found in this study will still be imposing. This study has tapped some deep-seated, gender-based values—and found them to be resistant to change, despite education. Only after this more difficult type of prejudice is eliminated, will *real* equal employment practices be attained. Making people aware of the pervasiveness of the problem, is the first step.

**Footnotes**

[1]These incidents were taken from an earlier survey conducted by Benson Rosen and Thomas Jerdee, published in 1974: "Sex Stereotyping in the Executive Suite," *Harvard Business Review*, March–April 1974.

[2]In the present study responses were tabulated by the sex of the fictitious individual involved in the incident, not by the sex of the respondent—although the number of respondents by sex was the same for both the male and female version of each incident. In a follow-up study, I intend to tabulate responses by the sex of the respondent.

[3]In this and certain subsequent situations, the responses do not total 100 percent, since more than one response was possible.

[4]Bureau of National Affairs, Inc., *Bulletin to Management*. Information on absenteeism and turnover is published quarterly in the bulletin.

## National Right-To-Work Law:
## An Affirmative Position

The historic Right of the States to outlaw the firing of employees who refuse to pay dues to labor unions is reaffirmed by Section 14(b) of the Taft-Hartley Act, which states that: "Nothing in this Act shall be construed as authorizing the execution or application of agreements requiring membership in a labor organization as a condition of employment in any State or Territory in which such executive or application is prohibited by State or Territorial Law."[1]

State laws forbidding this firing or refusal to pay dues are popularly known as Right-to-Work laws, because they safeguard the individual's right to work as either a voluntary union member or as a nonunion employee.

Because of the existence of Section 14(b), all 50 states are empowered to adopt Right-to-Work laws. Such statutes or constitutional provisions are now in effect in 20 states:

| | | |
|---|---|---|
| Alabama | Louisiana | South Dakota |
| Arizona | Mississippi | Tennessee |
| Arkansas | Nebraska | Texas |
| Florida | Nevada | Utah |
| Georgia | North Carolina | Virginia |
| Iowa | North Dakota | Wyoming |
| Kansas | South Carolina | |

In the remaining 30 states, workers can legally be compelled—and millions are being compelled—to join labor organizations in order to earn their livelihood. Union/company agreements requiring all employees to pay union dues are explicitly sanctioned by Sections 7 and 8(a)(3) of the National Labor Relations Act.

The battle over Right-to-Work laws has been raging since the enactment of Section 14(b) and arguments pro and con have been expressed and debated over the years. I would like to shed some light on this very complex issue by the following:

— present the problem (issue); that is, should Americans be compelled to join labor unions?

— discuss Right-to-Work support, including the National Right-to-Work Committee and its purposes and goals;

— present arguments on both sides of the issue with the view towards providing support for National Right-to-Work legislation; and

— present conclusions/justifications for a National Right-to-Work law.

### The Problem

Today, under the sanction of federal laws, unions and management can make agreements whereby employees can be forced into a union. Under compulsory "union shop" and "agency shop" agreements, the employee must either join or pay dues and fees to the union, or be fired from his job.

This situation exists in 30 states. Only in the 20 states which have enacted state Right-to-Work laws, authorized by the federal law, can employees exercise freedom of choice to join or not join, or pay agency fees to a union.

The right of workers to organize has been perverted to include the privilege of compelling men to join or pay fees to labor organizations against their will, and the privilege of forcing employers to herd their employees into unions. Right-to-Work laws seek to remedy these flagrant abuses of power.

Supporters of Right-to-Work laws believe that union democracy tends to be stifled under conditions of compulsory unionism, because there is little need for union leaders to be responsive to a captive membership. Right-to-Work simply means that an individual has the right to join or financially support a union, and a corollary right to refrain from joining or supporting a union, without losing a job.

The following practices are examples of what can, and often does, happen under compulsory unionism:

— Workers are subject to unlimited amounts of monthly dues and "assessments."

— A portion of workers' dues is used, without their approval, to support political parties to which they may be opposed.

— Union officials can call all employees out on strike without a "secret ballot" vote of the employees.

— Seniority of older workers means nothing when company-union agreements give "super-seniority" to union officials and committeemen.

— A worker can be discharged from a job, if late in paying monthly dues, regardless of the reason.

— The salaries of union officials can be raised to any amount without approval of the rank-and-file member, even though the member is compelled to contribute the money which pays the salaries.

— Local unions are dominated by the national and international unions through such gimmicks as "trusteeships" and the merging of several locals. The worker has no voice in such manipulations.[2]

## Support for Right-To-Work Laws

The supporters of Right-to-Work laws are many and varied, including the National Right-to-Work Committee, legislators, educators, authors, workers, and even some union officials.

The National Right-to-Work Committee, organized in 1955, is a public-interest organization, incorporated as a nonprofit corporation, for only one purpose: to protect the right of citizens to obtain and hold jobs, whether they belong or pay fees to unions or not. The Committee's more than one-half million supporters and members include employees—both union and nonunion—business firms, homemakers, clergymen, educators, and people from all walks of life.

Over the years, the Committee has won steadily increasing recognition for its work in exposing and combating the evils of compulsory unionism. Today, the Committee is widely regarded as the most effective organization in labor matters when the issue of compulsory unionism is involved. The Committee demonstrated its effectiveness by blocking an all-out drive by union officials in 1956 to repeal Section 14(b) of the Taft-Hartley Act, which affirms the right of states to enact Right-to-Work laws. In 1970, the Committee scored another very significant victory when the Congress voted to include Right-to-Work protection in the Postal Reform Bill. It has successfully fought off attempts since then to repeal that provision of the Law.

The Committee has helped defeat repeated attempts to repeal or emasculate state Right-to-Work laws, and has backed successful efforts to strengthen those laws in several states. It has blocked efforts to extend compulsory unionism to public employees in state after state, and at the federal level. It has been instrumental in the introduction of, and mobilization of grass roots support for, legislation providing for a national Right-to-Work law, guaranteeing freedom of choice for federal employees, and prohibiting the use of compulsory union dues for political purposes.

Details of the National Right-to-Work Committee's program are:

1. Conduct a national education program designed to alert the American people to the wrongfulness of compulsory unionism and to bring about understanding of the Right-to-Work principle.

2. Safeguard Section 14(b) of the Taft-Hartley Act (that section of the national labor law which reaffirms the right of states to have Right-to-Work laws).

3. Preserve all existing Right-to-Work guarantees for public employees.

4. Provide assistance in organizing statewide citizen movements to promote, enact, and protect state Right-to-Work laws.

5. Work to obtain legislation which will: curb the use of compulsory union dues for political activity; protect public employees at all levels of government against compulsory unionism; prevent compulsory unionization of farm workers; ultimately, provide national Right-to-Work protection covering all employees.[3]

There are a large number of other supporters of Right-to-Work, too numerous to discuss here. There follows, however, a small sampling of some of these supporters and selected statements they have made.

Jameson G. Campaigne, author of *American Might and Soviet Myth*, stated:

"The freedom of the checked-off man will not come from action by unions. It can only come through both Federal and state legislation. The most vital provision of any such law is the abolition of the compulsory check-off and the prohibition of compulsory union membership . . . only when the individual working man is free to decide for himself whether to support union policies, support union political candidates, support a strike or oppose it, and work to change his union leadership if he wishes—only when his human rights to these actions are protected by law will he be a free man again. The end of the check-off and the abolition of compulsory union membership are the key to the liberation of the American worker so that he can 'use his powers for himself and for the commonwealth.'"[4]

John McClellan, U.S. Senator, Arkansas, stated: "If I were a wage earner, I might well be inclined to join a union. I would not want to be compelled to join."

Everett M. Dirksen, former Minority Leader U.S. Senate, Illinois stated: "Is there a greater right? Is there a more important right? Is there a more fundamental right than the right to make a living for one's self and for one's family without being compelled to join a labor organization?"

David Lawrence, editor and columnist, stated: "No organization should have the privilege of keeping from their jobs any workers who wish to perform their services. The big question is whether individual liberty really prevails in America and whether every citizen is to be permitted to enjoy the freedom that is too often extolled."[5]

Samuel Gompers, courageous founder of the American labor movement, stated: "There may be here and there a worker who for certain reasons unexplainable to us does not join a union of labor. This is his right no matter how morally wrong he may be. It is his legal right and no one can dare question his exercise of that legal right."[6]

## Major Arguments

The issues involved in the Right-to-Work controversy are highly sensitive ones. Well-intentioned people on both sides are caught up in the wave of emotionalism. Proponents of Right-to-Work laws feel they are defending a basic individual liberty. On the other hand, opponents of Right-to-Work legislation feel they are fighting for the very lifeblood of the labor union movement. Add to this combination the traditional chasm between certain members of both unions and management who have not accepted the idea of accommodation and resolution of differences through negotiation, and the setting is perfect for a highly charged campaign.

The major arguments in behalf of compulsory unionism are as follows:

1. "Union security," that is, the strength of the union, depends upon universal acceptance of membership as a condition of employment.
2. Majority rule is a democratic principle, and a minority of workers who will not voluntarily support the union should be compelled to do so to solidify the power of the majority.
3. The union negotiates contracts for the benefit of all employees of a craft or class, and those who do not voluntarily contribute support to an organization which benefits them should be compelled to contribute.
4. The power of discipline over all workers should be available to the union so that it may insure the fulfillment of contracts and other assumed obligations.

Not one of the foregoing arguments can be maintained against the facts, nor can they justify the oppression and denial of individual liberty which is the inherent wrong of compulsory unionism.

## Union Security

Labor union leaders and other opponents of Right-to-Work laws argue that the inability of unions to arrive at union shop agreements with employers, strikes at the core of union security and strength. It is a simple historical fact that the unions have increased in numbers and economic and political power in the last twenty years as voluntary organizations and, under favoring national and state laws, they have no need to compel unwilling workers to join and pay dues.

Those in favor of Right-to-Work laws argue that unions do not need further strengthening, because they are adequately protected under present law.

In his book, *The Case for Right-to-Work Laws*, the Reverend Edward A. Keller, C.S.C., states that union security clauses are an effective way to exercise the right of unionism but they are not a necessary means. No one has proved that compulsory unionism is the only reasonable and normal means of security for labor unions today. The protective labor laws of both the federal and state governments can, should, and do give adequate and reasonable security to unions today in the United States.[7]

It is also hardly debatable that a voluntary organization of workers united for selfhelp is inherently a much stronger organization, than a union composed to a considerable extent of unwilling members. Many of the strongest friends of organized labor have pointed out on many occasions, that the strength of unions as voluntary organizations would be greatly weakened by converting them into compulsory monopolistic organizations. If legally permitted, these would inevitably require detailed regulation by government, which would otherwise be unnecessary.

Two members of the National Defense Mediation Board, Judge Charles E. Wyzanski (former Solicitor in the Department of Labor) and former Senator Frank P. Graham, both made this point in opposition to compulsory unionism. President Franklin D. Roosevelt made a similar public pronouncement. Mr. Justice Frankfurter in the state "right-to-work" cases (335 U.S. 538) quoted extensively from the late Justice Brandis, who held that:

> "The ideal condition for a union is to be strong and stable, and yet to have in the trade outside its own ranks an appreciable number of [men] who are non-unionists . . . Such a nucleus of unorganized labor will check oppression by the unions as the unions check oppression by the employer."[8]

## Majority Rule

Critics of Right-to-Work laws contend that democratic principles require the minority to support the majority.[9] This is an unnecessary argument, especially when applied to Right-to-Work, because our laws and customs already require the minority of employees who are not members of a labor union to accept the terms and work under the contract(s) of the majority. This is similar to the requirement that any minority or dissenting group in a community must accept the laws enacted by the majority representatives. But, even in the case of public laws, a dissenting minority or a political party in opposition, is not required to stop its opposition; nor is it required to contribute to the political support of the majority party. Even members of the majority are at liberty to withdraw from such an association.

Those who espouse compulsory unionism are essentially adopting the communist theory that there should be only one party to which everyone should give allegiance and support. Inside the party, there may be disagreements, but no one is permitted to go outside and support an opposition movement.

The claim of democratic majority rule by compulsory unionism is a pure fraud. Our democratic theory of majority rule is based on the preservation of minority opposition and the possibility of shifting the majority power. But when workers are required to join and support a union regardless of their desire to oppose it, the whole democratic basis of majority rule disappears. It is supplanted by a majority rule that has no place in a democratic society.

Issue can be taken with both the aforementioned points, by arguing that the legal privilege of majority or exclusive representation is more than just compensation for the union, because it denies the minority of nonunion employees the right to bargain with their employer, independently of the union. The fact they are denied this legal right makes absurd the union accusation of "free-riders" because they, as the minority in the bargaining unit, are compelled by law to bargain through the union. This is an important example, in this day of emphasis on civil rights, of a minority being legally denied the right of self-representation.

### Free Rider

Much public stress is laid on the argument that, since the union negotiates for the benefit of all workers of a class, all such workers should be compelled to contribute to the cost of maintaining the union activities. This argument has a superficial appeal, but it is both fundamentally unsound and highly deceptive in facts.

The argument is fundamentally unsound because, throughout our society, voluntary organizations carry on activities which benefit a great many who do not contribute any financial or other support. Fraternal organizations, churches, and civic and political organizations raise money, organize work and carry it on for the benefit of a large number of persons who contribute no support. It would be absurd to suggest that whenever a voluntary organization benefits any group of people, it should be empowered to compel them by law or by economic pressure to contribute support.

The argument is also highly deceptive for three reasons. First, only a part of the dues and assessments of the unions is devoted to negotiating contracts. The unions have a great many activities such as political campaigns, social and economic propaganda, insurance, etc., to which no one should be compelled to contribute, particularly when a member can gain no personal benefit. Second, the real objective of forcing all workers to join unions is, as the union leaders themselves admit, not so much to compel them to pay their share of an expense, as to compel them to accept the discipline of the organization. Workers who become members add to the economic and political power of the union.

Third, the unions sought and obtained by law a special privilege: the right to represent any minority of nonmember employees and to make contracts binding on any such minority. The unions took away, by law, the right and freedom of individual employees to contract for themselves—and now the unions demand that nonmembers be compelled to pay for having their freedom of contract taken away and exercised against their will. The nonmember is not a "free rider," but a captive passenger.

### Power of Discipline

The argument based on the need for an increased power of discipline, which is being made with increasing vehemence, rests on the theory that non-union employees, who cannot be disciplined by depriving them of their employment, are a menace both to the union and to the employer, because they will not live up to contract obligations. This is a fraudulent argument, because the nonunion employee is just as much bound as the union employee to carry out the obligations of the trade agreement.

Also, without being made a member of the union, the independent worker is subject to employer discipline to an even greater degree than a union member. If he breaks contract obligations or refuses to obey management orders, he can and will be disciplined by the employer, and he will not have any union backing to support him in a recalcitrant position. On the other hand, if a union member gets in difficulty with the management, the union is obligated to support, if it can.

What the unions really mean is that they want the power of discipline over all employees, particularly so they will all strike, or otherwise support the union officials in whatever position they may take that is antagonistic to management. The fact is that the increased power of discipline given to union officials by compulsory unionism, is contrary to the interest of both the employer and the free workers.

There are various other arguments brought forward by unions in an effort to prove that a worker is better off as a compulsory member, than as a voluntary nonmember. For instance, the American Federation of Labor contends that if the employee is not a union member, the employee has no voice at all in determining rate of pay, hours or other conditions of employment. Theoretically, this appears to be plausible. But as a practical fact, a union member in one of the huge unions today has as small a voice in determining union policies and programs, as the average citizen who is not active in politics has in making the laws.

The most effective voice anyone can have in an organization, unless part of the ruling hierarchy, is the voice of opposition, the voice of criticism. This may be a small voice, but one which can be made effective if it is coupled with the power to withdraw from the organization, to refuse to give it moral and financial support, and to threaten unwise or vicious leadership with the development of a rival faction or organization to challenge its authority.

The unions claim that Right-to-Work laws are an "antilabor weapon." How can a law be "antilabor", which provides only that an employee be free from coercion either to join or not to join a union? How can a law sustaining the freedom of individuals of the laboring class be honestly called an "antilabor" law?

In my opinion, the unions are, in effect, claiming that it is against the interests of the worker to be free from such coercion. They are claiming that if the union approves of such coercion, then it is "anti-labor" to insist that the employee be kept free from any tyrannical use of this power. It is the unions that have claimed to be the ancient, time-honored enemy of such coercive power in the employer. Is it any better for similar power to reside on the union side? Is the union's argument against what they feel is excessive power, one of principle or one of placement?

The agreement for a union shop is called a "union security" agreement. This very designation is a confession that it is not the worker who is made more secure by union shop agreements. Only the union itself—that is, the union officialdom—is made more "secure" by such agreements. These union shop contracts, these "one party" monopolies, make it practically impossible for dissenters, even for a substantial majority, in the union to successfully oppose the dictatorial control of a well-entrenched machine of labor bosses.[10]

## Public Opinion Poll

In December 1985, in an effort to determine public opinion on the Right-to-Work issue, the Opinion Research Corporation designed and conducted a comprehensive study to measure public attitudes on the controversy. The outstanding finding of the study was that, with or without the Right-to-Work label, and regardless of the argument presented, solid majorities of the public lined up on the side of voluntary union membership. The public's view on the nine aspects of the Right-to-Work controversy follows:

*The "Free-Rider" Argument.* (1) Even though they may benefit from the union, they should be allowed to decide for themselves whether to join or not. (66 % yes.) (2) Because they may benefit from the union, they should be required to join or lose their jobs. (28% yes.)

*Firing for Refusal to Join Union.* (1) A company should not be permitted to fire an employee refusing to join a union. (70% – yes.) (2) A company should be permitted to fire an employee refusing to join a union. (21% – yes.)

*Open Shop vs. Union Shop.* (1) A worker should be permitted to hold a job whether or not the worker belongs to a union. (60% – yes.) (2) A worker should be able to get a job if the worker doesn't already belong, but has to join after becoming hired. (32% – yes.)

*Right-to-Work Laws Without Definition.* (1) Are you in favor of Right-to-Work laws in states like this one or are you opposed to Right-to-Work laws? (58% in favor; 21% – opposed.)

*Right-to-Work Laws With Definition.* (1) Some states have passed Right-to-Work laws which provide that a worker cannot be discharded from a job for either joining or not joining a union. If you were asked to vote on such a law, would you vote, for or against it? (61% – for; 24% – against.)

*The States Rights Option.* (1) Whether you are personally for Right-to-Work laws or not, do you think the federal government should or should not allow each state to decide whether it wants to pass such a law? (63% – allow states; 22% – not allow states.)

*Contract Rights.* (1) In states with Right-to-Work laws, the company and the union cannot make a contract requiring workers to join the union in order to hold their jobs. (61% – prefer this.) (2) In states without Right-to-Work laws, the company and the union can make a contract requiring the workers involved to join the union in order to hold their jobs. (25% – prefer this.)

*Repeal of 14(b).* (1) If Congress keeps Section 14(b) of the Taft-Hartley Act, it means that states can continue to have Right-to-Work laws, if they want. If Congress repeals Section 14(b) of the Taft-Hartley Act, it means that states cannot have Right-to-Work laws. Which do you think Congress should do? (64% – keep section 14(b); 14% – repeal section 14(b).)

*National Voluntary vs. Compulsory Membership.* (1) Congress should pass a law making all union membership voluntary; thus, workers can hold their jobs whether or not they join a union. (63% – yes.) (2) Congress should pass a law that, where there is a union, all workers involved must join to keep their jobs. (25% – yes.)

## Summary

The right of workers to organize has been perverted to include the privilege of compelling them to join or pay fees to labor organizations against their will, and the privilege of forcing employers to herd their employees into unions. Right-to-Work laws seek to remedy these flagrant abuses of power; however, 30 states do not have such laws.

The only responsible action that would terminate compulsory unionism and the abuses associated with it while protecting the right of citizens to get and hold jobs (whether they belong or pay fees to unions or not), is the enactment of a National Right-to-Work Law. The sooner this happens, the better off all involved parties, including labor organizations, will be.

### Footnotes

[1]The National Right-to-Work Committee, "14(b) Is Not An Odd Shoe" (Arlington, VA: *The National Right-to-Work Committee*, January 1975), p. 2.

[2]The National Right-to-Work Committee, "What Happened to Liberty and Justice for All?" (Arlington, VA: *The National Right-to-Work Committee*, August 1976), p. 2.

[3]The National Right-to-Work Committee, "The Right-To-Work Issue: Should Americans Be Compelled to Join Labor Unions?" (Arlington, VA: *The National Right-to-Work Committee*, August 1976), p. 3.

[4]Campaigne, Jameson G., *Check-Off* (Chicago: Henry Regency Company, 1961), p. 20.

[5]Richberg, Donald R., *Labor Union Monopoly*, (Chicago: Henry Regency Company, 1966), p. 11.

[6]The National Right-to-Work Committee, "The Voluntarism of Samuel Gompers" (Arlington, VA: *The National Right-to-Work Committee*, August 1973), p. 3.

[7]Skibbins, Gerald J., and Weyman, Caroline S., "The Right-to-Work Controversy," *Harvard Business Review*, July–August 1966, p. 9.

[8]Richberg, Donald R., *Labor Union Monopoly* (Chicago: Henry Regency Company, 1966), p. 5.

[9]Skibbins, Gerald J., and Weyman, Caroline S., *op. cit.,* p. 9.

[10]Richberg, Donald R., *Labor Union Monopoly, op. cit.,* pp. 8–9.

# The Labor Position On Repeal
# Of Section 14(b) Of Taft-Hartley

## ABSTRACT

Labor arguments are presented concerning the "right-to-work" issues, in an attempt to understand both sides of the issue, make an intelligent assessment of the opposing viewpoints, and possibly, refine one's own arguments.

## Introduction

The basic federal law governing labor-management relations is the National Labor Relations (Wagner) Act of 1935, as amended by the 1947 Labor-Management Relations (Taft-Hartley) Act and subsequent laws. The depression-bred Wagner Act was highly favorable to labor organizations. The Taft-Hartley Act, which was bitterly opposed by labor, nullified and modified some of the Wagner Act guarantees and, in so doing, gave rise to state right-to-work laws through Section 14(b).

A right-to-work law is a law which prohibits labor-management agreements requiring union membership as a condition of getting or keeping a job.

This paper will examine the reasons why Section 14(b) should be repealed.

## Background

Since the 1940's, the issue of right-to-work laws has been an extremely emotional one. Labor unions bitterly resent the tag name of right-to-work, saying it is a misnomer for antiunion laws. Supporters of such laws say workers should be free to join or not to join unions.

The major amendments to the Wagner Act were contained in the Taft-Hartley Act, passed by a Republican Congress in 1947 over President Truman's veto. Passage of the bill followed the heaviest wave of major strikes in recent history, some of which had tied up entire industries like steel, coal and automobiles. The strikes reflected labor's desire to catch up with the rest of the economy after a long period of wartime wage controls, under which most unions had complied with a 1941 "no strike" pledge made by labor leaders.

The Taft-Hartley Act was, obviously, opposed by organized labor. The Act forbade, among other things, the closed shop and the closed shop hiring hall, a union-run employment service which referred only union members to employers. In addition, Section 14(b) of the Act essentially empowered the states and territories to pass right-to-work laws forbidding employers and unions from signing union shop contracts.

Ordinarily, state labor relations laws do not apply to unions and businesses which are involved in interstate commerce or activities affecting interstate commerce and which, therefore, are governed by federal labor laws. However, the 1947 Taft-Hartley Act created special rules with regard to state right-to-work laws. The Taft-Hartley Act itself forbade the closed shop. It permitted the union shop, however, with the proviso that union shop contracts would be legal only in states which did not forbid them. (A union shop contract requires employees to join a union within a specified time after being hired. Employees who refuse to do so must be dismissed.) The effect of this proviso Section 14(b) was to validate state right-to-work laws wherever they were passed, for unions covered by the Taft-Hartley Act and not normally subject to state laws.

As a result, existing state right-to-work laws are applicable to all unions and businesses (unless exempted by the state laws themselves), with one exception. The exception involves the Railway Labor Act. Railroads, airlines and other firms and their employees which are subject to the Railway Labor Act, rather than the Taft-Hartley Act, are not subject to state right-to-work laws.

## Legislative History of 14(b) of Taft-Hartley

The genesis of Section 14(b) was this: under the House bill, H.R. 3020, a new section 13 of the National Labor Relations Act was included to assure that nothing in the act was to be construed as authorizing any closed shop, union shop, maintenance of membership, or other form of compulsory unionism agreement, in any state where the execution of such agreement would be contrary to state law. Many states had by that time (1947) enacted laws or adopted constitutional provisions to make all forms of compulsory unionism in those states illegal. It was never the intention of the National Labor Relations Act, as is disclosed by the legislative history of that act, to preempt the field in this regard to deprive the states of their powers to prevent compulsory unionism. Neither the so-called "closed shop" proviso in Section 8(3) of the existing act, nor the union shop and maintenance of membership proviso in section 8(a)(3) of the conference agreement, could be said to authorize arrangements of this sort in states where such arrangements were contrary to the state policy. To make certain that there should be no question about this, section 13 was included in the House bill. The conference agreement, in section 14(b), contains a provision having the same effect and was the result of the conference committee's work.

## The Case For Repeal of Section 14(b)

The following are major labor arguments advocating the repeal of Section 14(b) of the Taft-Hartley Act:

### Union Security

The union security provision, which a union inserts, says a worker shall join the union—or commence paying a fee to it—after a certain period of time on the job.

Under the union shop, it is the employer rather than the union who decides what person shall be hired for a job. An applicant is hired only with the qualifications for the job. Then, and only then, is the requirement enforced to join the union holding the contract with the employer. Under the union shop contract, the union cannot say whom the employer will hire. Under a union shop agreement, an employee loses his union membership only for failure to pay normal fees and assessments.

As the bargaining representative of all the workers, the union can be most effective—and it can best represent all the attitudes of the workers—when all the workers are members. The strength of a union depends on what proportion of the workers belong. In some situations, it is impossible for a union to maintain itself without some sort of union security; and in all situations, union security gives added strength to a union.

Through an effective union representing all the workers, the individual employee achieves a more effective voice in determining the wages paid for work, and the conditions on the job. Labor-management agreements, in addition, provide an orderly procedure for the handling of grievances and lay-offs, and for the rehiring of workers.

Further, since under the Wagner Act a union, once certified as bargaining agent, must "represent equally all employees in the bargaining unit"—whether union members or not—it seems only fair that these employees be required to join the union.

Labor supporters of the repeal of 14(b) also argue that such repeal would not result in compulsory participation in union activities, because various court rulings have held that, although workers in a union shop must pay union dues, they need not participate in union activities. Furthermore, union shops would not automatically follow the repeal of 14(b), because management must agree to their establishment in the collectively bargained agreement.

On May 24, 1965, Labor Secretary W. Willard Wirtz testified in support of repeal of 14(b) when hearings were conducted on H.R. 77, a bill to repeal Section 14(b). Repeal of Section 14(b), Wirtz said, "is not—as some have attempted to suggest—a proposal to 'make the union shop mandatory' . . . for the point is that this is a matter which should be left to responsible private decisionmaking—to be resolved one way or the other in private collective bargaining. The central argument is that all who receive the benefits of union representation should contribute to its support, particularly its financial support," Wirtz stressed.[1]

Paul H. Douglas (D, IL) on October 6, 1965, in arguing for repeal during debate in the Senate, said that "an agreement for the union shop is not perpetual; it can be revoked at any time if a majority of the workers become dissatisfied with it." He said 14(b) gave states "a hunting license to prohibit employers and employees from coming to a voluntary agreement to establish the union shop under free collective bargaining." He added that under 14(b), states were "given a hunting license to weaken or break the unions." He added, "The repeal of 14(b) would not require the establishment of compulsory unionism or a union shop by law."[2]

### Individuals Rights

Some who oppose union security are apt to say that union security is undemocratic, when in fact, union security is simply an expression of our democratic concept of majority rule. Majority rule is the very basis of our society and civilization.

To argue against union security is, in effect, to argue that the minority has even more rights than the majority—and that goes counter to all the common sense rules for our democratic society. The union shop operates where a majority of the workers have decided in its favor, and where the employer has agreed with the union to a union security contract. Minority rights must always be protected, but minority rights cannot be allowed to take precedence over majority rights.

Certainly there have been abuses by unions as well as by governments. But few people are aware of the strict codes of democratic conduct which the government, by law, has imposed on unions. No other voluntary organization must meet such requirements of frequent secret ballot elections, freedom to criticize elected officials without reprisal, and democratic procedures for setting policy and making decisions.

Noting that public debate surrounding repeal has often been "extreme" and "even irrelevant," Secretary of Labor Wirtz, in testimony on May 24, 1965, stated that the real issue was not whether employees had the "right to work," but if a majority had the "right to decide," that all be represented by a union.[3]

## The Free Rider

The union's activities on behalf of the workers require funds. If the union is to represent properly all the workers in the group it must have their participation and financial support. Union dues are an obligation that workers owe to the union that serves them. People who do not join the union, nor support it financially, are known as free riders.

Under the Taft-Hartley law, unions are required to provide services for everyone in the plant or shop included in the bargaining unit, whether they are members of the union or not. These services—bargaining the basic contract, handling grievances, and representation at the state level to increase unemployment and workers' compensation benefits—cost money to provide. Someone has to pay for the time of the people who manage these things for workers in the plant. There is only one place the money can come from—the people who are getting the service. Since the law requires this service to be provided for all, it is only logical that all should help pay for the benefits received. Yet Section 14(b) is a license to make those services available and free to some. No other service organization is in this position. No one may be obliged to join such other organizations, but neither do those organizations have to provide service to those on the outside.

On May 26, 1965, in testimony on H.R. 77, A. C. Skinner, then president of the Mine, Mill and Smelter Workers Union, said that "when not bothered, pressured or influenced, the overwhelming majority of working men and women will join a union voluntarily." He said if right-to-work were a valid concept, then Americans should also be free to refuse payment of federal taxes and free to disregard scores of other obligations where majority rule prevails on every citizen in our society.

If the union, under the law, must represent all the workers, then it seems fair that all the workers should support the union by belonging to it.

## Uniform Application of National Law

Section 14(b) is the only provision of federal labor law that is not uniformly, nor evenly applied, to all states.

Willard Wirtz, in his testimony, stated that not applying Taft-Hartley uniformly to all states resulted in "disruptive competition" among states, by encouraging business to locate where there is less union activity, mainly in the South.

The House Education and Labor Committee has said "Section 14(b) was an explicit departure from the principle specifically recognized in the basic provisions of the National Labor Relations Act that a uniform national labor relations policy is necessary and desirable." It said, "The isolation of union security as a separate and severable issue to be considered wholly apart from all other matters, is no longer realistic, if indeed it ever was. The fact is that the special treatment given by the statute to this single matter has been the source of continued confusion and uncertainty with respect to a widening span of related matters . . ."[4]

It stands to reason that Taft-Hartley should be applied uniformly, lest its other provisions be haphazardly applied.

### Other Arguments

Union spokespeople believe that right-to-work laws are, to a large extent, responsible for the slow growth of unions in the South, and many other states with such laws. They further argue that in many parts of the South, right-to-work laws are only one of a battery of antilabor devices designed to keep unions weak, keep wages low and keep business taxes (for such items as unemployment insurance) low—thereby creating a favorable business climate to "pirate" industry from other areas.

Finally, unions contend that antiunion business groups often put forward right-to-work proposals in state legislatures not only for their own sake, but also to absorb the attentions and resources of unions in a fight against the proposals, thus diverting the unions from pushing favorable welfare and tax legislation through the state legislatures. Alluding to this allegation on May 25, 1965, in House testimony on H.R. 77, AFL-CIO President George Meany said, "In the last eight years alone—from the beginning of 1958 to the present time—we in the AFL-CIO have engaged in more than 40 significant battles over so-called 'right to work' laws . . . It is impossible to estimate how many millions of dollars and how many thousands of man-hours were thrown into these contests by both sides—a staggering waste of money and manpower."[5]

There is no doubt that these battles will continue.

### Summary

Given the reasons set forth above, it is easy to see that Section 14(b) of Taft-Hartley should be repealed. In the words of Samuel Gompers, "Organized labor's insistence upon and work for, not the 'closed shop,' as our opponents term it, but the union shop, in agreement with employers, mutually entered into for the advantage of both and the maintenance of industrial peace with equity and justice for both, is to the economic, social and moral advancement of all our people."[6]

The union shop, in agreement with employers, is the application of the principle that those who enjoy the benefits and advantages resulting from an agreement, shall also equally bear the moral and financial responsibilities involved.

## Footnotes

[1]Congressional Quarterly Almanac 1965, *Government Printing Office*, Washington, DC, February 1966, p. 824.

[2]*Ibid.*, p. 831.

[3]*Ibid.*, p. 824.

[4]Report of the House Education and Labor Committee on H.R. 77, *Government Printing Office*, Washington, DC, June 22, 1965, p. 3.

[5]Congressional Quarterly Almanac 1965, p. 820.

[6]"The Truth About 'Right-to-Work' Laws," *AFL-CIO News*, Washington, DC, January 1977, p. 2.

# The Agency Shop: Arguments Pro And Con

## ABSTRACT

The "agency shop" form of union security, whereby certain employees must pay union dues whether they are members or not, is one of the most detested contract clauses requested of management. The remarkable increase in the number of employers agreeing to such clauses causes the author to examine the issue from a union and management point of view.

A union security provision of collective bargaining agreements is a clause requiring employees to become members of a union or assume some financial obligation to the union. Among the more common forms of union security agreements are the union shop, agency shop, and maintenance-of-membership clauses. The union shop is a form of union security requiring membership in the labor organization as a condition of employment within a specified number of days after an individual begins work. Maintenance-of-membership is a type of union security arrangement demanding present union members to maintain their membership status for the duration of the contract as a condition of continued employment, but does not require other employees to join. The agency shop obligates all employees in the bargaining unit who do not join the union, to pay periodic dues and assessments, usually a monthly amount equivalent to the amount paid by union members, as a condition of employment to help defray the union's expenses when acting as a bargaining agent.

The agency shop provision was first introduced in 1946 at the Ford Motor Company in Ontario, Canada. Justice I. C. Rand stipulated that nonunion men in the bargaining unit should not be forced to join the union as a condition for holding their jobs, but should be obliged, instead, to contribute the equivalent of dues to the union for services rendered as bargaining agent.[1] Justice Rand gave as his main reason for imposing the agency-shop provision, the elimination of "free riders"—a name given to those nonunion workers in a bargaining unit who enjoy the benefits of union representation but make no financial contribution to the union. The existence of these free riders was made possible by the legal requirement that unions represent everyone in the bargaining unit, but the lack of a legal requirement that they join the union, once it is awarded recognition. Thus the union must represent everyone in the bargaining unit, but no individual in the unit is legally compelled to join the union. Those who do not join are known as free riders.

Unions in the United States showed little interest in the Canadian decision, however, since the Wagner Act of 1935 had declared the closed shop, in which union membership is required before the individual receives the job, legal. Consequently, U.S. unions could avoid the problem of free riders by negotiating for a closed shop provision. It was not until 1947 when Congress passed the Taft-Hartley Act, that U.S. unions started to investigate the provisions of the agency shop. The Taft-Hartley Act outlawed the closed shop provision and partially surrendered federal jurisdiction over union security clauses in labor-management agreements. Under Section 14(b) of the Taft-Hartley Act, the new law permitted the states to legislate in the field of union security, provided their laws were "more restrictive than Federal law."[2] Remember that in a **closed** shop, union membership is required before the individual can be offered employment, while in a **union** shop the individual has a specified number of days after beginning work to join the union. The distinction is important, because in a closed shop, the union has the first input into the hiring decision, since management can only accept applicants who have first been accepted by the union; while in the union shop, management can hire anyone they wish, since union membership is secondary.

Thus 14(b) of Taft-Hartley started the right-to-work laws, which stated that union membership could not be required by unions or employers as a condition for employment. This, in effect, made union shops illegal, at which point unions became interested in other ways to maintain union membership and dues, including agency shop clauses. As a result, labor unions in the U.S. turned to this device through the 1950's to dodge state right-to-work laws banning the union shop.

One of the first unions in the United States that tried to enforce the agency shop clause was a Florida local of the Retail Clerks' International Association. It succeeded in persuading an employer, a supermarket, to incorporate an agency shop clause in its contract. As might be expected, the nonunion workers who, up to this point had enjoyed the freedom of not having to pay union dues, objected to this new arrangement. These workers brought suit against the employer and union in the Florida State courts, and eventually the case went to the U.S. Supreme Court. The Retail Clerks argued that the Taft-Hartley grant of power to the states over union security clauses, did not extend to the agency shop.[3]

The Supreme Court ruled that a State court in Florida—where agency shops are not strictly prohibited by law—had the right to interpret the State's right-to-work laws to mean that an agency shop is illegal.[4] In other words, the Court held that the States' Rights provision of Taft-Hartley could be interpreted to permit banning the agency shop, as well as the union shop. This meant that agency shops are legal only in states that do not object to them. The unions' reaction was to combat the right-to-work movement more vigorously than ever before.

The National Right-to-Work Committee, a pro business group chartered to combat compulsory union membership, immediately hailed the new ruling as a boost to its drive to increase the number of right-to-work states, a drive the AFL-CIO called a "union-busting" campaign.[5] As of December 1989, there were 20 states with right-to-work laws: Alabama, Arizona, Arkansas, Florida, Georgia, Iowa, Indiana, Kansas, Louisiana, Mississippi, Nebraska, Nevada, North Carolina, South Carolina, South Dakota, Tennessee, Texas, Utah, Virginia, and Wyoming. Out of these states, Indiana is the only right-to-work state where the agency shop is declared legal.

The second case specifically dealing with the agency shop issue involved the United Auto Workers. In 1955, the UAW finally won a full union shop from General Motors. Later on, a problem arose in applying the national agreement to GM plants in Indiana. Although the Indiana Supreme Court had ruled that the State law did not extend to the agency shop, GM refused a UAW demand for it in Indiana. The corporation argued that, regardless of State law, federal law prohibited the agency shop. Company lawyers could not find in the Taft-Hartley Act's authorization of the union shop, any duty on the part of the employer to bargain on the agency shop. UAW then filed an unfair labor practice charge against GM, accusing it of refusal to bargain.[6]

The Supreme Court eventually ruled that GM did not have to bargain on the agency shop issue, stating that state courts had authority to "enforce" right-to-work laws in the states that have such laws.[7] The importance of the court decision lies in the fact that it places the enforcement of state right-to-work laws in the state, and not the federal government. As noted earlier, after this decision almost all right-to-work states prohibited the agency shop.

While it is important to review the legislative history of the agency shop question, it is equally important to understand why there has been so much controversy over this issue.

### Labor's Position

One of the main arguments for the agency shop is that Taft-Hartley requires a union that has been certified as a collective bargaining representative of the workers by the NLRB to represent all workers in the bargaining unit, whether they are union members or not. Unions feel that individual workers should not be able to receive benefits secured by their union, without having to pay some amount for the expenses involved. The facts show that unions spend large sums of money in negotiating better wages and working conditions in the bargaining unit. They are also compelled by law to process grievances and extend contract terms without discrimination to members or nonmembers. Under these circumstances, it seems unfair for a worker to refuse to pay dues, while taking advantage of the same benefits as union members.

As the reader might imagine, the free rider was very much resented by union workers. The agency shop tends to eliminate some of the hostility between dues-paying, nonunion workers and the union workers. The strong feeling of resentment toward the free rider is evident in the following quote from a union official in the oil industry:

> "You'll find a lot of hot numbers working in the oil industry. The time has come for them to join up, help pay the freight, quit hitchhiking. Persuasion should be used. If that doesn't work, then we'll have to think of something else. The government doesn't allow free loaders at tax time. The union shouldn't either."[8]

In defending the agency shop provision, George Harrison of the Railway Clerks said: "We have always felt that it is manifestly unfair that individual employees should be permitted to obtain all of the benefits which result from the collective bargaining process and be subject to none of the obligations of that process."[9] At the very least, the agency shop would require nonunion members to pay for benefits in the collective bargaining process.

### Management's Position

Those that object to the agency shop clause contend that it is a form of bribery: to keep a job an individual must pay money to the union. There is no good reason why a nonunion employee forced to pay dues under the agency shop clause, would decide not to become a member of that union. Hence, the practical effect of an agency shop is the same as a union shop. Right-to-work advocates have consistently argued that the union shop violates workers' rights of free association, by compelling them to join a union against their will. If agency shop clauses lead to union shop effects for the majority of workers, then an individual's right to free association has again been violated. It would seem almost foolish for an employee **not** to join the union, since dues are required, and the arrangement inadvertently forces a worker into making that decision.

Management also contend that, in some cases, an individual's religion might prevent joining a union or paying dues to a union. To answer this, some union contracts allow those people to pay union dues to a charity.

Another argument against the agency shop concerns the objection of many employees to having any portion of their dues expended for political purposes. Federal law has long forbidden the union to use dues to contribute directly to political campaigns. But even these provisions do not prevent labor organizations from drawing upon dues to defray the costs of lobbying, or to pay for political articles and radio and television advertisements for candidates they support. The Right-to-Work committee addressed this issue by stating, "major labor unions seek to hold American workers captive in compulsory unionism and use their money to enhance their political interests and economic issues."[10]

Such a statement is evidence of strong feelings by the anti-agency shop forces.

## Conclusion

Arguments on both sides of this issue are compelling and deserving of merit. As is usually the case, a compromise seems the most equitable solution. This compromise should take the form of a "service fee" clause whereby non-union members in the bargaining unit would pay only their share of the actual collective bargaining costs. All other union related expenses, such as general promotion, lobbying, political campaigns, etc., could be paid for by fees (dues) assessed on union members only. In this way, the stronger objections of both labor and management can be met most equitably.

## Footnotes

[1]Masse, Benjamin L., "Is the Agency Shop Legal?" *America*, Volume 107, December 15, 1962, p. 1244.

[2]*Ibid.*, p. 1245.

[3]"Victory for Right-to-Work Law: An Issue in 1964 Campaign?" *U.S. News & World Report*, Volume 55, December 16, 1963, p. 108.

[4]"Trouble with the Agency," *Time*, Volume 81, July 14, 1963, p. 91.

[5]"Labor Loses Agency Shop Case," *Engineering News*, Volume 171, December 12, 1963, p. 74.

[6]Masse, p. 1245.

[7]"Labor Loses Agency Shop Case," *loc. cit.*

[8]Barbash, Jack, *The Practice of Unionism*, (New York: Harper & Row Publishers, 1956) p. 159.

[9]*Ibid.*, p. 160.

[10]Bok, Kerek and Dunlop, John T., *Labor and the American Community*, (New York: Simon and Schuster) 1970, p. 103.

# Is Codetermination A Workable Idea
# For U.S. Labor-Management Relations?

*Kenneth A. Kovach*
*Ben F. Sands, Jr.*
*William W. Brooks*

## ABSTRACT

The German experience with worker participation since the early 1900's provides a basis of comparison to the situation in the United States.

Participation by employees in decision making at the upper levels of private industry has been the exception, rather than the rule in the United States, but there are indications this situation will change. Such diverse individuals as United Auto Workers' Vice-President Irving Bluestone, Undersecretary of Commerce Sidney Harman, and Federal Mediation Service Commissioner Samuel Sackman have spoken of the increasing need for worker involvement in decisionmaking. In addition, experiments with employee participation in such firms as Harman International Industries and Carborundum Co., and the current Chrysler-UAW agreement allowing union President Douglas Fraser a seat on the company's board of directors, are evidence that rhetoric is being replaced, at least in some instances, by action.

To evaluate the potential for this idea in the United States, it is necessary to define several terms and trace the history of one of the more highly developed, legally mandated systems of labor participation in an industrialized nation.

The degree of integration of all members of an organization into the decision making process ranges from zero (all decisions made by one person) to 100 percent (anarchy). The types of decisions (working conditions, societal responsibilities, production, financial matters marketing approach, etc.) form subsets within the overall system of decision making.

Originally, the major decisions affecting workers were made by religious leaders or the nobility. With the coming of industrialization, decisions were made by the owners of capital, who regarded workers as one of the means of production. For various reasons—increasing wealth of the workers, higher levels of education in the labor force, greater complexity of the technological means of production, organization among the workers, etc.—it became necessary and desirable to introduce a degree of industrial democracy, involving the labor force in the decisions affecting conditions of work, methods of production, and, ultimately, financial and investment decisions.

Research into the evolution of this development reveals many descriptive terms. Among the more popular are participative management, industrial democracy, *autogestion* (French for self-management), and *Mitbestimmung* (German for codetermination). It is interesting to note that one of the major indices used in the United States usually lumps these terms under participative management, although they mean entirely different things, insofar as management, labor, and society are concerned.[1] While it may be true that they are parts of a spectrum along which worker participation may be measured, the results of each can differ greatly, and the workability of each may be dependent upon exogenous factors such as culture, economic development, and other environmental conditions.

Labor leaders, industrialists, and society should be aware of the distinctions and differences among the various levels of organizational democracy, if for no other reason than that the subject cannot be discussed rationally unless the terms are well defined.

Henry Mintzberg pointed out that many movements (degrees of participation, in our terms) hardly touched the United States. He stated that what has instead received considerable attention here is "participative management." In discussing this concept, he distinguished two of its propositions. One of a factual—that is, testable—nature, is that participation leads to increased productivity: involve employees and they will produce more, management is told (e.g., Likert, 1961). The other, a value proposition not subject to verification, is that participation is a value worthy in and of itself: "In a 'democratic' society workers have the right to participate in the organizations that employ them." The American debate over participative management has focused almost exclusively on the first factual proposition (although the proponents really seem to be committed to the second value position).[2]

The latter concept, the right of workers to participate in decision making, forms the ideological base for the actions of many European unions. It also is the one that causes major concern among U.S. managers and, it may be added parenthetically, many U.S. unions. James Furlong said that "the theme of extending to economic life the principles of political democracy—the right of all citizens to help choose their leaders and to express their opinions freely on the choice and fulfillment of group goals—is the red thread that runs through all defenses of *Mitbestimmung* (codetermination)."[3]

## Codetermination in West Germany

One West German experiment is of particular interest. A combination of historical developments—a perception of common interests among industrialists and labor in dealing with an occupying army, and general cultural and social factors—has resulted in legislation that requires the participation of many West German workers in decision making at all levels. Since July 1976, West German law has given workers near parity with stockholders in controlling the management of approximately 625 major companies, employing about five million workers.[4]

In March 1979, West Germany's high court dismissed a suit brought by twenty-nine employers' associations and nine companies, asserting that the 1976 law undermined property rights and blurred the line between companies and unions in collective bargaining.[5]

The 1976 law, *Mitbestimmung in der Bundes Republic Deutschland* (codetermination in the Federal Republic of Germany) is the latest in a long series of legislative acts establishing and defining the rights of workers in German industry.

As early as 1848, political representatives of German labor demanded the establishment of factory committees to include workers. Although no legislation resulted from this first parliamentary discussion, worker committees were established in some companies on a voluntary basis. These were consulted primarily on social matters.[6] In 1905, mining companies with more than 100 employees were required to establish worker committees under the provisions of the Prussian Mining Law.[7] This law, and subsequent regulations in 1916 and 1920, established worker committees with full rights of participation in decisions concerning working conditions and limited rights in financial and personnel matters, although final decisions were made by management alone.

The Nazi regime dissolved all trade unions. Union headquarters were occupied by the military and their funds confiscated. Most of the leading trade unionists were arrested, and workers and employees were placed in the German work front.

Following World War II, German industrialists, in an attempt to prevent the decartelization of the steel industry, made common cause with German trade unions in dealing with the occupation authorities. Works councils were established along the lines of the Works Councils Act of 1920. The 1946 Allied Control Council Law No. 22 provided the basis for these councils. Finally, in 1951, the Act on the Codetermination of Workers in the Supervisory and Management Boards of Undertakings in the Mining Industry and the Iron and

Steel Production Industry was passed. This was, according to Furlong, the "high-water point in the *Mitbestimmung* movement."[8]

Current German law requires a works council *(Betriebsrat)* in any firm employing more than five workers. The council must represent both blue-collar and white-collar workers in proportion to their numbers in the company. Nationwide elections to the councils are held triennially. Ballots are secret, and only workers are allowed to vote. The number of representatives elected ranges from one (five to twenty employees) to thirty-one (7,001 to 9,000 employees). In companies with more than 9,000 employees, two additional works council members are required for every additional 3,000 employees or part thereof.

Companies with several plants or divisions must establish a central council for the firm. Normally, each works council furnishes two representatives to the central council. In conglomerates, a group works council may be established at the option of the separate councils.

Certain works council members must be released to devote all their time to council matters. The number released ranges from one (in units with more than 300 employees) to twelve (in units with more than 10,000 employees). All members are entitled to four weeks of paid vacation during the first year, to attend training courses and other educational functions related to the activities of the council. The firm must provide facilities, information and assistance to the council.

The works council does not bargain for wages and working conditions normally negotiated by the unions on a regional or national basis, but it has a right to codetermination—an equal say with management in deciding such issues as:

— job evaluation, piece rates, and wage structures;
— working hours, overtime arrangements, breaks, and holiday schedules;
— staffing policies, including guidelines for recruiting, assigning and dismissing workers;
— social plans, i.e., measures to mitigate the effect of layoffs on workers in the event of reduction;
— training, occupational safety and welfare schemes;
— allocation of company housing; and
— workers' conduct on the shop floor.[9]

Hiring, discharge, work allocation, promotion, and demotion decisions require the consent of the council. Unilateral action by the employer in these areas is not allowed.

In companies with more than 100 employees, an economic council (*Wirtschaftausschuss*) of four to eight members is appointed by the works council. The economic council has limited powers, but has the right to information on important issues, i.e., manufacturing methods, automation, production programs, and data concerning the financial condition of the firm. Analysis of this information is the responsibility of the economic council, while final approval of proposed actions of the firm rests with the works council.

Codetermination also functions at the management level. In German joint stock or incorporated public firms, a supervisory board (*Aufsichtsrat*) is elected by the shareholders and is generally comparable to the board of directors in U.S. firms. A management board (*Vorstand*) conducts the day-to-day business of the firm. No member of either board may serve on the other. Private, limited liability firms (the most popular form of organization in Germany) are not required to have a supervisory board, unless they have more than 500 employees. Smaller private firms with unlimited liability (partnerships, etc.) are outside the limits of the Codetermination Act.

The power of the supervisory board to appoint and supervise the management board, and to make major decisions concerning the goals and objectives of the firm, make membership on the board extremely important to the worker. Current law requires three general levels of worker representation on the supervisory boards:

1. parity with shareholders in coal, iron and steel producing industries employing more than 1,000 workers;

2. one-third representation in joint stock companies employing up to 2,000 workers and in other limited liability companies employing between 500 and 2,000 workers; and

3. equal representation (with a bias in favor of the shareholders) in firms with a work force of more than 2,000.[10]

The management board constitutes the lower half of the two-tier board system. In the steel industry, the workers choose the labor director (*Arbeitsdirektor*), although this power is not inherent in current law. The labor director (personnel director, in U.S. terms) has specific responsibilities in staff and social matters.

Experience has shown that, to fulfill the purpose and objectives of the Codetermination Act and in the interest of the undertaking, concerned persons appointed as labor directors should have the special confidence of the employees.[11] Furlong says that, "Whether the unions in fact control the post, will be left to capital and labor to thrash out."[12]

We are beginning to hear discussion of the desirability and practicality of implementing a codetermination system in the United States. It is important, then, to address the issue from the relative perspectives of U.S. management and labor organizations, since the latter most likely will be the structure through which employee involvement gained.

## The Union Perspective

Since most codetermination schemes already implemented in the United States include the particular labor organization and represent workers on the governing board instead of, or in addition to, unspecified employee representatives, it becomes imperative to discuss codetermination from a labor perspective.[13]

Before doing so, it is important to reemphasize the differences between U.S. unions and their West German counterparts which have embraced the concept of codetermination. As noted earlier, the works councils in West Germany have two main roles. They are responsible for plant bargaining over issues—job evaluation, working hours, training, etc.—not dealt with in collective agreements at regional or national levels. Many of these issues are also of primary interest to national unions in the United States. In addition, the works council is considered the first and fundamental forum for codetermination.

The wildcat strikes at the plant level that plague so many European industries are virtually unknown in Germany. Strikes can be called only at the regional or national level. If the works council and the employer are unable to agree on an issue, either may apply for arbitration by a committee of an equal number of worker and employee representatives and one neutral member.

Unlike members of shop steward committees in the United States, German works council members (with the exception of two or three members, depending on the size of the company) are not required to be union members. Any employee aged 18 or older may vote for council members; candidates must have been with the firm for at least six months.[14]

Much of the real power in unions in West Germany rests in small local units, rather than at the national level. Unions thus structured will be more receptive to ideas like codetermination, than will national unions like the U.S. system, which legally guarantees formal interaction with employers to discuss conditions of employment.

Many alleged experts, while acknowledging the success of codetermination or similar schemes in West Germany, Sweden, Israel, etc., contend that similar systems will not work in this country, due to the different role of labor organizations in the United States. The ultimate goal of organized labor in many countries where the industrial democracy experiments are working, has been to achieve an unspecified equal footing with management in the operation of the business. Thus, ideas such as codetermination have fit nicely into their long-range objectives. Government legislation of such schemes (e.g., West Germany) is viewed by labor as welcome assistance from an unexpected source. In the United States, however, organized labor has sought to fill a different role. Most U.S. unions think of themselves as the protectors of employees, as the intercessor variable between workers and management, serving as a safeguard against exploitive management action. The fact is that, after "economic gain," the reason given most frequently by new union members for joining is "protection against arbitrary management action." This is evidence of the popular perception of the degree to which unions fulfill this role.[15]

This being the case, many U.S. unions question the desirability of sitting with management on codetermination boards. They certainly must work with management, and they may wish their members to see them as interacting with management on an equal footing, but a checks-and-balances relationship still may be the more advantageous position, from organized labor's standpoint. As Albert Zack, AFL-CIO director of public relations, has said, it is preferable for U.S. unions to meet company representatives across the bargaining table, rather than try to get involved in traditional management functions.[16] The feeling of many union officials—that under the present collective bargaining arrangement labor probably bargains on as many, if not more, issues than the number they might have any effect on as members of a board of directors—adds to the conviction that the present way is the best. In addition, many in the labor movement feel that, unlike most European unions, they finally have won equality at the bargaining table, and they are reluctant to throw it away for the promise of equality in the boardroom.

Nevertheless, some unions in the public sector would welcome the introduction of codetermination. Richard Calistri of the American Federation of Government Employees has said that his organization would be delighted to have codetermination introduced, provided management genuinely cooperates and does not just look out for its own interests.[17] Part of the reason public sector unions are more positive about codetermination, may be that they have not been afforded the opportunity to bargain collectively on a range of issues, as have their private sector counterparts. Thus, for them, the prospect of sitting on a corporate board of directors may hold the promise of affecting an increased number of issues, a promise not as easily envisioned by private sector unions.

Another union perspective is represented by the International Brotherhood of Teamsters, Warehousemen, and Helpers of America, who regard the question of codetermination in U.S. industry as moot. While agreeing that it might benefit organized labor, the Teamsters contend that implementation in this country would be both impractical (the membership is not seen as favoring it) and counter to the free enterprise system.[18]

The only major private sector union to endorse the idea wholeheartedly appears to be the United Automobile Workers (UAW). As mentioned earlier, UAW Vice-President Irving Bluestone and Undersecretary of Commerce Sidney Harman have worked together to bring codetermination closer to implementation in the United States experimenting with its introduction in Bolivar, Tennessee (Harman), and Jamestown, New York (Carborundum). In both instances, the experiments have been reasonably successful.[19]

It is ironic that while many in the management sector of the federal government, such as Sidney Harman and Commissioner Sackman, have spoken favorably of codetermination, it is the increased involvement of such individuals in labor-management relations, necessitated by the new system, that may well be the major negative aspect of the plan, in the eyes of labor leaders. Based on experience in other countries, there is no doubt that the introduction of codetermination would, at least initially, mean increased government involvement in labor-management relations. It is generally accepted that more laws will be needed to govern the composition of these boards, as well as their jurisdiction over traditional collective bargaining subjects, their relationship to stockholders, etc. The of the federal government's imposing to this extent in private sector labor-management relations is outside the traditions and interests of the American labor movement. Most labor leaders would prefer to bargain with private employers, than to wrestle with government bureaucrats.

## The Management Perspective

From the perspective of American business owners and managers, industrial democracy represents both threat and promise. The perceived threat to managerial aims has been evidenced by more than a century of active struggle **against** organized labor—from resistance to early railroad strikes in the Midwest, to current textile industry boycotts and legal battles in the South. While steady inroads have been made into formerly management-determined conditions of employment such as employee benefits, health, and safety, resistance to workers' sharing in planning and operations decisions has remained strong and effective. Decision making in the American workplace is still viewed as management property.

Notwithstanding the threatening aspect of industrial democracy, its promise has received increasing emphasis, as concern about worker productivity has risen in the 1980's. Several recent studies have indicated that worker participation programs often have been successful in raising productivity.[20] Such venerable strategies to increase worker participation as the Scanlon Plan and the incentive plans at Kaiser Steel and Lincoln Electric Company, have been outdone in popularity by recent formulas for job enrichment, team projects, management by objectives, and other participative schemes. These latter attempts to involve American workers in the operation of the business do not envision participation in direction of the firm. The traditional role of management as paternalistic initiator has been altered very little.

In fact, many strategies of industrial democracy have been motivated by management's desire to deny union representation, or at least to limit its influence. Industrial democracy and worker participation programs have been used as planned, pre-emptive tactics by such management representative organizations as the National Association of Manufacturers.[21]

Codetermination, which represents the extreme form of industrial democracy—granting labor a formal voice in company decision making—is, of course, anathema to tradition-conscious American employers. It has been acknowledged as a threat in publications of the NAM.[22]

### Summary

The fact that U.S. unions have not generally endorsed codetermination seems to preclude its receiving significant support in the political arena at present. Since the "red thread" referred to by Furlong is a specter that alarms union leaders as well as managers, it appears political capital could not be made by backing codetermination. That fact probably accounts for the evident lack of enthusiasm on the U.S. legislative scene. There is no pending legislation in either House of Congress addressing the topic.[23]

In view of the reservations about worker participation in company decision making as expressed by American managers and labor representatives, it appears unlikely that any sweeping movement to include worker representatives in the management process is likely. No evidence of such a movement has surfaced in recent national political campaigns.

Since neither the legislative nor the electoral arena offers encouragement for proponents of codetermination in the United States, it would seem that the traditional political path to such a change is barred. Thus, any near-term adoption of a codetermination strategy for worker participation in American firms will take place in individually negotiated cases. Single organizations may agree with their labor representatives to incorporate some features of the *Mitbestimmung* model. Even as such beachheads are established, there is little likelihood that codetermination will become a major force furthering employee participation in U.S. management.

### Footnotes

[1]Jane Bettie, *Business Periodicals Index*, 3rd ed. (New York: The H. W. Wilson Co., January 1958, annual).

[2]Henry Mintzberg, *The Structure of Organizations* (Englewood Cliffs, NJ: Prentice-Hall, 1979), pp. 203–104.

[3]James Furlong, *Labor in the Boardroom* (Princeton, NJ: Dow Jones Books, 1977), p. 28.

[4]*Ibid*, p. 5.

[5]James Furlong, "Workers in the Boardroom," *Wall Street Journal*, March 12, 1979, p. 18.

[6]"Codetermination in the Federal Republic of Germany," translation, *International Labor Organization*, Geneva (Bonn: Refererat Presse-und Offentlichkeitsarbeit, 1976), p. 18.

[7]*Ibid*.

[8]Furlong, *Labor in the Boardroom*, p. 19.

[9]*Co-determination: Worker Participation in German Industry* (New York: German Information Center, 1977), p. 13.

[10]*Ibid.*, p. 18.

[11]"Codetermination in the Federal Republic of Germany," p. 18.

[12]Furlong, *Labor in the Boardroom*, p. 74.

[13]Meade Paper Co., Eaton Corp., Carborundum Co., and Harman International Industries are a few companies with such schemes.

[14]*Labor News and Social Policy*, no. 3, June–July 1978 (periodical pamphlet issued by the Embassy of the Federal Republic of Germany, 4645 Reservoir Road, NW, Washington, DC).

[15]Joel Seidman, Jack London, and Bernard Karsh, "Why Workers Join Unions," *Annals of the American Academy of Political and Social Science* 274 (January 1979), p. 84.

[16]Statement by Albert Zack, AFL-CIO Director of Public Relations, 18 April 1979, telephone conversation with author.

[17]Statement by Richard Calistri, Director of Public Relations, American Federation of Government Employees, April 16, 1979, telephone conversation with author.

[18]Statement by Bernard Henderson, Director of Public Relations, International Brotherhood of Teamsters, Warehousemen, and Helpers of America, April 14, 1979, telephone conversation with author.

[19]U.S. Department of Labor, Bureau of International Labor Affairs, *Industrial Democracy in 12 Nations*, (Monograph No. 2, January 1979), p. 4.

[20]Bruce Stokes, "Answered Prayers," *MBA* 12 (December 1978 – January 1979), p. 22.

[21]*Industrial Democracy in 12 Nations*, p. 2.

[22]National Association of Manufacturers, *Codetermination: Labor's Voice in Corporate Management* (Washington, DC: 1975).

[23]Telephone interview with Jeffrey E. Friedman, Office of the Subcommittee on Labor-Management Relations, U.S. House of Representatives, June 8, 1979.

# An Explanation Of Management's Obligation To Bargain In "Good Faith" Under Labor Law

## ABSTRACT

Today's manager is faced with an increasingly restrictive set of rules when dealing collectively with a labor organization. In an attempt to simplify certain of these obligations, today's managers will avoid being accused of lacking good faith.

In 1935, the National Labor Relations Act (Wagner Act), while stating that the policy of the United States was to encourage collective bargaining, defined several management labor practices that were prohibited, and established the National Labor Relations Board (NLRB) to administer the act.

Five major types of management activity were defined as "Unfair Labor Practices":

1. To interfere with, restrain or coerce employees in the exercise of their rights to self determination,
2. To dominate or interfere with the formation or administration of any labor organization, or contribute financial or other support to it,
3. To discriminate in regard to hire or tenure of employment, or any terms or condition of employment, to encourage or discourage membership in any labor organization,
4. To discharge or discriminate against an employee who files charges, or gives testimony before the NLRB with respect to alleged management violations, and
5. To refuse to bargain with the representative of its employees.

As a result of the Wagner Act, labor relations in the U.S. became very one-sided. No restrictions were placed on the right of unions to strike, boycott, or picket employers, nor were unions compelled to bargain with representatives of management or held accountable for contractual violation. Management, however, was required as a matter of public policy to bargain with the union and to do so in "Good Faith."[1]

It is important for today's managers to understand their rights and obligations with respect to organized labor under the law. The first thing management should realize is that collective bargaining under the Wagner Act does not require them to actually reach an agreement with their employee's representatives, it merely obligates them to make a good faith attempt to reach such an agreement. If, after numerous conferences and meetings, management and the union reach an impasse and cannot agree on the terms of a contract, the Board will not find management guilty of refusing to bargain collectively, merely because they have refused to accept the union's demands. In other words, management is not required to enter into an agreement with a union, if they cannot meet its terms. However, they must try their best to reach an agreement by bargaining back and forth, just as they would in negotiating with a business customer or supplier. Simply agreeing to recognize the union as the employee's exclusive bargaining representative and letting it go at that, is not enough. Nor is it enough to meet with those representatives as many times as they wish, merely to say "yes" or "no" to their terms. Even recognition *plus* such meeting, does not constitute collective bargaining by management. The essential element is a *bona fide* attempt by the employer to reach an agreement with the union. It is that good faith effort to reach some kind of an understanding with their employee's representatives, that is required of management by the Act's collective bargaining provisions. This good faith, or the lack of it, is something which the Board finds, after looking at all the evidence. It cannot be defined simply in terms of a state-of-mind, although that is important. But it can be analyzed by examining what facts and circumstances the Board considers evidence of good faith collective bargaining, or evidence of its absence.

As already indicated, management is not required to bargain collectively with every labor organization or employee representative requesting recognition. Only those organizations or individuals who are not company-dominated and who represent a majority of the employees in an appropriate bargaining unit, are entitled to collective bargaining under the Act. If they represent just a minority of these employees, they need not be recognized. Management can legally refuse to have anything to do with a minority union, but has to make it clear that the refusal is because of their minority status, and not because they are outsiders. If they refuse to meet with a minority union simply because they dislike unions, or because they prefer individual bargaining to collective bargaining, they will find themselves in difficulty with the Board.[2] Such a refusal, while not a violation of collective bargaining provisions, is considered interference with labor organizing under Unfair Labor Practice No. 1. On the other hand, management must be just as careful not to recognize such a minority union, when a majority representative is requesting recognition. Even if no majority union is present, management should not grant exclusive bargaining rights to a minority union. In such a case, the minority union can only represent its own members, and *not* serve as a bargaining representative for all employees. Any ensuing agreements should be made to expire, just as soon as a majority union appears on the scene and requests recognition. With this action, management effectively avoids any unfair labor practices under the Wagner Act's collective bargaining provisions, and also avoids any breach of contract suits with the minority union.

Management's duty to bargain collectively with a union, or individual representing a majority of their employees in an appropriate bargaining unit, does not begin until that representative asks for recognition and negotiation. The mere fact that a union represents a majority of employees, does not obligate management to seek it out for collective bargaining; that action is required only when that union requests recognition and a meeting. Then, however, management must agree to confer with the union at a time and place satisfactory to both. Refusal to do so is an unfair labor practice under item five of the "Unfair Labor Practices." This does not mean, however, that management must immediately recognize the union as exclusive bargaining agent for their employees, and proceed to negotiate a contract with it; as stated earlier, there is no obligation to bargain with everyone claiming to represent a majority. Management has the right to, and they should for their own protection, ask the union to prove its majority at the very first meeting. If the union refuses to do so and insists on collective bargaining on its own claim of majority representation, management can then refuse to recognize it.[3] Even if it should later turn out that the union did represent a majority, management will not be found guilty of refusing to bargain collectively, as long as the Board believes their doubt as to the union's majority, or the appropriateness of the bargaining unit, was genuine. "Reasonable doubt" as a defense will not work, however, when the union has recently been certified by the Board. Such certification is conclusive proof of its majority and the propriety of the bargaining unit, and it cannot be challenged by management. It is not given a specific duration by the Act, but the Board usually recognizes such certification for about a year in the ordinary case.[4] After that time, management can challenge such certification.

Once a labor organization, or individual, has proved that it represents a majority of the employees in an appropriate bargaining unit, management's obligation to bargain collectively becomes inclusive, and they cannot attach any conditions to this collective bargaining. For example, they cannot refuse to recognize and negotiate with the union until it organizes or signs contracts with their competitors, as such a condition constitutes a refusal to bargain collectively. This does not mean that they have to agree to terms which the union cannot, or does not, require of management's competitors. In other words, management may refuse to enter into a specific, proposed union agreement until their competitors do likewise, so long as they are willing to recognize and negotiate with the union a contract containing terms enabling them to compete with nonunion employers.[5] Similarly, management cannot refuse to bargain collectively with their employee's authorized representative, because something illegal has been requested, such as a closed shop. They have the right to refuse that demand, but cannot refuse to recognize the union and negotiate with it, merely because they do not like its terms. Nor can they refuse to bargain collectively when the union in question has called a strike against them, which means management cannot refuse to negotiate *unless or until* the union abandons its strike. Their obligation to bargain continues during and after the strike, so long as the union retains its majority. As a matter of fact, management must bargain with the union, even if it loses its majority during the strike, if such loss is caused by management's refusal to bargain, or any other unfair labor practice.

Likewise, the fact that the union and its members engage in violence or other unlawful conduct during the strike, does not excuse management from bargaining with them. Nor does a majority union lose its right to collective bargaining, because it strikes in violation of its existing agreement.[6] Such violence or illegality in a strike may cost the union members their right to reinstatement, but it does not deprive them of their right to collective bargaining, so long as they retain their majority.

Additionally, management cannot simply meet with union representatives and deny everything they propose. They must offer counter proposals, if asked to do so by the union, when they reject its terms.[7] Nor can they insist that the union accept, without any modification, terms which they themselves have drawn up. To present such a contract on a "take it or leave it" basis is to refuse to bargain collectively.[8] Management must be willing to talk things over with the union, and to discuss the proposals of both sides. After all, the whole question of good faith in collective bargaining is really a matter of evidence, since the Board looks at the entire record to see whether or not management engaged in good faith bargaining with the union. If it refused to make any counter offers, it will find them guilty of refusing to bargain in good faith. If, on the other hand, it finds that they made some concessions and offered counter proposals when they rejected union terms, it will not convict them of refusing to bargain collectively, even though they fail to agree with the union's proposals. In other words, it is not the actions or statements of management on a particular demand that determines their good faith, but their attitude and conduct during the entire negotiations.

Although counter-proposals are a key test in the Board's determination of good faith, there are other factors that indicate its presence or absence in collective bargaining. For example, a management that announces or changes any term or condition of employment while the matter is still under discussion with a majority union, will be found guilty of a refusal to bargain collectively.[9] Any such unilateral action or statement of policy is not only the very opposite of collective bargaining, but, according to the Board, also constitutes an attempt to undermine and discredit the union. Furthermore, as long as their employees are represented by a union or other bargaining agency, management cannot go over the head of such an agency to deal directly with the employees. This, again, is lack of good faith and is particularly important during strikes. As already pointed out, management can be compelled to reinstate striking employees with back pay, if the strike was caused or prolonged by their unfair labor practices. One unfair practice often producing to this result is when management attempts to get the strikers to return to work, despite the union's instructions not to.[10] If management offers to take them back or asks them to go back to work by appealing to them directly, instead of negotiating for their return with their union, they are guilty of refusing to bargain collectively, and, therefore, liable to a reinstatement order.[11] Any kind of refusal to bargain collectively before or during a strike will deprive management of their right to replace the strikers permanently, and will force them to reinstate the strikers, and, in many cases, award them back pay.

Additional examples of lack of good faith by management include:

1. Making a misleading statement at the bargaining table,[12]
2. Presenting vague and uncooperative attitude toward union demands,[13]
3. Refusing to consider a union demand,[14]
4. Refusing to budge on checkoff provisions,[15]
5. Retracting concessions previously granted,[16]
6. Demanding additional concessions, and[17]
7. Refusing to arbitrate bargaining differences.[18]

Because of the severity of the given by the Board for violations of the unfair labor practice and good faith bargaining provisions of the law, it is crucial that today's manager understand exactly what can and cannot be done under them. With an increasing number of unionized professional and white-collar employees, many managers who have never had to face this issue in the past, will find themselves confronting it in the near future. Since it has long been established in this country that ignorance of the law is no excuse, today's managers must familiarize themselves with these issues. Failure to do so could beome a costly and inexcusable mistake.

## Footnotes

[1]J. T. Dunlop, "Structure of Collective Bargaining," in G. G. Somers (ed.), *The Next Twenty-Five Years of Industrial Relations*, Madison, Wisconsin, Industrial Relations Research Association, 1973.

[2]*Berkshire Knitting Mills*, NLRB No. 17.

[3]*Texarkana Bus Co. vs. NLRB*, CCA-8, April 30, 1941.

[4]*Whittier Mill Company*, 15 NLRB No. 47.

[5]*Aronsson Printing Co.*, 13 NLRB No. 799.

[6]*NLRB vs. Highland Shoe Co.*, 119 F. (2nd) 218.

[7]*NLRB vs. Geo. P. Pilling & Son, Co.*, CCA-5, March 18, 1941.

[8]H. S. Roberts, *Roberts' Dictionary of Industrial Relations*, (Washington, DC: Bureau of National Affairs, Inc., 1971).

[9]*Inland Lime & Stone Co. vs. NLRB*, CCA-7, March 13, 1941.

[10]*NLRB vs. Lightner Publishing Co.*, 113 F. (2nd), 621.

[11]*Manville Jenekes Corp.*, 30 NLRB No. 60.

[12]*Rangaire Corp.*, 157 NLRB No. 62 (1966), 61 LRRM 1429.

[13]*Adler Metal Products Corp.*, 79 NLRB No. 33 (1948), 22 LRRM 1359.

[14]*V-0 Milling Co.*, 43 NLRB No. 59 (1942), 11 LRRM.

[15]*H. K. Porter Co., Inc., vs. NLRB*, U.S. Sup. Ct. (1970).

[16]*Tomlinson of High Point, Inc.*, 74 NLRB No. 127 (1947), 20 LRRM 1203.

[17]*Franklin Hosiery Mills, Inc.*, 83 NLRB No. 37 (1949).

[18]*Mechanical Contractors, Assn.*, 202 NLRB No. 1, 82 LRRM 1438.

# The Plant Closing Issue Arrives At The Bargaining Table

*Kenneth A. Kovach*
*Peter E. Millspaugh*

During the last decade, the United States has watched its economy undergo immense dislocations. Technological obsolescence, declining competitiveness in world markets, a severe recession, and other factors have combined to force drastic structural changes in many sectors, particularly in the heavy industries. Steel, automobiles, machine tools, textiles, and rubber have provided a strong foundation for the American economy for over half a century, but now they find their very survival is at stake. Associated with these industries' efforts to adjust is the movement of capital in pursuit of new priorities, and the consequent economic disruption associated with plant closings.

## The Central Issues

Traditionally, organized labor and management in the United States have perceived their interests as opposed, in relation to plant closings. Viewing plant shutdowns as a threat to job security, union membership, union territorial prerogatives, and wage and benefit achievements, organized labor has vigorously pressed for a voice in the closing decision. Management has just as vigorously resisted, contending that such decisions are management's prerogative, and are necessary to the effective operation of a profitable business enterprise.

In recent years, a public interest dimension has been introduced into the plant closing debate. Greater recognition exists that a shutdown can injure those beyond the worker and family, to the small businesses dependent on the plant, to the economic and social fiber of the community, and even to the viability of local government. All are now strongly promoted by a number of public interest groups.[1] Also gaining advocacy is the public interest thesis of corporate accountability, which would place the responsibility for plant closing at the corporation doorstep.[2]

## The Institutional Settings

The plant closing combatants are waging their struggle primarily within the framework of three institutions: the courts, the legislatures and the collective bargaining process. The federal judiciary has been engaged in the plant closing debate primarily due to labor's contention that the terms of the National Labor Relations Act (NLRA) bring management shutdown decisions within the ambit of mandatory bargaining.[3] Although the National Labor Relations Board appears to favor this interpretation, the courts have been considerably more cautious.[4] Through a small number of recent opinions, the Supreme Court has provided a degree of protection against mandatory decision bargaining in plant closing situations.[5] The Court's inclinations were reaffirmed last summer in its ruling that management had no duty to bargain over an economically motivated decision to partially terminate a business.[6]

Sensitive to entrepreneurial freedom, the courts generally have given little indication that decision bargaining requirements about plant closings will be enlarged under NLRA interpretations, in the foreseeable future. A partial judicial success can be reserved for labor, however, as the requirement for "effects" bargaining in plant closing situations under the amended NLRA appears now to be firmly in place.[7]

Over the years, judicial initiative in plant closing situations has been solicited on other grounds as well. For a brief interlude, the courts seemed to be on the verge of accepting job protection from a shutdown, based on the theory that seniority rights established in a labor contract were "vested," thereby surviving termination of the agreement and following the job to a subsequent facility.[8]

The courts have also been asked to use interpretation of the terms of labor contracts to find an unwritten intent that worker job entitlements would continue beyond a plant closing.[9] Theories favoring the perception of a job as a legally protectable property interest, rather than a mere contract right, have also been advanced.[10] Even the public interest arguments of the corporate accountability lobby have appeared in the courtroom in opposition to plant closings.[11] One conclusion, however, is inescapable: no theory has succeeded in securing any significant judicial intervention in plant closing situations.[12]

What, then, can be anticipated from the second institutional arena in which plant closing issues are being played out, i.e., the legislatures? In recent years, certain segments of organized labor, along with various public interest groups, have taken their case for plant closing relief to both the state legislatures and the Congress.[13] Compaigning since the mid–1970's, these groups have prompted the introduction of plant closing legislation in some twenty-one states, as well as the U.S. House of Representatives and the Senate.[14]

Although the legislative proposals at the state level vary widely, requirements for prenotification, severance benefits and the establishment of a community action fund are the most universal.[15] A major stumbling block to the passage of such state proposals is the fear that such laws would create a strong disincentive to state economic and industrial development efforts.

Sweeping plant closing relief proposals have appeared at the federal level, generating considerable fact finding activity through public hearings.[16] Ambitious requirements for governmental intervention before and after the closing decision, along with other controversial features, have thus far prevented federal proposals from gaining the support necessary for enactment. In addition, in light of a generally unfavorable political climate, the prognosis for a legislative response in the near term is not encouraging.

## Collective Bargaining Developments

In contrast to the lack of responsiveness within the courts and legislatures, plant closing issues are gaining stature within the collective bargaining process. It can be argued that because the courts and the legislatures have failed to respond, the collective bargaining arena is showing activity. Whatever its cause, the emergence of plant closing issues in the bargaining process could be a driving force shaping labor-management relations in the future. This development is not, however, without its ironies.

For half a century or more, management has resisted union involvement in plant closing decisions. Although required to "effects" bargain, management's discretion to close in the first instance has been practiced by the business community and has been largely protected by the courts.[17] Hard pressed to survive the forces of a new economic order, management has necessarily intensified its interest in plant shutdown bargaining. Ironically, the management that is now more willing to bargain over the ultimate job security question, is less able to guarantee the jobs in question. There is also evidence that, although plant closing considerations are appearing at the bargaining table with increasing frequency, it is not at the pleasure of either party. As a result of such bargaining, labor must often sacrifice major "givebacks,"[18] while management surrenders a degree of entrepreneurial control, and often must guarantee against future shutdowns.

The precise extent to which plant closing considerations have invaded the collective bargaining process can only be a matter of conjecture. Some indication of the extent to which they have penetrated specific industries in recent years, however, is demonstrated in Table I.

During 1990, plant closing bargaining became evident in many industrial sectors. In the meatpacking and processing industries, for example, plant closing considerations became a major component in recent labor contracts.[19] A similar outcome was experienced in the tire industry's pacts with the United Rubber Workers.[20] Other industries have followed suit. Nowhere, however, has the issue gained the prominence it experienced in the beleaguered auto industry.

### Table I
### Plant Movement Limitations by Industry*

| | Total Agreements | | Agreements having plant movement limitations | |
|---|---|---|---|---|
| | Agreements | Workers (in '000s) | Agreements | Workers (in '000s) |
| Total, all unions | 1,823 | 7,339.2 | 392 | 2,873.1 |
| Total, 9 unions | 764 | 3,654.9 | 271 | 2,277.3 |
| Autoworkers | 118 | 995.2 | 39 | 738.2 |
| Clothing workers | 19 | 165.3 | 12 | 143.3 |
| Electrical workers | 110 | 295.8 | 16 | 29.0 |
| Garment workers | 42 | 257.0 | 36 | 242.8 |
| Machinists | 89 | 285.7 | 16 | 76.0 |
| Meat cutters | 50 | 142.8 | 19 | 66.7 |
| Retail clerks | 48 | 137.0 | 18 | 64.0 |
| Steelworkers | 120 | 587.8 | 42 | 430.7 |
| Teamsters | 168 | 748.4 | 73 | 486.6 |
| Other | 1,059 | 3,724.3 | 121 | 595.8 |

*Because of rounding, sums of individual items may not equal totals.

Source: "Characteristics of Major Collective Bargaining Agreements," *Bureau of Labor Statistics Bulletin*, 2065, 1990. (Note that these figures reflect only "plant movement" limitations. This should be distinguished from an agreement pertaining to a plant shutdown where no relocation is contemplated.)

### The Automobile Manufacturing Industry

Perhaps hardest hit of the major industries, the autoworkers have initiated large-scale, industry-wide plant closings. With management working for company survival[21] and unions fighting for job preservation, plant closing bargaining has been suddenly stripped of its previous forms of gamesmanship. A negotiating process is emerging, dominated by the plant closing issue which now presents a credible and practical problem on both sides of the bargaining table.

An explicit plant closing component first appeared in the auto industries' labor-management arrangements, in connection with the loan guarantee measures taken by the federal government to assist the Chrysler Corporation in

1974. At the government's insistence, both the union and the company were required to make concessions designed ultimately to keep the doors open at Chrysler plants. The United Auto Workers ratified an enormous $1.068 billion giveback in the form of direct wages and various economic supplements, in return for a seat on the Chrysler Board of Directors for UAW president Douglas Frazier, and a voice in layoff decisions.[22]

The agreement contained such radical concessions from both sides, in comparison with other recent industry agreements, that it was initially perceived as merely a temporary aberration. Union givebacks of such magnitude and the unprecedented codetermination concessions[23] by Chrysler management, could only be attributed to governmental third-party pressure and the unique circumstances surrounding the pact. This generalization, however, proved to be premature.

In 1981, some ten months before the union contracts were to expire, both the General Motors Corporation and Ford Motor Company approached the UAW to begin negotiations on new agreements. Talks were initiated with General Motors, where it soon became apparent that plant closing considerations could not be ignored, and, indeed, would be a significant factor in shaping any agreement. Although talks subsequently broke down, they centered primarily on marketing strategy considerations, in an effort to minimize the necessity of anticipated plant closings. For example, the concept of tying union economic givebacks to reduced auto prices was seriously explored for the first time in recent memory in the auto industry.[24]

With the union and General Motors at an impasse, talks with Ford began. In time, these talks may enter the annals of United States labor negotiations, as the most innovative dealings ever undertaken in a major industry. In a sweeping agreement concluded in February 1982 and subsequently ratified by local unions and the UAW bargaining committee, the parties culminated a prodigious good-faith effort to restructure their relationship, as it pertained to job preservation. One need look no further than the basic terms of this agreement to appreciate the extent to which plant closing considerations permeated the bargaining. Union givebacks included a 3-percent annual improvement factor, cost-of-living allowances for nine months, and considerable reductions in the twenty-six personal and forty-three general holidays over the three-year contract.

In return, Ford granted the union a form of profit sharing for its members, along with both "decision" and "effects" bargaining rights for any future plant closings. The company guaranteed the union against plant closings for two years, that work force reductions would be accomplished through normal attrition, and that laid off workers with over 15 years seniority would receive a severance benefit, equal to 50 percent of their present salary, until reaching retirement age.

The major significance of the 1982 Ford-UAW contract resides within its precedent-setting impact within the industry. General Motors' announced intention in late February 1982 to close seven more plants, coupled with the success of the Ford negotiations, sent General Motors and the UAW back to the bargaining table. The parties reached agreement on a pact comparable to the Ford contract in breadth and basic structure. The G. M. Pact cleared the local union ratification process by a bare 52 percent margin. In return for a company pledge not to close the seven plants, the union conceded some fundamental gains in improvement factors and cost-of-living adjustments in the wage package.

## Conclusions

Unable to obtain legislative and judicial support for the increasingly serious problem of plant closings, labor unions are bringing the issue to the bargaining table. The influence of plant closing considerations on the collective bargaining process may be shown to correlate with the business conditions under which the bargaining is conducted. Certainly, the potency of plant closing considerations has been evident in the recent round of negotiations in the ailing automobile industry.

As a matter of national labor policy, the desirability of addressing plant closing problems exclusively within the collective bargaining process will surely be debated in the years ahead. There are those who contend that the bargaining process called for under the NLRA, as interpreted by the courts, provides the appropriate mechanism for resolving such an issue. They point to the recent plant closing bargaining developments to support their position. Others hold the view that the existing bargaining structure is weighted against union interests, and will continue to seek legislative or judicial intervention to right the imbalance. However appropriate, adequate, or inadequate this bargaining response is, it appears that labor and management, within the limits of their own resources, have begun to grapple with the problem.

The advent of bargaining over spreading plant shutdown raises related questions that only time can answer. The extent to which this development marks a watershed in the history of United States labor-management bargaining is uncertain. It is tempting to conclude that the contract innovations, reflected in the recent auto pacts, will usher in a new era of labor-management relations, and that the former relationship will be irreversibly altered. To conclude that future relations will soon embrace principles of codetermination, and abandon their adversarial moorings, would be unrealistic. It would be more prudent to suggest that some residue of the good faith and cooperation, forced on the parties by these distressed conditions, may survive the return to better times.

## Footnotes

[1]B. Bluestone and B. Harrison, *Capital and Communities* (Washington, DC: The Progressive Alliance, April 9, 1980); M. Green, J. Bernstein, V. Kamber and A. Teper-Marlin, *The Case for a Corporate Democracy Act of 1980* (Washington, DC: Americans Concerned About Corporate Power, December 1, 1979).

[2]R. Nadar, *Taming the Giant Corporation* (New York: Norton Publishing Company, 1979); M. Green, *et. al.*

[3]This is based most frequently on the argument that the plant closing decision is a "term" or "condition" of employment by the Act's definition. See 29 U.S.Code 158(d) which characterizes collective bargaining as "the performance of the mutual obligation of the employer and the representative of the employees to . . . confer in good faith with respect to wages, hours, and other terms and conditions of employment . . ."

[4]The difference between the National Labor Relations Board and the courts in this area has been apparent for some time. See analysis in T. Schwartz, "Plant Relocation or Partial Termination: The Duty to Decision-Bargain," 39 *Fordham Law Review* 81, 86 (1970).

[5]Although the Court has required bargaining on a decision to subcontract work previously done by union employees in *Fibreboard Paper Products Corp. vs. NLRB*, 379 U.S. 203 (1964), the decision to terminate an entire business for whatever reason has been protected from bargaining in *Textile Workers Union vs. Darlington Manufacturing Co.*, 380 U.S. 263 (1965), as has an economically motivated decision to partially terminate in *First National Maintenance vs. NLRB*, 452 U.S. 666 (1981).

[6]*First National Maintenance vs. NLRB*, 452 U.S. 666 (1981).

[7]*NLRB vs. Adams Dairy, Inc.*, 350 F. 2d 108 (CA8, 1965), cert denied, 382 U.S. 1011 (1965). Acknowledged in *First National Maintenance*, "effects" bargaining, as the term implies, requires the parties to bargain in good faith over the effects of a management decision; in this case, the decision to shut down.

[8]*Zdanok vs. Glidden Co.*, 288 F. 2d 99 (2nd Cir, 1961). This ruling was extremely controversial, little followed, and eventually overruled. For a critical analysis of the case see Aaron, "Reflections on the Legal Nature and Enforceability of Seniority Rights," 75 *Harvard Law Review* 1532 (1962);

*contra,* see Blumrosen, "Seniority Rights and Industrial Change: *Zdanok vs. Glidden Co.*," 47 *Minnesota Law Review* 505 (1962).

[9]The *Zdanok* holding again provides an excellent example of the application of broad interpretation of the terms of a bargaining agreement to achieve this purpose. It has been argued that broader "contextual" interpretations are warranted, because the workers of today "are caught up in a system of industrial relations that transcends the immediate contracting situation." See Blumrosen, "Seniority Rights," p. 528.

[10]The perception of a job as a legally protectable property interest has had its advocates in this country for many years. See P. Drucker, "The Job as Property Right," *Wall Street Journal*, March 4, 1980. This concept was explored in the major plant closing case of *United Steel Workers vs. U.S. Steel Corp.*, 492, F. Supp. 1 (1980).

[11]*United Steel Workers vs. U.S. Steel Corp.*, 492 F. Supp. 1 (1980), Brief *Amici Curiae.*

[12]P. Millspaugh, "Plant Closings and the Prospects for a Judicial Response," *Journal of Corporation Law* (Spring 1983).

[13]See description of these efforts in Bluestone and Harrison, *Capital and Communities*, note 1; Labor Union Study Tour Participants, Economic Dislocation; Plant Closings, Plant Relocation and Plant Conversion (Washington, DC: UAW, USA, IAM, Washington, DC, May 1, 1979), a report on plant closing laws in Sweden, West Germany, and Great Britain with recommendations for similar laws in the United States.

[14]B. Bolle, "Overview of Plant Closings and Industrial Migration Issues in the U.S.," Economics Division, *Congressional Research Services of the Library of Congress*, May 15, 1980; P. Millspaugh, "The Campaign for Plant Closing Laws in the United States: An Assessment," *The Corporation Law Review* (Fall 1982).

[15]The contents of the legislative proposals, both state and federal, are examined in Millspaugh, *ibid.*

[16]Most of the public hearings on plant closing legislative proposals in recent years have been conducted outside of Washington, DC, in areas experiencing plant shutdowns. They have been held under the auspices of the Senate Committee on Education, Labor, and Human Resources, and the House Committee on Education and Labor, or a respective subcommittee.

[17]See "Major Collective Bargaining Agreements, Management Rights and Union-Management Cooperation," *Bureau of Labor Statistics Bulletin*, 1425–5, 1990, pp. 15–16.

Various clauses in labor agreements giving management specific rights to shutdown decisions have become quite standard, such as:

(1) Without intending by the language of this section to limit the functions and prerogatives of management, or to define all of such functions and prerog-

atives, it is agreed that the following are the exclusive functions of the employers . . . the right to decide the number and location of its plants, the creation of new departments and the elimination of existing departments in a plant . . .

(2) The union recognizes other rights and responsibilities belonging solely to the company, prominent among which is the right to decide the number and location of plants . . .

(3) It shall be the sole right of the company to diminish operations in whole or part, or to remove a plant for operation or business of same or any part thereof, to any location as circumstances may require.

[18] A term that connotes a union bargaining concession in the form of "giving-back" to management those contract rights that were previously secured.

[19] Especially noteworthy was the United Food and Commercial Workers pact with Armour Meats. In return for security against unannounced future shutdowns, the union agreed to a production line speed-up and a wage and cost-of-living freeze.

[20] Under the fear of imminent shutdowns, the union agreed to $9.9 million in wage concessions, representing a 13 percent increase in labor costs over the life of the contract in its pact with Uniroyal.

[21] In the case of General Motors, its automaking subsidiaries.

[22] The company also agreed to establish a profit sharing plan for its blue-collar workers and to allow access to the company books by union auditors, as part of the total arrangement.

[23] Codetermination connotes the sharing of decision making authority between labor and management. It is representative of a growing trend in the United States seemingly patterned after the European model. For a further discussion of codetermination in general, and the Chrysler agreement in particular, see Kenneth A. Kovach, Ben Sands, and William Brooks, "Is Co-Determination a Workable Idea For U.S. Labor-Management Relations?" *MSU Business Topics* (Winter, 1979).

[24] It was announced that for every $1-per-hour give-back in labor costs, a $150-per-car production savings could be realized, and that this would subsequently equate to a $250–$300 reduction in the retail price. Dealers were to be asked for concessions also.

# New Directions In Fringe Benefits

Employee benefits, or fringe benefits, are compensation other than wages or salaries. Such benefits comprise more than 35 percent of the compensation of the typical U.S. employee today, and the proportion is increasing annually. In recent years, fringe benefits have grown twice as fast as wages and salaries. During the early 1930's, however, benefits comprised less than 4 percent of typical payroll costs. Since World War II, fringe benefits have increased dramatically, and in the last ten years, they nearly tripled in cost.

Clearly, today the term "fringe" is a misnomer. Fringes are no longer extras. The great majority of Americans rely on them as their first line of defense against illness, unemployment and old age. Currently fringe benefits provide protection against the contingencies of life from the first day of employment to retirement and beyond. Many of these benefits are not new to the compensation package; some were introduced unilaterally by employers as early as the turn of the century. Fringe benefits, however, now play a far more important role in labor relations than has been the case in the past. A great variety of fringe benefits can be found in industry today, with some labor agreements containing special (and often unique) benefits.

There appear to be several reasons for this growing emphasis on fringe benefits. As this country has grown richer and more self-assured, the desire to eliminate risk and increase personal security has grown stronger. Employees have shown a strong tendency to want to eliminate insecurity of every conceivable kind. While employees could buy most benefits directly, they seem generally to find it more convenient to have their contribution for benefits deducted from their paychecks. In most cases, too, fringes provide important income tax savings. When the company pays for the benefits, the employee does not have to pay tax on them. Furthermore, employees often recognize that an organization's mass purchasing power can buy various insurance and benefit plans more inexpensively.

Collective bargaining has also contributed to the growth of fringes. Unions do compete with each other, and there is considerable prestige attached to being the first union to win a new type of fringe. Union members may give their union more credit for a new benefit, than for an equally costly increase in pay. When one union wins such a benefit, other unions will usually follow suit, with nonunion firms then feeling compelled to join the parade to continue attracting good, new employees.

Employers provide fringe benefits partly to raise employee morale, partly to meet their social responsibilities, and partly to make more effective use of their workforce. With the possible exception of profit-sharing plans, however, it would be unrealistic to expect benefit plans to motivate higher productivity. The idealistic belief that employees will be grateful for the organization's beneficence and will, in turn, express their appreciation by harder work has largely disappeared today. Fringe benefits may improve employee morale and make both unions and employers look good, but they do not generally contribute to increased productivity.

## New Influences on Fringe Benefits

Given that fringe benefits are important to employees, labor unions and employers, why are they changing and what is the direction for the future to be? Many companies are concluding that they must offer a range of benefits to match the changed realities of the new life-styles that abound today. Benefits have traditionally been designed to fit the needs of the breadwinner, dependent spouse and family. Several current trends have transformed this life-style.

— Fewer male employees are now the sole support of the family.
— More couples are remaining childless; those who have children, have fewer children.
— Marriage is not as popular as it once was.
— Work spans are more discontinuous, especially among women with children.
— Retirement is no longer expected at age 65.

The work force is thus characterized by a greater variety of family and behavior patterns than ever before. In fact, traditional families consisting of a working husband with dependent wife and children now constitute less than 15 percent of the nation's work force. Roughly half of all workers belong to families that have two or more incomes, and another 14 percent live alone. The number of unmarried couples living together is more than double what it was ten years ago. Most conventional benefit programs provide a single worker with some unwanted coverage, like life insurance. At the same time, the value of the total benefit package is generally far less than that for a married worker at the same salary and seniority level. Furthermore, members of two-income families may duplicate their spouse's benefits in areas such as health insurance, while unmarried couples who live together often cannot obtain coverage.

The general trend in fringe benefits for the future, then, is toward more flexibility in meeting the needs and wants of the employees. While most companies still maintain conventional benefit plans, the flexible plan is an idea whose time has come. Despite concerns over the difficulties and cost, corporate interest in the idea is growing. There are dissenters, however, with labor unions being one of the most vocal critics of flexible benefits. Union leaders have expressed the fear that employees, given a choice, may eliminate benefits they need. Unions thus generally favor a comprehensive plan that covers every contingency.

Even though most companies are not yet ready for sweeping changes, fringe benefits may be repackaged in several different mixes. Such packages may address needs of single workers, those who are married with no children, employees with young dependents, parents facing college expenses, and "empty-nesters" interested in retirement. Many companies may substitute defined contribution plans for defined benefit plans (called the *cafeteria* approach), thus providing the opportunity for a benefit package more tailored to a particular employee at the same cost to the employer. To date, the most common corporate response to new trends has been the rewriting of health insurance plans, so that workers covered under both their own and their spouse's plan cannot collect more than 100 percent of any cost. This, however, is only the beginning.

## The Cafeteria Approach

Under the cafeteria approach, every employee receives a core of essential benefits. Then employees can "buy" other benefits with credits earned on the basis of wages and seniority. Few companies have these plans today, mainly because of the administrative costs involved and their pessimistic assessment of the employees' capability to make intelligent choices. Neither of these reasons should be roadblocks. After an initial investment to program the various choices available, the cost of administering the cafeteria plan is not prohibitive, particularly in light of its potential returns. The argument about employees not being capable of making intelligent choices is another example of management confusing education level with intelligence. Thus, I believe that the cafeteria-style benefit plan could become more prevalent in the future as a way to satisfy the needs of an increasingly diverse work force.

## New Directions

The typical benefits package today is made up of four main components:

1. **Pay for time not worked.** The demand for leisure is being met with more holidays, longer vacations and shorter workweeks. The number of celebrated holidays keeps increasing, with half the union contracts specifying ten or more paid holidays per year. The trend for the future is certain to include even more

paid holidays, including such holidays as the employee's birthday, the date on which the employee joined the union, and personal days off. The trend for the future is also certain to include longer paid vacations. Employees in the future will get longer vacations than before, have them earlier in their careers, and be freer to choose when to take them. Although the two-week vacation after one year of service is still typical, workers are beginning to qualify for longer vacations sooner. The maximum amount of vacation time that a worker may receive has also been increasing and should continue to do so.

In comparison to most European countries, the American worker gets very little vacation. Many European countries set legal minimums on vacation time, and nowhere is the legal minimum as little as two weeks a year. Since many of the more generous vacation plans in this country result from pressure by organized labor, and since many large labor unions are becoming international in scope, pressure for more vacation time can be expected to continue. Even today, many countries have adopted "floating" days off, and others have instituted vacation banking systems that allow workers to save and withdraw days off throughout their employment.

Another kind of pay for time not worked is dismissal pay. Such pay is still not a common product of collective bargaining, but it is likely to become more prevalent in the future as unemployment, due to both economic and technological causes, continues to be a problem. Supplementary unemployment benefit plans also address the problem of unemployment, and over 5 million employees are now covered by such plans.

2. **Insurance.** Most organizations now provide several forms of protection against the loss of income and extra expense caused by sickness. Companies in more than a dozen different geographic areas have formed groups to plan and carry out cost-cutting strategies for health-care benefits. These programs include efforts to curb excessive use of hospitals through utilization reviews, outpatient and surgicenter care, insurance coverage of second and even third opinions on elective surgery, reimbursement for health services at home, greater use of pre-admission testing, and increased private use of professional standards review organizations. Trends in recent years involve an increase in the amount and duration of benefits; extension of benefits to retired workers as well as to those dependents not yet covered; defrayal of costs for some medically related drugs; protection against catastrophic illness and accidents; dental, visual and mental health benefits, and, preventive health-care plans. There has also been a strong trend toward exclusive employer financing of the health-benefit package. While continuing union emphasis on health-expense defrayal may cause one to conclude that this trend will continue, one must keep

in mind the effects of a depressed economy on the firm's ability and willingness to pay for such coverage. And the fact that the insurance package has increased in cost faster than other fringe benefits have over the last five years, means that this area will be one of the troublespots in collective bargaining in the years ahead.

3. **Retirement.** Rising inflation has reversed a recent trend toward early retirement, resulting in a heightened awareness within American corporations of the importance of retirement planning and education programs. Most pension plans relate benefits to past earnings, but there is a trend to weigh more heavily the income received in the last years of employment. Today, in the more liberal companies, pensions and Social Security benefits together may total as much as 80 percent of an employee's after-tax preretirement income, whereas 25 percent was much more common a decade ago. There is a trend toward having the employer pay the full cost of a pension plan, as well as a trend toward a fully funded and actuarially sound plan.

There has also been a marked increase in the vesting allowances for workers covered by pension plans. Under normal economic conditions these would be expected to continue in the future but more and more employers have recently been trying to reverse this trend, by shifting more of the burden of financing the program and keeping it actuarially sound back to the individual employee. Whether this is the start of a new long-term trend or simply a temporary concession, depends on the performance of the U.S. economy over the next few years.

While most private pensions do not include a cost-of-living allowance, more and more companies are making *ad hoc* pension adjustment every two to three years, with the trend toward routine adjustments. Most companies compute pensions on final pay, with a trend toward a smaller number of years being the basis for the computation, thus increasing the pension amount. But some base the computation on career averaging rather than final pay, thus softening the effects of changing jobs in midcareer. Some top executives are even able to negotiate a supplemental executive retirement plan when changing jobs, so that they lose nothing in the switch, a practice that can be expected to continue in the next decade as employers compete for proven, upper-level human resources.

Another relatively new idea that should catch on in a big way in the near future is for the company to provide retirement planning for each employee. Today, many companies, well aware of the innumerable pitfalls awaiting the unprepared retiree, are making preretirement counseling—a new and vital benefit for employees—just as important to many of them as their insurance and pensions. The more responsible companies now offer corporatewide, multihour seminars, that in the aggregate involve thousands of employees and usually their spouses. As recently as 1960, preretirement planning was largely looked on as the prerogative of top executives. In the last five years, however, retirement counseling in companies has doubled, with great variation in the scope of the programs offered. A few give only the information that the law requires and call that preretirement planning, but many voluntarily go much further. The typical corporate program is less than four years old, was purchased outside the company, and was then tailored to its own needs. Participants spend a minimum of 15 hours in group sessions, which make use of printed and audiovisual materials, lectures, and some seminar-type discussions. It is clear to me that in the future, corporate America will take more responsibility than ever before for the retirement lives of its employees.

4. **Service and perquisites.** A variety of other fringe benefits are also available to employees today. Some employers provide amenities such as recreation rooms, jogging tracks, saunas, and picnic facilities for use by employees. Because of land costs, most elaborate amenities of this type are confined to suburban locations. Tuition-aid plans are available to many workers, but only three to five percent of white-collar workers and a lower percentage of blue-collar workers take advantage of them. Younger workers use these plans more than older workers do, although men and women use them about equally. Participation increases with previous educational attainment and with income. Professional and technical workers use them more than others, and people in the West participate more than those who live elsewhere.

Versatile tuition-aid programs are offered by some companies. Others provide adoption benefits. These generally range from $800 to $1,000 per adoption, but some companies pay the same amount that an employee would receive through a medical plan for a normal delivery. In addition to the adoption benefits, some companies allow the adoptive mother to stay home with her child for weeks or months, during which time her job is held for her and her insurance benefits are continued.

Given the lifestyle trends discussed earlier regarding children, marriage, work spans, etc., these types of benefits can only increase in appeal in the next ten years. If profit and loss statements dictate a reduction in the number of dollars a company will give for fringe benefits, items in this miscellaneous category will be the first to go, for workers have not become as accustomed to the newer fringes as they have to the old standbys.

## Other Developments

Some innovative benefits being explored by companies today will likely be common place later in the decade. One such benefit is the Tax Reduction Act Stock Ownership Plan (TRASOP). Under this plan, the company establishes a tax-qualified trust for employees, and contributes employer stock equal in value to 10 percent of the amount taken by the company as an investment tax credit. Such a plan can benefit both the employees and the company.

Another new idea is the Matching Charitable Contribution Plan. Under this plan, the company makes contributions up to a specified limit to qualifying charities of the employee's choice in an amount equal to that contributed by the employee. Advantages of this plan include social value and employee morale boosting.

Some firms have a sick-leave pool: a portion of the employee's sick leave is pooled, to be used by those who need it. Other companies are experimenting with varying work hours such as flexitime, summer working hours, four-day weeks, split days, and a floating schedule. Each of these ideas is indicative of the innovative thinking that will lead fringe benefits in entirely new directions in the next ten years. Such innovative ideas do not necessarily have to increase the cost of the fringe-benefit package to the employer.

## The Cost of Coverage

A U.S. Chamber of Commerce survey that showed employers spent an annual average of $7,560 per worker on fringe benefits in 1989, also showed the rise in benefits was topping out. Surveys for several previous years indicated a leveling off in the rate of increase in benefit plans, perhaps due to better understanding of the real cost of benefit programs. Such a trend may well continue, as the current recession decreases many firms' abilities to pay for the fringe package.

Despite substantial concern over the increasing cost of providing employee benefits, a majority of top management indicated in a national underwriters' survey that they had no plans to scale back their benefit program in the future. Fifty-nine percent of those surveyed said they planned to expand their benefit programs in the future, while 38 percent said they would maintain their programs at current levels. According to this survey:

— 92 percent of executives believed the rising cost of benefits was one of the most pressing problems they faced.

— 46 percent felt internal pressure for expansion of benefits would come from middle management, while external pressure was anticipated from unions and the federal government.
— 70 percent said the rising cost of benefits was the most pressing problem in the benefit field for the future.

Approximately half of those responding to the survey cited potential increased federal regulation of the pension system, the introduction of some form of national health plan, and increases in the Social Security tax rate as among the most pressing problems, in addition to benefit cost. Fifty-one percent indicated they would like to see benefits play an increasingly larger role in the total employee compensation picture, while half indicated that the major development they would like to see in pensions and employee benefits in the future is a relaxation of government regulation and interference, with more emphasis placed on individual savings, including tax incentives, and more flexibility and options in the plans. Fifty-three percent said they planned to pass along to their employees some of the increased costs of providing benefits, and 51 percent plan to pass costs along to the consumer. A quarter of the respondents said the fundamental change they would make in their employee benefit program would be to have employees share more of the costs. It is reasonable to assume that the continued depressed economy, and the resultant depressed financial condition of many employers, will not only continue this trend but actually accelerate it in the near future.

Today's focus is on ways to maintain employee morale while keeping the cost of benefits down to a manageable level. This emphasis is sure to continue in the future.

### Conclusion

In conclusion factors affecting the direction of fringe benefits in the future can be summarized as follows:

— Benefits have risen as a direct result of union-won demands over the years. When companies consider basic pay demands too high, they move to the benefits area as an additional negotiating chip.
— Successful experimentation with "cafeteria plans" has shown that employees regard the option of picking and choosing benefit alternatives as an extremely attractive addition to traditional compensation programs.
— People do have different needs according to their age, financial and family position, attitudes, and life style. Younger employees tend to favor benefits that can be of frequent or immediate use, such as vaca-

tion days, holidays and flexible working hours. Older employees are usually security conscious, preferring life insurance and retirement-related benefits.

— For certain employees, extra vacation days or the opportunity to take a leave of absence is of enormous psychological value, far beyond its actual cost to the company.

— Increasingly, organizations with well-constructed benefit programs are gaining a competitive edge in the recruiting process. The swing elements, however, are not the traditional benefits but, rather, the additional special coverages.

— Whether the employer continues to pay the lion's share of the cost of these new packages, or shifts more responsibility to the employee, is directly related to the performance of the economy and its resultant influence on company profit and lost statements.

— Fringe-benefit packages are undergoing their most radical change since World War II, with emphasis placed on coming up with new ideas and tailoring the system to individual employees, rather than increasing the level of existing benefits and offering one package to all. This will, in turn, give fringe benefits more "bang for the bucks" and increase their importance in the total compensation scheme beyond their already sizable, and constantly growing, 35 percent. Fringe benefits will be "where the action is" in the near future.

# Strategic Human Resource Mandates For The 1990's

*Kenneth A. Kovach*
*John A. Pearce II*

As we begin the 1990's, it is evident that significant demographic shifts are taking place in U.S. society that will profoundly impact corporate human resource management in the decade ahead. While strategic managers are being alerted to the general nature of the changes, little progress has been made in identifying their HRM consequences. Since new demographics will dictate bold new initiatives for planners, it is imperative that they be aware of what the coming changes are and begin to formulate strategies to deal with them. From the perspective of HRM, this article looks at some of the best available information on the most imposing changes of the 1990's, and suggests coping and proactive strategies for succeeding in the highly dynamic environment of the new decade that is upon us.

## The Changes

Dramatic transformations are occurring in the U.S. labor force. Changes in participant age, sex, race, ethnic origin and geographic location must be understood and analyzed separately, for each will dictate a separate response by corporate human resource planners.

### Age: Younger Workers

The segment of the labor force under 25-years of age will decrease by 3.4 percent during the 1990's, a drastic reversal from what was experienced during the 1970's and early 1980's. As a result, human resource managers will be faced with a two-pronged problem. On one hand, less pressure will come from employee ranks for those jobs with the characteristics typically favored most by younger workers, e.g., incentive pay systems tied to personal performance, task related programs including job enlargement and job enrichment etc. This is not to say that these factors will cease to be influential in determining employee attitudes, but rather that they will be less emphasized, due to the decreasing percentage of employees in the age group typically most influenced by them.

On the other hand, the smaller pool of younger workers will experience increased attention from recruiters seeking to fill entry-level positions. To attract these employees, human resource planners will be forced to place a greater emphasis on inhouse training and development programs. The younger age group's opportunity for rapid advancement is going to be somewhat limited by the bulge in baby-boom, middle-age workers who are ahead of them in the corporate hierarchies. The availability of inhouse training and development programs which will enable younger employees to distinguish themselves from their peers when competing for the limited number of mid-level positions, will be a valuable recruiting tool in the coming decade.

### Age: Middle-Aged Workers

The 25–54-year age group will be the fastest growing age segment of the labor force from now until the year 2000, increasing 27 percent. When compared with the decrease in the percentage of younger workers and a slight increase in older workers, the 25–54-year olds will be "where the action is" for human resource managers in the 1990's. The baby boomers of post-World War II are the subgroup most responsible for this increase, as evidenced by the fact that by the year 2000, the 40–54-year-old group will comprise 25 percent of the U.S. population.

A major challenge for human resource managers will be to prepare for the probable job displacement of many of these workers as a result of automation. The 25-to-40 segment of this age group will not be covered by the provisions of the 1967 Age Discrimination in Employment Act and the 40–54 segment will have less seniority than the traditionally more job-stable 55-and-over sector. Therefore, 25-to-54-year old employees will be most susceptible to job displacement. Additionally, when automation impacts workers in this age group, they will be forced to continue employment, either with the same employer or elsewhere, whereas younger workers will be denied employment originally and older workers may choose early retirement. As a result, job displacement due to automation will hit middle-aged workers harder than any other.

Human resource managers must thus be prepared to introduce policies in company programs and union contracts that address the issue of job displacement due to automation. Job security as a trade-off for wage increases became an increasingly accepted idea in the late 1980's, and will continue. The "deals" in this regard between management and labor in the automobile, steel, and general manufacturing sectors in the past decade are only a trickle compared to the flood of such arrangements one can expect to see due to technological advances in the 1990's. Such arrangements will be born of economic necessity by both employees and employers. For example, one of the most popular forms of job security is likely to be a clause wherein employees above a certain seniority level will be retrained for another position within the company.

Pension portability will also be a response to automation's impact on middle-aged workers over the next ten years. The older of the baby boomers will be of an age where they must begin long-term retirement planning. Increased solvency problems with Social Security, and E.R.I.S.A. restrictions on options for vesting of private pensions, will make portability of seniority for pension rights a major issue in the near future. Intercorporate and inter-industry agreements for pension portability will become commonplace by the turn of the century, with combined employer funding of such plans expected to be a major concern of human resource experts.

"Attrition" arrangements, whereby the employer reduces the labor force by agreeing to replace employees who leave through normal attrition rather than by layoffs prompted by automation, will likewise gain wide acceptance. Such arrangements will often be palatable to middle-aged workers faced with the alternative of job loss and will allow employers to address the issue of technology and displacement in a socially acceptable way.

For employees who are displaced due to automation, the employer is likely to have some type of supplemental unemployment coverage. Over 5 million employees now receive coverage where the company finances a private unemployment plan to supplement state plans for workers above a certain seniority level. The middle-aged workers of the 1990's will be drawing from such plans since they will have a qualifying level of seniority to be eligible, but—as opposed to older workers—will not have enough seniority to avoid the technologically induced layoff. As a result, supplemental unemployment costs will rise as the number of covered employees goes to an estimated 1 million during the 1990's.

### Age: Older Workers

The segment of the labor force aged 55 and older will increase by 3.4 percent during the 1990's, exactly offsetting the decrease in the percentage of younger workers. While the increase in this age segment will be dwarfed by the growth of the middle-aged group, older workers will present unique and serious problems for human resource managers. Nowhere will these problems be more acute than in the areas of retirement and health care costs.

By the turn of the century a number of factors will have come together to drastically increase retirement costs for the typical U.S. employer. The increase in older workers eligible to receive retirement benefits does not begin to tell the story of the approaching problem with retirement financing. More and more employers will be forced to offer early retirement options as a result of 1986 changes in the Age Discrimination Act, whereby the upper age of the protected group went from 70 to infinity for many employers. Such options will be offered in an attempt to replace older workers with younger ones, as a means to save on wage costs (where seniority is a wage factor within jobs) and insurance costs (when age profiles influence company premiums). Moderating the widespread use of such policies will be increased retirement costs and rapidly rising starting wage rates for the undersized pool of younger workers.

Additionally, the practice started in the middle 1980's of using later employment years, as opposed to income averaging, when figuring income for pension purposes can be expected to continue and to further increase pension costs.

Cost containment managers should anticipate yet another major negative factor that will influence retirement costs. The introduction of cost-of-living adjustments to pension payments is presently done by only a small segment of employers and even there takes place on an *ad hoc* basis. Starting with the organized labor sector and gradually spreading to the rest of the labor force, C.O.L.A. clauses in pension plans will begin to appear during the 1990's, with regularly scheduled rather than sporadic adjustments. Such adjustments already take place in Social Security and federal and military pensions, but the federal government has found it possible to operate with huge deficit budgets. Such a luxury is not available to the private sector and the financial implications of C.O.L.A. clauses in the pension plans of major employers are staggering. Current estimates are that even a weak C.O.L.A. clause, one that adjusts for only 50 percent of the inflation rate, will increase the cost of the average private-sector plan by 30–33 percent over the next decade. Yet a dramatic increase in the number of these clauses seems probable, meaning that human resource managers and cost containment specialists should prepare accordingly.

Anyone who doubts that the above factors (older work force, early retirement options, later years for income calculations, and C.O.L.A. clauses) do not add up to a serious cost problem for the 1990's, needs only to contemplate the fact that in 1983 a Health, Education and Welfare Department study found that unfunded vested pension liabilities of all public and private pension systems exceeded $600 billion, while Standard and Poors Compustat Services found that such liabilities exceeded the net worth in some companies. *Business Week* found that underfunding was almost $22 billion among their top 100 corporations (AFL-CIO News, 1989). The factors discussed above will only exacerbate the solvency problem in the 1990's.

In addition to pension issues, the larger segment of older workers will cause problems in the area of health-care costs. In 1988, 10 percent of the U.S. GNP went to medical expenses. By the year 2000, the figure will rise to 15 percent. From the corporate perspective, this escalation raises serious questions about health-care cost containment. Since people typically incur 85 percent of their health care expenses during the last two years of life, it is easy to see why even a modest percentage increase in the older segment of the labor force foretells a drastic increase in health care costs. Also to be remembered is that since 1967, health care has been the area of the U.S. economy hit hardest by inflation. The average employer now spends $2,200 per employee, per year on health care, an expenditure that is expected to increase 15–20 percent this year alone!

As a result of the aging labor force and the impact of inflation, budget analysts, corporate planners, and human resource managers will need to devise a corporate strategy for health care cost containment. They should be looking at policies to curb excessive use of hospitals through utilization reviews, outpatient and surgicenter care, insurance coverage of second and even third opinions on elective surgery, reimbursement for health services at home, greater use of preadmission testing, and increased private use of professional standards review organizations. Health maintenance organizations (H.M.O.'s) also offer significant cost advantages when required as part of the employers' insurance package. Today only 13 percent of employer-provided health coverage includes use of a H.M.O. By the year 2000, almost 60 percent of such plans will have use of a specified H.M.O. as a component.

Finally, it can be expected that more of the cost for health care will be passed on to the employee. In 1980, 50 percent of employer health care plans were contributory. In 1988, the figure rose to 62 percent and by the year 2000, it may well approach 80 percent.

Obviously, containment of retirement and health care costs will be a major area of activity in the near future as a result of the increase in older employees.

### Sex: Female Employees

There can be no doubt that one of the most striking changes experienced in the labor force during this decade will be the increasing participation of women in full-time jobs. By the year 2000, women will comprise 65 percent of the entering labor force—their percentage of the labor force will have increased 27 points from 1989 levels—and they will comprise 47 percent of all U.S. workers.

The stereotypical family unit of a generation ago, with the male breadwinner, the female housewife, and one or more children, applies to less than 15 percent of the U.S. families today. At present in the U.S., nearly 50 percent of married women with children under two-years old are working, with 62 percent of all mothers working outside the home. If the present trend of an annual three percent increase in working mothers continues, by 1995 over 80 percent of all mothers with children at home will be working. Only part of this increase will come from women seeking self-fulfillment through careers; the rest will be the result of economic necessity.

From 1960 to 1973, family income increased every year, but the purchasing power achieved in 1973 has not been matched since, with the decline hitting families with young children particularly hard. In 1973, households headed by over-30-year-old males earned $25,253 (in 1988 dollars), while in 1988 that figure had dropped to $18,763. Of the married women who worked outside the home, 40 percent had husbands whose annual incomes were less than $15,000 (AFL-CIO News, 1989). Thus, more and more women are working simply to maintain an economic standard of living equal to their counterparts of 15 or 20 years ago.

As these trends continue through the next decade, they can be expected to elicit a different set of responses than those occasioned by the age shifts discussed earlier. While changes in labor force composition by age can be dealt with through internal company policies, the increasing number of women in the full-time labor force can be expected to draw a legislative response. The most important Congressional initiative is the proposed Family and Medical Leave Bill (H.R. 770), a key item on the agenda of the Congressional Democratic leadership. This bill, already approved by the House Education and Labor Committee and with over 200 sponsors in the House, will require all companies with 50 or more employees to provide unpaid leave of up to ten weeks every two years for parents of newborn or newly adopted children, up to ten weeks to care for a seriously ill child or elderly parent, and up to fifteen weeks for the employee's own serious illness. Three years after enactment, the bill would apply to employers with 35 or more employees (U.S. Congress, 1988). This bill, in its present or amended form, can be expected to pass sometime during the 1990's. Magnifying the cost impact of this legislation is the fact that as a result of the age trend discussed earlier, women entering the work force in the greatest number will be those of childbearing age, who will disproportionately seek the benefits made available under the new law.

Another legislative response that seems likely is the Act for Better Child Care Bill (S5). Having already cleared the Senate Labor and Human Resource Committee, and with a large number of congressional sponsors, this bill would set federal standards for child-care facilities, establish a referral system, provide financial assistance to low-income families who need such care, and help fund the expansion of existing facilities. When one considers that at present there are 36.2 million children with one or both parents working, and only 2.5 million child-care slots in licensed facilities (U.S. Congress, 1988), there is reason to believe that employers will be playing a major role in establishing such facilities during this decade.

Thus, on the two big issues tied to female labor force participation, family and medical leave and child care, the human resource manager of the 1990's should implement company policies similar to those just discussed, rather than wait for legislative dictates and then assume a passive role of compliance. In addition, companies should implement other adjustments to the needs of their female labor force through internal initiatives such as pooled sick leave, flexitime, summer working hours, four-day weeks, split days, job sharing, and telecommuting for "number crunching" jobs that can be done at home.

## Race and Ethnic Origin: Blacks, Hispanics

Although caucasians will remain the major labor group in the U.S. through the year 2000, their absolute numbers will increase only 15 percent, compared with a 20 percent increase for blacks and a 74 percent increase for Hispanics. The fertility rate among Hispanic women is presently 96 births per 1,000, compared with 83 for blacks and 69 for whites. These facts, coupled with heavy immigration, will make the Hispanic growth rate faster than that of any other race or ethnic group in this country.

Present projections indicate that Hispanics will comprise 10.5 percent of the work force by the turn of the century and will surpass blacks as the largest racial minority in the next 20–25 years. Thus, human resource planners and recruiters will have to adjust their mindset on minority employment from simply *black* to *Hispanic* and *black.* As the relative number of each of these groups increases in the next ten years, their skills and productivity are likely to be an increasingly important element in determining a corporations' future prosperity.

The problems to be faced when dealing with this growing segment of the work force stem from the deprived backgrounds and low education levels that characterize a disproportionate number of these employees. While 86 percent of white workers presently have at least a high school diploma, only 60 percent of Hispanics and 73 percent of blacks have this level of formal education. With the fastest-growing occupations requiring a college degree or extensive training beyond high school (e.g., computer analyst and processor, increase 75.6 percent by year 2000; medical assistant, increase 90.4 percent; paralegal personnel, increase 103 percent, etc.) the lack of highly educated and trained personnel among the fastest-growing racial and ethnic groups will dictate a greater emphasis on inhouse training programs. Such programs will by necessity be job-specific and targeted toward expediting the employment of the least-educated personnel in entry-level, nonsupervisory jobs. Recall our earlier findings that the decrease in the number of younger workers and the bottleneck created by the baby boomers will increase the importance of training for the under-25 age group. Now we see that an increasing share of this young age group will consist of lesser-educated black and Hispanic workers. The conclusion is that during the 1990's such training programs should be of the job specific, entry-level nature for many workers.

## Geographic Location: South and West

Since the late 1950's, the North's population growth has slowed, while growth in the South and West has increased rapidly. Between now and 2000, the North's population will increase 4 percent, while that of the South and West will exceed 20 percent. Current trends indicate that by the year 2030, the population of the South will overtake that of the Northeast and Midwest combined. Of the 32.5 million new jobs created by the year 2000, 18 million will be in the South, 10 million in the West, and under 5 million in the North. Among the 50 fastest growing metropolitan areas over the next ten years, 20 will be in the South and 16 in the West with 11 in California, six in Florida, and five in Texas. Furthermore, the Far West, especially California and Washington, with their extensive production facilities, will dominate the production sector of the economy as more and more businesses relocate. The shift of industry follows the population movement, which, in turn, attracts more industry. The cycle is already in motion and is irreversible in the foreseeable future. The result of these shifts will be an HRM troublespot in the 1990's. Plant closings and relocations from the North, Northeast and Midwest will become more common as a result of the population shifts just discussed.

The fact that industry is and will continue to relocate to the South and West seems indisputable. If one agrees that the shift will continue, and then contemplates the number of citizens affected and the resultant political pressure for regulation of such an industrial movement, it is clear that this geographic shift of population and industry will occasion a legislative response.

Thusfar, organized labor has forced the issue of plant closings in three arenas. At the bargaining table, they have been moderately successful in getting contract clauses that require management to deal with labor on the effects of plant closings (advance notice, retraining, relocation allowances, and reinstatement rights), though not on the closing decision itself. The second arena is the court system where the U.S. Supreme Court has recognized a management duty to bargain over the effects of plant closings *(First National Maintenance Corp. v. N.L.R.B.*, 1981), but has removed the actual decision to close from mandatory bargaining *(N.L.R.B. v. Adams Dairy, Inc.* 1965). Finally, in the Congressional arena, bills have been introduced to eliminate or cushion the impact of employee dislocation in every session since 1974. It is in Congress that the definitive word on plant closings and relocations can be expected to surface sometime in the next few years. Congress is presently awaiting a report on plant closing from the Task Force on Economic Adjustment and Worker Dislocation, formed by the Secretary of Labor. The report is expected to recommend legislation that would require the following actions by companies contemplating closing and relocation:

— Employers will be required to give three months advance notice of a plant closing.

— Closings will be prohibited unless and until the employer has met with representatives, if any, of employees and consulted in good faith for the purpose of reaching a mutually satisfactory alternative or modification to the plant closing plan.

— A 15–member National Commission on Plant Closings and Worker Dislocation will be established to study and report legislative recommendations concerning closings.

Thus, employers can be expected to continue the rush to the South and West, but will be required to comply with soon-to-be passed legislation regulating conditions of relocations.

## Conclusion

The labor force trends discussed in this article will all have major implications for human resource managers during the 1990's. Only by being aware of such trends can responsible individuals begin to formulate intelligent corporate responses. The responses discussed can serve as a starting point for strategic human resource planning. In some cases, bold corporate initiatives are called for, while in others, simple legislative compliance will suffice. In any event, the labor force changes over the next decade will have serious negative repercussions for those caught unaware. This article has been an attempt to help planners avoid such situations and to begin to think about their reactions to the coming demographic changes of the 1990's. The time to begin was yesterday.

## References

*AFL-CIO News*. 1989: 3–6. For a fascinating look at the solvency problem with many pension plans, see *Business Week*, 1981. Pension Liabilities: Improvement Is Illusory: 114–118.

*First National Maintenance Corp. v. N.L.R.B.* 1981. 452 U.S. 666.

*N.L.R.B. v. Adams Dairy, Inc.* 1965. 350F. 2d, 108. For an overview of what Congress, the Supreme Court, and present collective bargaining patterns are doing in the area of plant closings see *Business Horizons*, 1987. Is the American Industrial Relations System Failing? 44–49.

United States Congress, House, Committee on Education and Labor. 1988. Parental and Medical Leave Act, Hearing. Washington, D.C., U.S.G.P.O.: 15–16.

United States Congress, House, Committee on Education and Labor. 1988. *Summary of Committee Action. The Family and Medical Leave Act*. For a detailed discussion of the Act see *Labor Law Journal*. 1987. Creeping Socialism or Good Public Policy? What You Should Know About the Proposed Parental and Medical Leave Act: 427–432.

# The Case Against Litton Industries

In August of 1982, lawyers representing a number of unions approached the National Labor Relations Board to ask that Litton Industries be treated as a single employer for purposes of unfair labor practice cases brought against the company.[1] Until that time, the Board had treated each individual Litton division as a separate entity on most labor relations matters, including unfair labor practice charges. The unions contended that this practice of the Board needed to be changed since the conglomerate had, in their opinion, a history of willful, repeated labor law violations that was not evident when each division was treated separately.

Litton Industries is a multinational conglomerate headquartered in Beverly Hills, California, with ninety divisions and wholly-owned subsidiaries. Its products include business and office machines, data automation equipment, marine and aircraft electronics, medical and electrical equipment, machine tools, microwave cooking products, resource exploration, and shipbuilding. Litton has 77,000 employees, twenty percent of whom are unionized, in 80 major plants in thirty states. In fiscal year 1984, it had revenues of 4.94 billion dollars, including 1.5 billion dollars in Department of Defense contracts.

Over the last twenty years, the NLRB has lodged over 50 major unfair labor practice charges against Litton, but since many include multiple counts of illegal activity, the actual number of violations of labor law runs well into the hundreds. The board and/or courts have found Litton guilty on over twenty of these counts, with the company settling before trial by offering remedial action (reinstatement, back pay, etc.) in another twenty.

A case can be built based on charges filed that the company has systematically used plant closings, layoffs, and the threat of same to discourage future unionization and to rid itself of existing unions. For example, when the microwave factory in Minneapolis went union, the number of jobs fell from 1400 to 300 as positions were shifted to a new plant in South Dakota. When union troubles started at the Jefferson Electric plant near Chicago, 500 jobs were suddenly shifted to Alabama. Ten plants have been closed, each after undergoing some form of organizing activity. In one case, by the time the NLRB ruled that Litton had to offer employees from a recently closed plant jobs at a new plant because the old one had been closed to "bust" the union, the new plant had been closed and the jobs relocated again.[2] At the McBee Systems plant in Athens, Ohio, the company violated the terms of an NLRB ruling by initiating a decertification election against the Graphic Arts International Union.

The company has been found guilty on a number of occasions of intimidating and spying on employees, of unlawful refusals to bargain in good faith, and of eliminating health and medical benefits unilaterally. Four workers who were trying to organize a local of the International Union of Electrical, Radio, and Machine Workers at the Triad-Utrad plant in Indiana were fired for their part in the organizing activities. By the time they were ordered reinstated, the organizing drive had failed. After the Aluminum Workers' Union won a certification election at the Jefferson Electric plant in Alabama, the top organizers were fired. Other union supporters were moved to the dirtiest jobs in the plant, and two first-line supervisors who refused to harass union activists testified that they were fired for their refusal. For over two years after the Printers' Union won a certification election at the plant in Santa Clara, California, the company refused to bargain. Faced with an NLRB final order to bargain with the union, the company closed the plant. And, finally, an eight-month strike resulted when the company demanded that the Machinists' Union surrender seniority rights and unilaterally attempted to set wage rates and eliminate or reduce health and medical benefits.[3]

Litton officials continue to insist that each division administers its own labor relations program without direction from headquarters, and that because of this, the unions' contention that the NLRB treat the company as a single entity for purposes of handling unfair labor practice complaints is inappropriate. These officials deny charges of anti-union bias and continually emphasize the fact that twenty percent of Litton's work force is organized (the same as the national average) and that, in the last fourteen months, twelve new collective bargaining agreements have been signed without a work stoppage.

### Sioux Falls Plant

As stated earlier, Litton's labor troubles go back to the early 1960's, yet the situation began to reach its present untenable position in 1980 at the company's microwave cooking products plant in Sioux Falls, South Dakota. The majority of the company's microwave oven production had recently been moved there from Minneapolis, after the latter had experienced union trouble. After a somewhat bitter organizing drive, the small, independent United Electrical, Radio, and Machine Workers of America was certified at the Sioux Falls plant. After months of futile negotiations, the union filed an unfair labor practice charge with the NLRB, charging the company with refusing to bargain in good faith. After investigating, the General Counsel saw fit to file a complaint with the Board, charging Litton with seventy counts of unfair labor practices.[4]

The case was tried before Administrative Law Judge David L. Evans on 67 different dates between March 9, 1982, and January 26, 1983. It produced the following examples of company violations of the National Labor Relations Act: Company officials violated Section 8(a)(1) of the Act five times by interfering with legitimate union-organizing efforts. Company officials violated Section 8(a)(3) of the Act five times by issuing improper warning notices to employees engaged in legitimate union business. And the company refused to bargain collectively in good faith concerning wages, hours, and other terms and conditions of employment, specifically by: having an overall intent not to reach an agreement; refusing to negotiate on the issue of a checkoff; insisting on an unusually harsh absence-control program; providing false and misleading reasons for wage proposals; taking unilateral actions concerning the length of breaks and lunch periods, and, finally; refusing to furnish required information to the union concerning the company's financial position and, in one instance, providing false information in this area.[5]

In this particular case, Litton received a recommended order from Judge Evans, subject to NLRB approval and court challenges. It required that Litton cease and desist from these unlawful practices, begin good faith negotiations, and post an NLRB notice stating what the company will and will not do to rectify the situation.

While the specific trouble at Sioux Falls, detailed above, is illustrative of Litton's overall labor policy, it at least appears headed for a satisfactory resolution. This particular situation, however, is most important in that it was the incident that galvanized union resistance to Litton's practices and forced the various unions at Litton to unite and seek a long-term, general resolution covering the conglomerate's companywide labor policy.

## Campaign Against Litton

The union campaign to stop Litton's unfair labor practices took two main thrusts. The first of these was the formation of a coalition of unions to oppose Litton's practices. The actions of Litton at Sioux Falls caused the union there to seek a partnership with other unions representing different plants and/or divisions of the conglomerate, based on a proven pattern in the company's actions that affected all unions.

In November 1983, Howard D. Samuel, president of the AFL-CIO's Industrial Union Department, took control of this union partnership and began directing the campaign against Litton. It was this coalition, presently consisting of eleven unions, that has asked the NLRB to declare Litton a single employer with a unified labor policy.

I feel that the success of the coalition in achieving this goal is crucial in the continuing fight against Litton. While getting the NLRB to declare Litton a single employer will not make unfair labor practices any easier to prove, or cut down on company delaying tactics, it will provide for stronger and more far-reaching remedies covering the whole company, rather than specific installations. From a union perspective, when dealing with an employer as large and diverse as Litton, such a situation is not only desirable, it is, in fact, essential. Conversely, I must caution the reader that, given the present composition of the NLRB as appointed by President Reagan, it is by no means certain that the Board will rule in favor of the coalition of unions and declare Litton a single entity. (This should be taken as a simple statement of fact, not a value judgment as to what the Board's decision should be.) The coalition has also organized protests at various Litton plants, NLRB regional offices and at the annual Litton stockholders' meeting.[6]

The second thrust of the campaign against Litton is legislative. In April 1983, Representative Paul Simon (D, MO) introduced legislation (H.R. 174) that would bar consistent labor law violators from receiving federal contracts. This bill presently has over 130 cosponsors and has given rise to a similar bill in the Senate (S. 1079), introduced by Senator Edward Kennedy (D MA). Called the Federal Debarment Bill, it would apply to companies or unions that establish a pattern of willful violations of final NLRB orders. Relief from debarment would only be granted upon affirmative corrective action or for national security considerations.

Litton would be especially vulnerable to such legislation, due to its 1.5 billion dollars in Department of Defense contracts and its recent purchases of the Itek Corporation and the Laser Weapons Systems Division of Martin Marietta, both of which are involved in laser weapons development and production under President Reagan's "Star Wars" space defense proposals. In light of these recent purchases, Litton's present $1.5 billion in Defense contracts may soon grow to a considerably larger figure. Hence, the company is vulnerable to this legislative thrust. As is to be expected, Litton is actively campaigning against the Federal Debarment Bill, claiming that thousands of workers could be severely hurt by a debarment action. The composition of Congress after the November, 1986 elections goes a long way toward determining the success of this second, legislative thrust against Litton.

On November 1, 1983, William A. Lubbers, then General Counsel of the NLRB, announced a plan to monitor Litton's subsidiaries as a group to determine if the parent company controlled their labor relations. He instructed the NLRB's thirty-three Regional Directors to identify all Litton subsidiaries in their regions and keep a list of all Board and court orders against them. The appropriate unions were informed that they had a right to name Litton in addition to the subsidiary, when filing unfair labor practice charges. Lubbers also established a special committee within the NLRB to review all charges against Litton subsidiaries.[7]

While such actions are a necessary first step, as stated earlier, I feel that with the present composition of the Board itself (as opposed to its General Counsel), it would be best to withhold judgment as to the effectiveness of the union coalition and its influence on the Board, until such time as actual decisions are rendered in the numerous Litton cases. The reader can then see if the Board's decision(s) are directed at Litton as an entity, or simply a subsidiary thereof.

Perhaps as a result of this movement by the Board, Mathias J. Diederick, chief labor negotiator for Litton, and James C. Allen, Director of Coordinated Bargaining, Industrial Union Division, AFL-CIO, have recently agreed to enter into a continuing dialogue to discuss all pertinent labor issues at Litton and to refrain from any future inflammatory statements.[8] (Sometimes you do not actually have to hit people over the head with a club; the threat of doing so is enough!)

On the legislative side of the issue, the House debarment bill was approved by the House Labor-Management Relations Subcommittee and is presently before the full House Education and Labor Committee. There appears to be a very good chance that the bill will pass the House, but it faces strong opposition from the Republican majority in the Senate.[9]

Shortly after the debarment legislation was introduced, Litton Chairman Fred O'Green made a surprising public statement suggesting that the company and the union coalition enter direct talks, through a joint panel, to resolve the escalating labor disputes. While the statement caught the unions by surprise, Mr. Samuel of the AFL-CIO's Industrial Union Department stated that the coalition welcomed the proposal.[10]

## Conclusion

Although the final results are not yet in, the early returns show progress for organized labor in its confrontation with Litton Industries. The actions of the General Counsel of the National Labor Relations Board and the Congressional Subcommittee on the debarment bill both hold promise that Litton's lawlessness will not be allowed to continue indefinitely.

However, the reader should take note that, in both instances, these are intermediate and not final steps. The full board still has to act on the General

Counsel's lead and issue appropriate decisions in cases involving Litton subsidiaries, and the full Congress still must act on the debarment bill before it really means anything.

In the case of the NLRB, the crucial battles are being fought in Senate confirmation hearings of Board members and, with one exception, President Reagan's nominees have survived. In the case of Congress, much will be determined by the political party composition of both the House and the Senate after the 1986 elections.

The reader would do well to keep in mind the outcome of the 1978 "labor law reform bill" presented by President Carter to a Congress with a Democratic majority in both Houses. It also had a provision similar to the present debarment bill and went down to defeat by one vote in the Senate after passing the House.

I would advise against holding your breath until either the Board acts on the General Counsel's groundwork, or until Congress sends the debarment bill to the President. The fact, while I do feel that Litton is systematically and willfully violating the law with direction from the top, it will probably be able to continue to do so for the foreseeable future. Nobody said life was fair.

### Footnotes

[1]Tamar Lewin, "Conglomerates: Test for Labor," *New York Times*, January 11, 1983, p. D2.

[2]George C. Higgins, "The Litton Campaign: Unions United," *America* (August 27, 1983), p. 85.

[3]Lance Compa, "How to Fight a Union-Busting Conglomerate," *The Nation* (July 9–16, 1983), p. 40.

[4]"Testing a New Weapon Against Litton," *Business Week* (December 27, 1982), p. 32.

[5]*Litton Microwave Cooking Products, Division of Litton Systems, Inc., vs. United Electrical, Radio, and Machine Workers of America*, JD-77-84, pp. 174–176.

[6]"Labor Escalates its Campaign Against Litton," *Business Week* (November 21, 1984), p. 47.

[7]*Ibid.*, p. 51.

[8]Telephone interview with James C. Allen, April 10, 1984.

[9]Telephone interview with Joseph Jerel, Legislative Assistant to Rep. Paul Simon (D. Mo.), April 11, 1984.

[10]Thomas C. Hayes, "Litton Asks Panel on Labor," *New York Times* (December 12, 1983), p. D14.

# The National Labor Relations Board

## Current Problems and Suggested Changes

The United States system of labor relations is the most legalistic in the Free World today. Pressures applied to change national labor policy in the past can be expected to continue in the future. Involved in this struggle is the basic issue of how the economy should function. The outcome of the battle will influence many of the basic economic decisions made in society—how the economy should function and for whom. Positioned in the middle of this constant struggle is the National Labor Relations Board. To discuss its current influence upon labor-management relations and vice versa, one must briefly examine the roles played by management and labor and the role of the Board in implementing the National Labor Relations Act of 1935.

The National Labor Relations Board was created by Congress for the sole purpose of administering the Wagner Act in accordance with public policy. Public policy in 1935, as now, was declared to be: "to eliminate the causes of certain substantial obstructions to the free flow of commerce and to mitigate and eliminate these obstructions when they have occurred by encouraging the practice and procedure of collective bargaining and by protecting the exercise by workers of full freedom of association, self-organization, and designation of representatives of their own choosing, for the purpose of negotiating the terms and conditions of their employment or other mutual aid or protection."[1] The achievement of this aim through even-handed administration and judicious interpretation and enforcement of the Act is the overall job of the Board. In its statutory assignment, the Board has two primary functions: (1) to determine and implement, through secret-ballot elections, the free democratic choice by employees as to whether they wish to be represented by a union and, if so, by which one; and (2) to prevent and remedy unlawful acts, called unfair labor practices, by either employers or unions. It consists of five members appointed by the President for five-year staggered terms. Any three members may constitute a panel for the purpose of rendering a decision. But the Board does not initiate a case; it must wait until a charge or petition is filed and certain other procedures are complied with, before any disputes may come before it for decision.

No other quasi-judicial agency exhibits to the same extent a separation of the powers of prosecution and decision. Judicial power resides in the Board proper, but the function of prosecution is lodged in the Board's General Counsel, an independent officer appointed by the President for a four-year term. The functions of the General Counsel flow partly from the statute and partly from powers delegated by the Board. Under the statute, this officer's basic duties are: (1) to determine whether, when, and upon what basis charges of unfair labor practices should be prosecuted—this determination is final with no appeal either to the Board or the courts is permitted; and (2) to supervise all employees in the regional offices and all attorneys except those serving as Administrative Law Judges and legal assistants to the Board members. With these powers and responsibilities in mind, I will examine some of the present problems with, and restrictions of, the National Labor Relations Board.

Public policy toward organized labor has changed significantly over the years. Every law since The Federal Anti-Injunction Act has expanded the scope of government regulation of the labor-management arena. Legislative control over collective bargaining started in 1932 (Norris-LaGuardia) when the judiciary was limited in the use of injunctions to deal with labor disputes. In 1935 (Wagner), Congress was concerned primarily with restricting employer conduct. The legislative branch attempted to balance the scales in collective bargaining in 1947 (Taft-Hartley), by placing limitations on union conduct, and in 1959 (Landrum-Griffin), it moved forward again by enacting legislation to deal with internal union affairs, with employee rights being the main issue. All of these changes in the nation's labor policy were brought into being by the introduction of new areas of labor-management relations, realignment of political power, public dissatisfaction with the power of employers and unions, serious economic problems, or marked alterations in the labor force. The Board, in its implementation of the NLRA, has acted as a barometer for legislative change in national labor policy, brought about by labor or management-backed forces.

It has become obvious to many parties that the Board has outlived some of its usefulness, in regard to the most important areas of its unfair labor practice jurisdiction. These areas include contract interpretation, arbitration, racial and sexual discrimination, and relations between employees and their unions. Legislation and/or other agencies which have come into existence since the Board's formation have taken over these functions. The Board is still viable, however, in the area of traditional conflicts concerning efforts of employees and unions to organize, and the achievement of collective bargaining. It is these areas, where the Board is still the main force, that are most glaringly in need of procedural change. Over the years, a major complaint made by unions against the Board has been the time lag involved from the date of filing petitions for representation elections, to the final holding of elections to determine employee choice. The essential element for labor unions is the ability to expedite election proceedings to sustain bargaining unit enthusiasm when voting for union representation. The theory of the law is that NLRB-conducted elections will be promptly held, and where the vote is for a union, employers will accept the majority decision of their employees. But under the protection of the Board and NLRA, an employer may challenge the validity of the pre-election investigation to determine, for instance, whether the employer's operations meet the Board's jurisdictional standards, or which employees constitute the bargaining unit the union is representing. Either course of action can result in time-consuming delays before a Board decision is reached and an election held. In the mind of organized labor, this delay produces an unfair advantage to unscrupulous employers who could use this time to influence employees' affiliation through implicit threats of job loss, or more explicitly by reprimanding or discharging union activists in hopes of swinging future election outcomes in their favor. These delays can be prolonged for periods of 200 days or more, from the initial filing to final Board decision.[2] It is a known fact that some employers practice these tactics to avoid elections and union involvement, with coaching from consultants employed specifically to preserve nonunion status in their companies. Delay is regarded as an employer weapon; the longer the period between initiation of an organization attempt and an election, the more discouraged employees become. Surely questions of Board jurisdiction and bargaining unit definition are valid ones and should be dealt with; but as one views the abnormally long delays with certain employer organizations, any rational person must wonder if the questions are raised out of legitimate concern or merely as a stalling tactic.

Another weakness of the Board is the enforcement of its decisions. Unions argue that remedies provided by the labor laws are inadequate to enforce the national labor policy. Unions prefer more severe penalties for flagrant violations of the national labor laws, criminal penalties, triple back pay and withdrawal of governmental contracts from firms engaged in activities calculated to destroy unions. But it must be pointed out again that the Board does not act on its own motion in charges of unfair labor practices or petitions for employee elections. Injured parties must file their claim with one of the Board's 47 regional, subregional, or resident offices. In handling unfair labor cases, the Board is concerned with the adjustment of labor disputes, either by settlements or through its quasi-judicial proceedings. The Board has no independent statutory power of enforcement of its decisions or orders. It must seek enforcement in the U.S. Court of Appeals, and herein lies what one side calls the "power of due process under the law" and the other calls "premeditated attempts at continued delay". An employer found guilty of an unfair labor practice may appeal the regional Board's decision to a Court of Appeals where the time involved in processing the appeal can result, according to NLRB statistics, in a median delay of approximately 365 days.[3] If an issue can be raised that will call for a decision by the full Board in Washington and not just an NLRB regional office, an even longer delay is guaranteed.

A good example of the ineffectiveness of Board decisions and the NLRA itself is the continued violations perpetrated by J. P. Stevens Co. on its employees and the union trying to represent them. A decade of Stevens litigation questions the ability of the courts to make the provisions of the federal labor law work in the face of persistent violations. Simply stated, Stevens would rather incur the punitive measures passed down by the Board and courts, than deal with unionism and collective bargaining.

These procedural delays are of no wonder me, when the rising number of cases filed with the Board each year and the increasing backlog pending at the end of each year are considered. The Board itself is naturally concerned about this increase and especially the 10 percent which are not disposed of at the regional level. As Board Chairman John L. Fanning pondered in his 1977 State-of-the-Board Address, "the basic question is how do we handle that volume of business in a way that does not, through delay, diminish the effectiveness of our administration of the statute?"[4] "No one should ever be content with the time lapses that accompany our decisions, even when no criticism generated by it flourishes. No matter how fast disputes are resolved, room for improvement should always be explored. The best justice is the speediest, within the ambit of our jurisprudential heritage of fairness, of due process."[5] Upon examination of the current caseload, one will notice new types of cases awaiting Board decision, e.g., whether an employer must respond to a union's request for information in the EEO area or jurisdictional applicability in the health care and educational fields. A look at the time involved in processing these cases shows a need for more Administrative Law Judges at the regional level. The trial docket, as of August 1984, stood almost where it did eight months previously, and nearly triple what it was less than three years earlier. To compound this situation, the Agency has projected a trial docket of almost 1,800 cases for the end of fiscal year 1985, unless they are able to get additional Administrative Law Judges.

If all parties are aware of the problems with the current law and the inabilities of the Board to deal with the violators and injured parties involved, the question then becomes: what is being done to relieve this pressure? On August 16, 1977, the Board took what chairman Fanning termed "a significant step to speed election procedures" under which workers voted by secret ballot to select or reject a union as their collective bargaining representative. The Board revised its rules to establish a "vote and impound" procedure enabling employee elections to be held on the date scheduled by an NLRB Regional Director. Previously, voting was postponed whenever the five-member Board in Washington granted an employer's or a union's request to review a Regional Director's rulings. Under the new procedure, the election is held as scheduled without regard to any challenges to the Regional Director's ruling and the employee ballots will be impounded, to be tallied only after the Board disposes of the request for review. Chairman Fanning said the rules revision "provides an important procedural change, one which will enable parties to our elections to plan their campaigns with greater certainty and afford employees the chance to cast their ballots at a time when they are most familiar with the issues involved."[6]

Another change, in addition to the "vote and impound" revision, is H.R. 8410 which easily passed a House of Representatives vote on October 6, 1984, and will be heard in the Senate during the Spring 1985 session. Commonly referred to as the Labor Reform Act of 1985, the labor-backed bill would amend the National Labor Relations Act by setting timetables for the holding of representation elections. The bill provides that where a majority of employees in a clearly appropriate bargaining unit petition for a representation election, the election would be held within 25 days. Where a petition presents issues of exceptional novelty, the time limitation before final Board action would be 75 days. These time limits would apply to decertification elections, as well as certification elections.

The Act would also provide for double back-pay to employees illegally fired during an organizing campaign, up to the signing of an initial contract. Although labor forces were hoping otherwise, House opponents of the bill added an amendment to allow for deductions from the back-pay period for wages earned in the interim. Included in the bill is additional authorization to the Board, allowing it to seek an injunction to stop stranger picketing when it is in violation of a collectively-bargained agreement. Additionally, any person or company found to have willfully violated a final Board order would be barred from participation in Federal contracts for a period not to exceed three years, although the Secretary of Labor may use discretion in lifting the ban in cases of national necessity. The bill also requires that if during an election campaign an employer addressed the employees on its premises or during working hours, the employees would be assured an opportunity to hear the union side in an equivalent manner.

Reaction to the House action ranged from statements that the legislation represents a "giant step toward justice and equity" to assertions that it represents an "outrageous demonstration of unchecked union power."[7] Despite the encouragement of AFL-CIO President Lane Kirkland, who feels the bill will correct the "current imbalance in the nation's labor laws in favor of those employers who willfully and repeatedly violate the law," this legislation makes no proposals that would affect collective-bargaining relationships, strikes, picket lines, boycotts, union security or section 14(b) of Taft-Hartley.

Another proposal for reform, of a more drastic measure than H.R. 8410, has been suggested in some corners. This is the establishment of a United States Labor Court, whose jurisdictional powers would be all-inclusive, formed by the unification of several existing administrative agencies. This "unitary system," as proposed by Charles J. Morris, would give the new Labor Court jurisdiction to enforce rights and duties under several major federal statutes.[8] Principal functions would include the ability to pass judgment on unfair labor practice cases under Section 8 (NLRA), contract enforcement actions under Section 301 (NLRA), private secondary boycott actions under Section 303 (NLRA), and injunctions under the national emergency provision of Title II under the Labor-Management Act. The court would also claim jurisdiction currently exercised by federal district courts under the Railway Labor Act and Title VII of the 1964 and 1972 Civil Rights Act. Should the Court attain an acceptable level of performance, Morris would see its jurisdiction expanded to include decisions under the Labor-Management Reporting and Disclosure Act, the Age Discrimination in Employment Act, the Fair Labor Standards Act, the Occupational Safety and Health Act, and the new Pension Reform Act. The administrative structure of the new Court would consist of three components: first, a board responsible for NLRA and RLA representation questions; second, a mediation agency providing conciliation and mediation under Taft-Hartley and the RLA, and; third, a general counsel to investigate and prosecute under the NLRA, RLA and Title VII of the Civil Rights Act.

It is anticipated that the courts' broad jurisdiction over both the collective bargaining process and the resultant contract would allow for more flexible and effective remedies, and result in a less litigious and chaotic state of labor-management relations.

On a smaller scale and in the area of representation elections, it has been suggested that the NLRB need not supervise these elections at all. Based upon a study he conducted, Julius G. Getman concluded that neither the union nor the company is overly successful in changing workers' predispositions when voting time comes around.[9] Current NLRB restrictions on union and employer campaign speeches, as well as the Board's practice of rerunning many contested elections, could be eliminated under Getman's proposal. Getman questions the Board's long-held assumptions about worker's attitudes and how they are affected by an election campaign. Currently, the Board can void an election for infractions of election procedures under the NLRA, but in doing so is working under the assumption that an "unfair" company or union tactic actually affected the vote. Until Getman's study, there was no empirical data to test this assumption. His study showed conclusively that the majority of workers were not attentive to the issues presented by either side in a campaign, and that while unions may contend that management is able to sway 17 percent of the employee votes during a campaign, the evidence shows that this attrition is due mainly to a lack of faith in unionism, and not due to any employer action or tactic.

While accepting the Board's important contributions and assets, everyone would like to eliminate its lengthy delays, its inadequate remedies, its multiple jurisdictional conflicts, and the recurrent changes in its members. However, unless this country were to experience chaotic changes, such as economic depression or marked political realignments in the legislature, no sweeping Board changes are likely. Management and union organizations are shaped by economic markets and are only modestly affected by labor law. The Board and its administration of the National Labor Relations Act will continue to change only on an incremental basis to meet the need for refinements in national labor law. The latest refinement will go before the Senate in their next session in the form of H.R. 8410. Of the proposals for change presented above, I consider this one both the most reasonable and the one with the best chance of implementation. It is obvious a change is needed. H.R. 8410 may well be the answer.

*Some time after publication of this article H.R. 8410 was debated in the U.S. Senate. Proponents of the bill contend there were 61–63 votes for passage, while opponents put the number at 52–55. In either case, the necessary majority for passage was present. When it became obvious that the bill would be passed in a floor vote, a filibuster was launched that lasted for almost a week. Under Senate rules a simple majority is needed to pass legislation, but 60 votes are needed to cut off debate (i.e., stop the filibuster). Three such votes were taken; the one coming close to the number needed to stop the filibuster being the last—when 59 votes were cast to bring the issue to a floor vote. As a result of this failure to limit the debate, the bill was killed. I still contend that the bill was, and still is, needed, and, I hope that some day a similar piece of legislation will finally be passed.

## Footnotes

[1]Benjamin J. Taylor, Fred Witney, *Labor Relations Law*, 1971, p. 217.

[2]*The AFL-CIO American Federationist*, September 1977, p. 13.

[3]*Ibid.*

[4]Bureau of National Affairs, Inc., *Labor Relations Reporter*, August 22, 1977, p. 95, LRR 382.

[5]*Ibid.*, p. 95, LRR 383.

[6]National Labor Relations Board, Release in AM Papers, October 7, 1977.

[7]Bureau of National Affairs, Inc., *Labor Relations Reporter*, October 17, 1984, p. 96 LRR 124.

[8]Charles J. Morris, "The National Labor Relations Board: Its Future," *Labor Law Journal*, June, 1975, p. 334.

[9]Julius G. Getman, "Do Representation Elections Need the NLRB?" *Business Week*, March 21, 1977, p. 54.

# Should The Davis–Bacon Act Be Repealed?

Fifty-plus years ago, Congress passed the Davis-Bacon Act in order to correct a serious labor abuse caused by two factors: a huge federal construction program and a chaotic labor market. Unscrupulous contractors were winning government contracts by employing itinerant bands of unskilled laborers and paying them exploitive wages. This widespread practice had two results: it took contracts away from local contractors, and it resulted in work of lower quality, since the laborers were, at best, only marginally skilled. The Davis-Bacon Act successfully corrected this abuse.

Today, however, it is questionable whether the Act is viable and effective under current economic conditions, and a move is clearly afoot to repeal the Act or to amend it radically. The champion of the Act is organized labor—primarily the Building and Construction Trades of the AFL-CIO—in tandem with the Department of Labor. Together they have joined to provide almost every work in defense of the Act. The foes of Davis-Bacon are far more diversified and include nine separate Government Accounting Office reports, a Reagan Administration Office of Management and Budget report, and a report by the Congressional Budget Office, to name only a few.[1] As could be expected, management organizations, such as the Association of General Contractors and the U.S. Chamber of Commerce, are also quite vocal in their support for repeal. It is interesting to note that no professional economists have testified in favor of the Davis-Bacon Act.[2]

Ultimately, the fate of the Davis-Bacon Act will be decided by Congress, not necessarily as a result of a rational decision about what is right or wrong, effective or obsolete, but as a clear function of political power. Whether organized labor retains the political potency to stave off the demise of the Act remains to be seen.

I would like to clarify the issue of whether the Davis-Bacon Act remains viable, through a discussion of the historic need for the Act and its present administration; an exploration of some of the major problems attributed to the Act, and; a critical evaluation of some of the recurring arguments favoring the Act.

## Problems of Interpretation

Incongruous as it may seem, the very simplicity of the law has created problems of interpretation. The body of the law states simply that "contractors constructing any building for the United States that costs more than $5,000 must pay to all workers at least the rate of pay prevailing in the locality." An amendment in 1935 lowered the minimum cost to $2,000 and gave the Secretary of Labor the responsibility for determining the prevailing rate of pay. In ensuing years, some sixty statutes have come into being that effectively apply the Davis-Bacon requirements to almost any construction project where federal funds are used.

The Department of Labor has had to evolve a system for determining several factors which affect the rate of pay. They begin by making these three determinations:

- Scope of the market area — how geographically far from the construction project the sample wage levels will be gathered.
- Classification of the project — ranging from heavy construction (highest wage rate) to highway, building, and residential construction (lowest wage rate).
- Designation of job classification and job structure — what specific trade (such as plumber) and experience level are required.

Once these steps are completed, the target group has been identified. The only thing that remains is to compare the wages of the individuals in the group and determine the prevailing wage for this specific project.

Determination of prevailing wage is easiest when at least 50 percent of the target group make the same wage (in both pay and benefits, to the penny). If that is not the case, the Department invokes what is called the "30-percent rule:" when 50 percent of the target group do not make the same wage, then the wage common (again, to the penny) to the largest group representing over 30 percent of the target group shall be the prevailing wage. If this requirement is not met, then a straight average of all wages shall prevail.

It does not take a profound intellect to realize that in most cases where 30 to 50 percent of a group earn exactly the same wage, it is because of a union contract. So today, instead of what the act originally intended — "to guarantee that Federal construction labor be paid the going rate for a particular locality" — prevailing wage has become synonymous with union scale. Even if 70 percent of a target group are earning less than union wage, the government will pay an artificially-high wage, if the remaining 30 percent are earning union scale. In fact, according to the GAO, over one-half of the project determinations that they had reviewed were not even based on wage surveys — they were based on union-negotiated contracts![3]

### Inflation and Price

The application of the Davis-Bacon Act artificially raises the cost of 22 percent of the construction projects undertaken in this country.[4] Quite simply, in those cases where the prevailing wage is in excess of the normal wage, costs are raised without a corresponding raise in productivity—a classic example of a cause of inflation. Estimates on the cost added by Davis-Bacon range from $400 to $900 million per year.[5] Basic administrative improvements could lower the rate of inflation by .3 percent.[6]

Side effects of Davis-Bacon have serious implications for nonunion contractors working on private projects as well. The prospect of ending work on a public project and returning to the previous wage rate, which in many cases is half what the employees earn under Davis-Bacon, can be disastrous to employee morale. It also creates tremendous conflict within companies where only a part of the work force is on a public project. End results are that worker morale decreases, agitation to unionize increases, and pay must be increased to retain personnel. It is estimated that the "spillover" costs of Davis-Bacon to private construction firms are approximately $1.8 billion per year.[7]

The federal level is not the only level of government to suffer the inefficiency and inflationary impact of this law. In 1981, forty-one states still had "little Davis-Bacon Laws" in effect, causing nearly every political subdivision in the country to be faced with the prospect of artificially-high costs on any construction project.[8]

An example will illustrate the magnitude of the cost/inflation problem. In Carson City, Nevada, a federal project required a painter. Department of Labor surveys found eleven similar projects with eight painters as follows: 2 @ $6.25 per hour (25%); 2 @ $7.74 per hour (25%); 1 @ $9.00 per hour (12.5%); and 3 @ $12.40 per hour (37.5%)—prevailing wage. If the two painters who usually work for $6.25 per hour get the contract for the job, the government will spend $6.15 **more** per hour, than is necessary to hire these workers. The price for this one small aspect of the project nearly doubles, and this does not account for the added administrative costs inherent in the Act. By far the most moving argument for repeal of this law is that we can ill afford to continue such an inflationary policy.

## Local Contractors/Small Businesses

The effect of the Department of Labor's fifty-year administration of the law has not been to protect local contractors, but to protect unionized contractors and unions.[9] In 1987, contractors in nonmetropolitan areas were used on 47 percent of private construction projects, but on only 27 percent of public, Davis-Bacon projects. On those projects, the contractors came from adjacent counties 40 percent of the time, and from even farther away the remaining 32 percent.[10] Since the Act was designed to aid the local contractor, it has obviously missed the mark.

In their zeal to find a prevailing wage in a nonmetropolitan area, the Department of Labor has often expanded the area of the wage survey to unrealistic proportions (or until it covers a metropolitan area with a union scale). The resultant prevailing wage is totally unindicative of the local wage structure and consequently scares local contractors away from the bidding. For example, the wage survey undertaken before hiring a steamroller operator in Cape May, NJ (extreme southern end of the state) extended to Newark (extreme northern end), the most heavily-unionized city in the State.[11] The wage more than doubled; the local contractor was not willing to pay it; the local town council could not afford it—and the project was scrapped.

Studies show that the size of the survey area is inversely proportional to the population density. A rural area is five times less likely to have a local contractor than an urban area would be.[12] Would it not be logical to expect that, in a town of 1,000, the rate charged by the only plumber in the county is the prevailing wage?

The problem of morale is the primary reason that many small businesses choose not to bid on government contracts. This problem is compounded by administrative procedures that eliminate the local contractor who does bid, more than 70 percent of the time. Even if the law had no inflationary effect, the fact that it is doing the most harm to the very group it is designed to aid, is more than ample reason to repeal Davis-Bacon.

### Administration

The administrative nightmare that is Davis-Bacon boggles the mind. More than $200 million in administrative and compliance costs is incurred annually by both contractors and the Department of Labor. This cost is ultimately born by the taxpayer.[13] Private contractors must adjust bids to allow for a 3 to 4 percent cost increase caused by regulatory overhead. This cost is particularly burdensome to small contractors who pay, proportionately, three to four times more than a larger firm. Once again, the greatest adverse impact falls on those whom the Act should be assisting.

Reactions to the administrative performance of the Department of Labor range from astounded to appalled. Consider the magnitude of the administration of the Act: 3,000 possible counties, nineteen trades, and four different types of construction, making 228,000 possible combinations. What is astounding is that these determinations are made by less than thirty government employees, and they are done manually—the system is not computerized![14] Small wonder the Department opts for union scale so readily. The weekly compliance reports, required of all contractors working under the Act, are collecting dust in a warehouse. The forms are never reviewed, unless some action is taken to draw attention to a specific contractor. The waste of manpower, funds and resources is inexcusable.

## Position of Organized Labor

Robert A. Georgine, President of the Building and Construction Trades of the AFL-CIO, stated that organized labor "has no intention of permitting this law (Davis-Bacon) to be emasculated. Those who would repeal these laws would adamantly oppose restricting the profits of contractors, yet they propose to restrict the wages of workers. If cutting personal income is such an effective weapon in fighting inflation, let them start with Henry Ford's $900,000 a year. Start with those who have a lot before they nickel-and-dime workers to death."[15]

Three defenses of the Act appear frequently in organized labor's presentations in support of Davis-Bacon. They are that: (1) the law assures quality (union) work; (2) it prevents exploitation of women and minorities; and (3) it helps to protect local contractors by making them more competitive. A fourth defense is that the law does not have any inflationary impact, but this is an unrealistic response to empirical data which prove otherwise.

The concept that the quality of work is higher under Davis-Bacon poses an intriguing question: does the quality of work performed by the Nevada painter increase, if his wages go from $6.25 to $12.40 per hour? If we look at process theories of motivation, we see that this pay will have no effect on the work output, since no desired behavior is being rewarded. And the content theories of Herzberg and Maslow agree that this wage jump will not motivate the worker. One can only wonder what new theories of motivation the AFL-CIO have discovered.

Claiming that Davis-Bacon prevents exploitation of women and minorities is an interesting way of defending the law, since it is probably most effective in keeping these two groups underemployed in the construction trades. The apprenticeship requirements in unions that currently employ only 10 percent blacks and Hispanics, compounded by fixed ratios of skilled workers to journeymen that are as high as 14 to 1, make it extremely difficult for minorities to benefit from this law. The situation of nonunion contractors under Davis-Bacon is not much better. I believe that employers who must pay such inflated wage rates will not hire marginally- or semi-skilled workers. The law also excludes minority-owned businesses because they are primarily small, nonunion contractors who, as we have seen, do not benefit from the law's provisions.

I have already demonstrated that the law does not, in fact, protect local contractors. Arguments concerning the efficiency of small contractors relative to their large urban counterparts, or the social and economic desirability of awarding work to the former as opposed to the latter, can be discounted, if most of the small contractors refuse to bid on Davis-Bacon projects.

The position of organized labor on Davis-Bacon is summed up in one sentence by the AFL-CIO: "If Davis-Bacon is weakened in Congress, it could well set off a chain-reaction assault by anti-worker conservatives upon the entire fabric of federal labor law."[16] Stripped of its rhetoric, this statement reveals the true story for union support: organized labor cannot afford a political loss of this magnitude. The merits or faults of this law have little bearing on the stand of labor; their considerations are purely political.

The Davis-Bacon Act was a remarkable success fifty-five years ago, but since then other laws have been passed that guard against wage losses, exploitation by employers, and adverse working conditions. Davis-Bacon has outlived its usefulness and is no longer serving the purpose for which it was intended.

Repeal is the most viable course to take in correcting the inequities of this law. Major administrative modification would go far to correct the problems with the Act, but I have no confidence that improving some aspects of the law through administrative change will correct the fundamental problem for more than a short time; in a few years, we will again have yesterday's law in today's economy.

Legislatively and politically, repealing Davis-Bacon will not be an easy course to take. There is sure to be some backsliding of union wages in the construction industry, but this should be a short-term problem. The option of labor action will continue to exist as a primary means of minimizing losses, and in the long run, if the fall of wages is more than workers will tolerate, the building trade unions may find themselves both larger and stronger than they are today. Several states have repealed their "little Davis-Bacon" laws, and to date there has been no tremendous collapse of the wage scale in those localities. Neither has there been a return to the chaotic exploitive labor practices of the early 1930's.

The Davis-Bacon Act has proven itself to be neither necessary nor viable in today's economy. As it exists today, it is a law of organized labor, administered by the Department of Labor, for organized labor. The losers are taxpayers, consumers, nonunion labor, and the unemployed. These groups have a lower average income than the beneficiaries, who are predominently white and male. Davis-Bacon, therefore, not only shrinks the size of the economic pie, but it also redistributes slices toward the top-half of the income distribution. Davis-Bacon enriches a minority of high-income people with political clout and deprives low-income people who have no political clout.

It is difficult to conceive of a more inequitable situation. The time to repeal Davis-Bacon was yesterday!

## Footnotes

[1]"In Search of a Cure for Davis-Bacon," *Nation's Business*, July 1981, p. 60.

[2]Armand J. Thieblot, Jr., *The Davis-Bacon Act* (Philadelphia: The Wharton School, University of Pennsylvania, 1975), p. 27.

[3]U.S. Comptroller General, *The Davis-Bacon Act Should Be Repealed*, (HRD-79-18; Washington, DC: GPO, April 27, 1979), p. iv.

[4]*The Davis-Bacon Act Should Be Repealed*, p. 3.

[5]Committee on Small Business (U.S. Senate), *The Impact of the Davis-Bacon Threshold on Small Business Construction Contractors*, 99th Congress, 2nd session, (Washington, DC: GPO, February 2, 1982), p. 638.

[6]"Hidden Report Points Way to Wage Reform," *Nation's Business*, May 1981, p. 22.

[7]Committee on Banking, Housing and Urban Affairs (U.S. Senate), *Oversight Hearings to Examine the Administration of the Davis-Bacon Act*, 96th Congress, 1st session, (Washington, DC: GPO, May 2, 1979), p. 171.

[8]"In Search of a Cure for Davis-Bacon," *Nation's Business*, July 1981, p. 61.

[9]Morgan O. Reynolds, "Understanding the Political Pricing of Labor Services: The Davis-Bacon Act," *Journal of Labor Research*, Summer 1982, p. 299.

[10]Bureau of National Affairs, "Small Business Spokesmen Attack Davis-Bacon," *Daily Labor Report* No. 22 (Washington, DC, February 2, 1983), E–1.

[11]Gregg Easterbrook, "How Big Labor Brings Home the Bacon," *The Washington Monthly*, February 1981, p. 46.

[12]John P. Gould, *The Economics of Prevailing Wage Laws* (Washington, DC; American Enterprise Institute for Public Research, 1971), p. 19.

[13]Jeffrey L. Sheler, "Test for Unions' Waning Strength In Congress," *U.S. News & World Report*, October 19, 1981, p. 72.

[14]"In Search of a Cure for Davis-Bacon," p. 61.

[15]Fern Schumer, "Fighting Words in Washington," *Forbes*, May 14, 1979, p. 93.

[16]AFL-CIO Issue Alert, "The Davis-Bacon Act Under Attack," *Fact Sheet No. 3* (Washington, DC, March 5, 1982), p. 2.

# An Assessment Of The National Emergency Strike Provisions Of The Taft-Hartley Act

## ABSTRACT

The national emergency strike provisions made available to the president under the Taft-Hartley Act are one of the most vital parts of our labor legislation structure. In the absence of government-imposed arbitration, they represent the "bottom line" in dealing with major labor disputes. As both the largest labor organizations and the employers they deal with both continue to grow, the ramifications of unsettled labor problems among these parties permeate every sector of our society. It is, therefore, vital that we realistically assess our last line of defense against economic chaos caused by major labor problems—the emergency provisions of Taft-Hartley.

## I. Introduction and Explanation of the Act

The Labor Management Relations Act, effective June 23, 1947 and amended in 1959, known as the Taft-Hartley Act, provides the necessary machinery for the investigation of labor disputes, and hopefully, to resolve them before they become a national emergency.

The machinery is put in motion whenever the president of the United States considers a threatened (or actual) strike or lockout within an entire industry, or a substantial part of it, to imperil national health or safety.

The first step the president takes is to appoint a board of inquiry, composed of a chairman and other members deemed necessary. The board has the power to act and conduct hearings anywhere in the United States, either in public or in private, as the occasion may warrant, to investigate the issues in dispute and to marshal relevant facts. The board submits to the president a written report within a pre-established time and includes statements from labor and management, but will not any recommendations. The president files a copy of the report with the Federal Mediation and Conciliation Service, known as the Service, and makes the facts available to the public.

After reviewing the report, the president may direct the attorney general to petition the District Court of the United States appropriate jurisdictional for a 60-day injunction to prohibit or end the strike or lockout. If the court finds that a threatened or actual strike or lockout is of sufficient severity that it will imperil national health or safety, it will issue a temporary restraining order.

During the 60-day injunction, each party involved in the labor dispute has to make every effort to adjust and settle their differences with the assistance of the Service. Neither party, however, is under any obligation to accept all or any part of settlement proposals made by the Service.

After the court order has been issued, the president reconvenes the same board of inquiry. If the dispute has not been settled by the end of the 60-day period, a 20-day extension is usually granted. During this time, the board reports to the president the positions of the parties, efforts made by each party for settlement and the employer's "last offer" of settlement. This report is also made available to the public. The National Labor Relations Board (NLRB) takes, within the next 15 days, a secret ballot of the employees involved in the dispute, questioning whether they wish to accept or reject the final, offered settlement. Within five days thereafter, the results are certified and forwarded to the attorney general. Following the balloting or settlement, whichever happens sooner, the attorney general requests the court to terminate the injunction. When the termination is granted, the president submits to Congress a full and comprehensive report of the proceedings, specifically the findings of the Board, results of the vote taken by the NLRB, and presidential recommendations in the case.

## II. Application of the Act

During the period since enactment of the Labor-Management Relations Act in 1947, every president has considered at least one labor dispute serious enough to require emergency action, Totalling 34 disputes, and the attorney general has submitted petitions for each injunction.

In large part, the act was passed in response to the industrial turmoil that occurred after World War II. Its necessity was dramatized when the national emergency provisions were used in seven disputes in 1948, a year after its passage. The use of the emergency section has varied considerably during the life of the act, and only the five national emergency disputes in 1971, involving grain elevators and stevedoring neared the number in 1948. The other disputes were distributed as follows: one each in 1951, 1952, 1953, 1956, 1957, 1961, 1963, 1964, 1967, and 1968; two each in 1954 and 1959; three in 1966; and four in 1962. In nine of the 25 years, there were no national disputes with sufficient economic impact to warrant calling the act into operation.

## III. Use of the Injunction

During the 40-year period, the attorney general submitted 34 petitions for an 80-day injunction to the Federal District Court to prevent or end a strike, but only 29 were granted. In 1971 the court rejected the government's contention that a strike of 200 Chicago grain elevator employees would "imperil the national health and safety," making it the first refusal to issue an injunction since the emergency provisions were enacted. Strikes occurred at some stage of the national emergency procedure in 29 of the 34 national emergency disputes, and where the 80-day injunctions were issued, the strikes were effectively halted or prevented in all of the 29 cases, with the exception of the 1949–50 bituminous coal dispute. In that case, the injunction was issued, but in contempt proceedings the union was found not guilty of ordering continuation of the strike.

The 29 stoppages affected 1.8 million workers who were idle for a total of 88 million work days. It is worth noting that the single 116-day steel strike of 1959–1960, involving more than one-half million workers, accounted for about one-half of the idle work days.

## IV. Industries Affected and Issues

The national emergency machinery is limited to strikes that affect an entire industry or a substantial part of one. The criteria for activating the national emergency provisions of the act are intended to limit its use; hence, they have been applied to a relatively small proportion of the industries and establishments in the U.S. economy. Eight organizations involved in 13 strikes had fewer than 10,000 workers, which indicates that the act is not used exclusively against large employers or industries employing a large number of individuals.

Former presidents have decided that extended strikes in the following list of industries would have a drastic effect on the nation's health or safety, if allowed to continue without some control:

| | Number of Disputes | Number of Strikes |
|---|---|---|
| stevedoring | 10 | 10 |
| aircraft – aerospace | 5 | 4 |
| atomic energy | 4 | 2 |
| bituminous coal mining | 3 | 2 |
| maritime | 3 | 3 |
| nonferrous smelting | 2 | 2 |
| grain elevators | 2 | 2 |
| meatpacking | 1 | 1 |
| fabricated metals | 1 | 1 |
| basic steel | 1 | 1 |
| shipbuilding | 1 | 1 |
| telephone | 1 | 0 |
| | 34 | 29 |

The most frequent issue in dispute—28 times—was wage rates. In a number of cases, wages combined with other issues caused an impasse. The national emergency provisions have also been invoked in disputes where the establishment of a union shop was one of the issues. This occurred in the aircraft-aerospace industry, January–May 1963, with no strike. The 1959 long-shore dispute and the 1961 maritime dispute were over the scope of the bargaining unit, along with other issues: problems related to job security, seniority, severance pay, supplementary benefits, hours of work, pension plans, etc.

## V. Shortcomings of the Existing Act

Though the emergency strike provisions of the Taft-Hartley Act were intended to serve the national interest, it is clearly recognized that there are inherent weaknesses in the existing law. The provisions have been unsuccessful in preserving the institution of collective bargaining, while at the same time protecting the public interest in the flow of goods and services.

Our presidents have invoked the emergency provisions of Taft-Hartley on numerous occasions, and yet in cases where an 80-day injunction was actually issued, the provisions have failed to resolve labor disputes in over half the instances (15 out of 29).

Probably the most widespread objection to the provisions is that they serve to postpone settlement, and offer no assistance or pressure toward reaching an agreement before they are invoked. The provisions seem to ignore the fact that bargaining representatives for both management and labor usually compromise their positions only when confronted with a rigid deadline. Knowing that a strike will likely be postponed with the invocation of the emergency procedures, management and labor representatives often intentionally delay a settlement, with the knowledge that they will be afforded an extra eighty days to reach a settlement. It is unfortunate that the act provides no pressure for either side to reach an agreement before the eighty-day period. Neither does it provide for additional remedies after this period, if no settlement has been reached.

There seems to be general agreement that the existing law should be amended to give the government increased prestige and effectiveness in handling labor disputes constituting a national emergency. The problem lies in moving beyond this point to that of adopting new provisions which would be acceptable to the concerned parties—labor, management, Congress, the administration, and the public. Over the years, several legislative proposals have been offered. However, it is inevitable that conflicts of opinion and interest concerning any public policy change would arise. In fact, it has been the political influence of labor and management that has proven to be a stumbling block to the adoption of legislative proposals amending the provisions.

## VI. Proposed Efforts to Amend the Act

I concede there is no easy solution. Lloyd G. Reynolds has expressed this dificulty, "The objective of public policy is not just to prevent strikes in essential industries. The objective is rather to prevent strikes by methods which are orderly and uniform in their application, which involve a minimum of direct compulsion, which do not impose greater hardships on one party than on another, and which leave maximum scope for settlements to be reached through direct negotiations between the parties."[1] Mr. Reynolds has suggested that anyone who could devise a policy within the above criteria, would deserve a Nobel Prize for industrial peace.

However difficult the problem is, it seems inevitable that it will have to be confronted in the future. Let us then examine some major, existing proposals that have tried to be fair and reasonable to labor, management, and the American public.

## A. The Administration's Proposal – S. 560

The administration's proposal—S. 560—was first put forth by ex-president Reagan. This bill would repeal Section 10 of the Railway Labor Act and put all transportation industries under the national emergency provisions of Taft-Hartley. Following the expiration of the present 80-day period, this bill would provide for either an additional 30-day cooling-off period, the appointment of an impartial three-member special board to determine if a partial operation of the involved industry is feasible, and/or appointment of a panel to select and order binding the most reasonable final offer made by a party in the dispute.

The addition of these new options to the existing law has been referred to as an arsenal of weapons, or choice-of-procedures approach. The uncertainty as to which procedure might be invoked and the unwillingness to risk the adoption of one of the procedures in place of a negotiated settlement, would likely lead to greater efforts by both parties to settle their differences through collective bargaining. The availability of these additional procedures to the executive branch would provide a tremendous influence to both parties to seek a solution to their differences without resorting to a prolonged strike.

During the additional 30-day period, the president could order both parties not to make any additional changes in the terms and conditions of employment, except by mutual agreement. Both sides would be required to continue bargaining with the board of inquiry, previously appointed by the president mediating the dispute. The argument against such a cooling-off period is that if both parties were close to reaching an agreement, they would be likely to agree to such an extension anyway, and if they were far apart, the extension would be unlikely to effect an agreement.

The second procedure of the administration's proposal S. 560, partial operations, is quite complicated and gives rise to confusion in its terminology and interpretation. A special board of three impartial members would be appointed by the president. This board would determine if and how the partial operation of an entire industry could continue without imperiling national health or safety, and if a partial strike would pose a serious enough economic burden on both parties to encourage them to seek settlement of their differences. If a partial operation were feasible, the board could present an order detailing the extent and conditions of operations to be maintained. The board could not present an order constituting a greater economic burden on any party, than that caused by a total cessation of operations. If a decision were reached to permit partial operations, the parties would be required to proceed without a strike or lockout, for a period not to exceed 180 days.

Those who would support a partial operation procedure, see it as a compromise between the right to strike and the public's right to receive essential goods and services. Though perhaps sound in theory, if partial operation is ordered, problems of implementation arise. These include questions concerning administration, enforcement and fairness. This procedure in its present form seems to provide a potential roadblock to effective settlement of emergency strike issues, inasmuch as the particulars of what constitutes "partial" operation is especially troublesome, from both a theoretical and practical point of view.

The last provision of this proposal calls for final-offer selection. Each party would be directed by the president within three days to propose two alternative offers to the secretary of labor, who then makes these offers available to both parties and mediates a five-day bargaining session. If still no agreement is reached, the parties would be given two days to appoint a three-member panel to select one of the final offers in its entirety. The president appoints a panel in the event the parties cannot agree on a selection.

As guidelines to reaching their selection, the panel is permitted to consider: (1) past collective bargaining and contracts between the parties; (2) comparison of wages, hours and conditions of employment peculiar to the industry in general; (3) security and tenure of employment with regard for the effect of technological changes on employment practices, or on utilization of particular operations; and (4) the public interest and any other factors normally considered in the determination of wages, hours and conditions of employment.[2] Unless found to be arbitrary and capricious by a reviewing court, the panel's decision is final and would become the binding labor agreement between the parties.

Supporters of final-offer selection argue that it discourages an extreme position by either party, as both are trying to gain the endorsement of the panel. It also encourages swift settlement of differences and provides a contract free from the influences of the arbitrators.

Those who argue against final-offer selection say that it is unfair and inflexible. They contend that each side will offer counterbalancing terms, that issues put forth by both sides should be considered and weighed carefully, and that a combination of the two would likely make up the best contract. It is also argued that the party who feels its offer will be accepted is likely to include minor advantages in its offer that could not be had through negotiation and arbitration.

## B. Recommendations from the American Bar Association

In 1989 a Special Committee on National Strikes in the Transportations Industries was appointed by the American Bar Association. Its purpose was to examine the present provisions of Taft-Hartley for dispute settlement and to make appropriate recommendations. The committee concluded that any amended legislation should include maritime, airline, railroad, and trucking industries.

The committee recommended that upon the recommendation of the National Mediation Board of an impending strike which would threaten the interruption of an essential transportation service, the president would be authorized to appoint a presidential Mediation Board. During its 60-day life, the board would investigate the dispute and act as a mediator. Just prior to the expiration of this 60-day period, the board would recommend to the president that the choices of one of four procedures for settling the dispute.

The first of these recommendations is that the president direct the board to make public its recommendations for settlement of the dispute. With the release of these recommendations, an additional 30-day *status quo* period would be allowed in the hopes that public opinion would persuade the parties to settle their differences. In the event no such agreement could be reached within 30 days, the parties would be permitted to resort to the strike or lockout.

The second recommendation is the appointment of a presidential Arbitration Board. This board would be given authority to conduct an investigation of the dispute and issue a final award to be binding on all parties in the dispute. The following factors would be considered by the board in arriving at its award: (1) the public interest; (2) industrywide comparison of wages, hours and conditions of employment; (3) nationwide comparison of wages, hours and conditions of employment; (4) security and tenure of employment with due regard for the effect of technological changes on employment practices, or the utilization of particular occupations; and (5) other normal considerations in determining wages, hours and conditions of employment.

The American Bar Association reluctantly included compulsory arbitration, while fully realizing its unfavorable connotations. It was felt that this, more than any other procedure, recognized the public interest.

The third and most controversial procedure presented by the American Bar Association is the presidential creation of an executive receivership of the carrier or carriers involved. The president would consider the public interest in deciding the length of time and conditions of the receivership. The government receiver would be allowed to adjust wage conditions during the seizure period, but would be required to keep any adjustments at a minimum, equitable level. The suspension of union security and checkoff arrangements was also recommended.

Critics of this procedure argue that it is unconstitutional, that government operation is no guarantee against strikes, and that the procedure does not really pressure the parties to seek an immediate termination of the strike or lockout.

The final procedure recommended is that the board be dismissed and that no further governmental action be taken. It seems unlikely that this action would be chosen, considering the implications of a true national emergency strike. However, the board felt that this procedure would deter the parties from delaying predictable emergency procedures.

### C. The Kennedy Bill – S. 594

Under Senator Edward Kennedy's proposal, the president would appoint a Board of Inquiry whose purpose would be to recommend procedures for resolving national emergency disputes. The board's report would be forthcoming before any injunction period. If an 80-day injunction period were granted, it would be done by a three-judge district court. Any appeal would be taken to the Supreme Court. If no agreement had been reached within 60 days, the president could issue an executive order detailing the procedures to be followed. This order would be effective only as long as an emergency was considered to exist. Congress could veto an Executive Order within 15 days. After 60 days of the injunction period, the president could direct the NLRB to take a secret ballot of the employees concerning the employer's final offer.

I feel that the Kennedy Bill is too broad-based, extending jurisdiction to a threatened/actual strike or lockout/other labor dispute in an industry affecting commerce. Such language could give rise to unlimited government intervention.

## D. Authors Proposed Change

The use of the emergency provisions of the Taft-Hartley Act in settling emergency disputes has failed nine times since the machinery was invoked in 1947, resulting either in a strike or lockout following the 80-day cooling-off period. In each of these cases, the president's personal intervention and use of invoked remedies failed to resolve the differences between the parties. The failure of presidential involvement, resulting economic losses, damages to other industries and services, and the suffering of tens of thousands who were not party to the dispute, call for more effective legislation and comprehensive solutions.

In the context of the Taft-Hartley Act, the term *emergency* is used to describe the effects of a threatened or actual strike that would imperil our national health and safety. I feel that prior proposals have not really effectively dealt with the heart of the issue: a timely settlement, in the interest of the public, to avert an emergency. There is no denying that the affected industries and labor unions have a great deal at stake in the event of a strike; however, the interest of the public should take precedence. Collective bargaining is a fair and proper way to settle disputes, but when such bargaining is dragged on and on with little or no effort and/or movement toward an agreement, the government should be given the power to render a final and binding settlement upon the parties to the dispute.

I propose the establishment of industrial commissions upon recommendation and periodic review by a congressional arbitration committee. An industrial commission would be set up for each industry considered essential to national health and safety. The industries identified here seem to constitute an acceptable list. The commissions would include high-level personnel from labor, management and government. Their task would be to forewarn management, labor, government and the public of any areas which might lead to serious disputes and the potential effect on the national health, safety and defense, these disputes were to lead to an actual strike. They would also be required to submit to management, labor, the congressional arbitration committee, and the media, suggestions which might lead to an early solution of the problem.

Thirdly, I propose the establishment of the aforementioned Congressional Arbitration Committee. One member from each of the House and Senate Committees involved in Labor, Agriculture, Defense, Commerce, and Manufacturing would make up the committee. This committee, with the assistance of the Industrial Commissions of each industry, would decide whether an actual emergency existed. They would then notify the president of all issues involved in the dispute. If the president concurred with their assessment, a 60-day injunction period could be granted. During this time, the parties of the dispute would be required to collectively bargain with the Congressional Arbitration Committee sitting in on the bargaining, but taking no active role in the actual negotiations. If no agreement could be reached within the 60-day injunction period, the parties of the dispute would be ordered by the president to prepare and submit a final offer to both the president and the Congressional Arbitration Committee. The committee would make available these final offers to each party and the media. The parties would then be given a final 25 days in which to collectively bargain towards an agreement. The committee would sit in on this bargaining also. If at the end of this period the parties had still not reached an agreement, the president would order a halt to any further negotiation. The committee would then be given 30 days in which to present to the parties and the president a final and binding contract. This contract would be a compromise of the issues of each final offer and the judgments of the committee. Upon favorable review and final approval of the president, this contract would be considered legal and binding.

I feel that this proposal allows management and labor sufficient time, in light of an actual emergency, to come to terms through collective bargaining. The threat of intervention by the Industrial Commissions and the Congressional Arbitration Committee would provide pressure for the parties to bargain in good faith in hopes of reaching an early settlement. And, in the event no settlement could be reached through collective bargaining, the settlement imposed by the Congressional Arbitration Committee and the president would protect the public interest, by not allowing the dispute to continue to drag on indefinitely. Under these circumstances, the final order would likely be as fair a representation of both sides of the issues as possible, without actual settlement by the parties.

This proposal has necessarily been rather broad based, and I fully realize that many minute details would have to be ironed out before it could be put into use. However, I feel it offers a fair and attainable solution to the still unresolved convinced that there will come a time in the not too distant future when the nation will benefit if its legislators and president enact such a proposal.

### Footnotes

[1]Lloyd G. Reynolds, *Labor Economics & Labor Relations*, 4th ed. (Englewood Cliffs, N.J.; Prentice-Hall, Inc., 1964), p. 285.

[2]Thomas A. Woodley, *Saint Louis University Law Journal*, 47–106 (Fall 1982).

# The Case For Government-Imposed
# Compulsory Arbitration

## ABSTRACT

Under present law, the president can prohibit a job action for up to eighty days if it will imperil national health or safety. A case is presented for legislation providing for government-imposed compulsory arbitration, to handle job actions not settled within the eighty-day period. Based on the growth in size of both employer and employee organizations and the increasing interdependence within the economy, this legislation is needed immediately.

Most lawmakers are of the opinion that laws should serve as deterrents to prevent dangerous or despicable acts by members of society. Labor laws, when they were enacted, were no exception. The Wagner Act was supposed to prevent the oppression of labor unions by employers, who seemingly had the upper hand at the time. When unions, through the provisions of this statute, began to gain the advantage, the Wagner Act was amended by Taft-Hartley. Finally, union members and society were protected from the unions' internal misbehavior by Landrum-Griffin.

The history of labor relations is liberally sprinkled with protections like these. All were designed by well-meaning lawmakers to regulate the labor movement. Only one avenue remains unpoliced: crippling strikes or lockouts that could have a devastating effect on the country. A half-hearted attempt was made to provide such protection in the Labor-Management Relations Act of 1947, which gives the president the authority to ask, through the attorney general, for a court injunction for a total of eighty days when a strike/lockout or threatened strike/lockout " ... if permitted to occur or to continue, will imperil the national health or safety."[1]

The question then becomes, what happens at the end of the eighty-day "cooling off" period? The parties involved are free to continue whatever it was they were doing to imperil the national health or safety prior to the injunction!

The president has seen fit to ask for a board of inquiry (the first step of emergency action) on thirty-two occasions since the enactment of the Labor-Management Relations Act. On four of these occasions, the president did not request court injunctions after reviewing the inquiry boards' reports. An injunction was requested for the other twenty-eight and was issued in all instances, save one. After the injunctions were discharged at the expiration of the emergency provisions, strikes continued in five cases.[2]

Although many individuals believe union leaderships are too responsible to permit any job action that might harm the majority of our citizens, on five occasions a difference of opinion has occurred between union leaderships and the president on what constituted peril to the health and safety of the nation. Thus, the question of labor leaders' responsibility is not the key consideration at all. A situation exists in this country where the most well-intentioned, public-spirited labor leaders may still, in the president's opinion, imperil the public health or safety because of the way they interpret Section 206 of the Taft-Hartley.

Under Taft-Hartley emergency provisions, the president does not have sole authority to issue an injunction. The president must first appoint a board of inquiry and review its report. If the board of inquiry's report indicates that the "health and safety of the nation is imperiled," the president may request the courts to issue an injunction. The court has the option of denying the injunction request, if it concludes no peril exists.

If such safeguards protect labor against arbitrary government action, why then is union leadership afforded the unchecked option of imperiling the nation after the expiration of a "cooling-off period"?

The president may take only one action under the statute when an injunction has been discharged—a report, with recommendations for future action, to the Congress. Section 210 of the Labor-Management Relations Act states, in part, ". . . the president shall submit to the Congress a full and comprehensive report of the proceedings, including the findings of the board of inquiry and the ballot taken by the National Labor Relations Board, together with such recommendations as he (sic) may see fit to make for consideration and appropriate action."[3] The time between the implementation of this procedure and any appropriate action could prove lengthy, even if Congress were in session at the time the injunction was discharged. Should Congress be in recess at the time, the delay would be that much longer.

One possible solution may be in the precedent set by actions taken under the Railway Labor Act. The emergency provisions of that act are virtually the same as those contained in the Labor-Management Relations Act. There is a similar "cooling-off period," after which the disputing parties are free to strike or to continue to strike. On three occasions, the president has asked the Congress to take legislative action. On all of these occasions, the Congress passed joint resolutions directing the parties to settle their differences, through arbitration based on the president's recommendations. Outlawing the railroad strikes in 1963, 1967, and 1970 by forcing the parties to arbitration, established a clear precedent as to what could be expected, should a similar situation occur in the future. The question to be answered is whether similar action can and will be taken in industries other than the rails—in other words, under Taft-Hartley.

President Reagan, during his administration, realized the inadequacies of Section 206 of Taft-Hartley and proposed an amendment to the emergency provisions prior to his resignation. In his proposal, there were three additional options to those already in the Act:

The first option would give the president the power to extend the court-imposed injunction. This would be used when the disputing parties were close to a settlement at the end of the eighty days already authorized.

Secondly, the president could opt to appoint a board to study the industry in question. The study would determine what portion of the industry would be allowed to continue operation to relieve the peril to the nation, and which, if allowed to stop, would cause some hardships to management or the union. This would provide either management or the union with some leverage, depending on the particulars, but the country would be out of danger.

The third alternative would allow the president to invoke a procedure for final-offer selection. If invoked, each party would be given three days to submit one or two final offers to the secretary of labor. After five days of additional bargaining without settlement, a final-offer selector group of three neutral members would select a binding final offer from those submitted by the parties.

No action was taken by Congress on then-President Reagan's proposals, mainly because of the negative feelings many individuals had about government-issued settlements of private-sector labor disputes. Thus, it was not the first alternative that was objected to, but rather the second and third. Yet the instances of third-party-imposed settlements, whether they're called arbitrated settlements or some other name, are becoming more frequent in our country.

The process of arbitration is firmly entrenched in the overall art of collective bargaining. The provision for arbitration as the method of resolving grievances is included in 97 percent of all labor-management contracts. It is an established and accepted practice in the industrial community.

The U.S. Supreme Court handed down decisions in the now-famous "Trilogy Cases" that eliminated any question as to validity of imposed arbitration.[4] No reason is evident why this method of resolving grievance impasses cannot be equally effective, if applied to collective job actions.

It is clear, however, that many would view such a legislative change as contradictory to our free-enterprise system. There are those who voice (loudly) their opinion that arbitration as a method of resolving labor disputes is "undemocratic."

There are also those who claim that compulsory, government-imposed arbitration destroys the collective-bargaining process. On this point, Seinsheimer stated:

> Almost everyone favors voluntary arbitration and almost everyone opposes compulsory arbitration. But seldom are feasible alternatives to compulsory arbitration in the public sector offered. Without denying that compulsion is less than an ideal state of affairs, the author argues that the alternative—depriving the public of vital services—is worse.[5]

To paraphrase Seinsheimer's words and twist them a bit, it might be said perhaps the alternative—to imperil the health and safety of the nation—is worse. This altered quote, could then be applied to both the public and private sectors.

Either the precedent set under the Railway Labor Act should be extended to all other industries under Taft-Hartley, or former-President Reagan's proposal should be adopted. In either case, the provision for government-imposed compulsory arbitration must be included as an extension of the emergency provisions of the Labor-Management Relations Act of 1947. The power to impose arbitration must be delegated to the president, as a last resort, to protect this nation against arbitrary actions by either labor or management. As our management and labor institutions become bigger, and as a result our entire industrial society becomes more interdependent, the alternative is possible economic disaster.

### Footnotes

[1]*Labor-Management Relations Act*, 1947, Section 206, National Emergencies.

[2]B. J. Taylor and F. Witney, *Labor Relations Law*, Englewood Cliffs, NJ: Prentice Hall, Inc., 1975, pp. 478–480.

[3]*Labor-Management Relations Act*, 1947, Section 210.

[4]*United Steelworkers of America vs. American Manufacturing Co.*, 363 U.S. 564 (1960); *United Steelworkers of America vs. Warrior and Gulf Navigation Co.*, 363 U.S. 574 (1960), and; *United Steelworkers of America vs. Enterprise Wheel and Car Corp.*, 363 U.S. 593 (1960).

[5]W. G. Seinsheimer, "What's So Terrible About Compulsory Arbitration?" *The Arbitration Journal*, 26:4, 1981.

# Is It Time To Amend The Overtime
# Provisions Of The FLSA?

## Abstract

The Fair Labor Standards Act (FLSA) was passed in 1938 to boost a
sagging economy by limiting working hours and establishing a
minimum wage. Advocates contend that, if administered properly, it
can serve the same function today. Views as to how the act should be
amended/administered so as to bring rhetoric closer to reality are
considered.

The Fair Labor Standards Act was enacted in 1938, during a period of
economic crisis, to regulate employers in interstate commerce by establishing a
minimum hourly wage, a standard work week's maximum number of hours (40
hours), and the rate of premium pay to be paid for those hours worked in excess
of the fair work week (time-and-one-half). There were both humanitarian and
economic reasons for passage of FLSA. The minimum wage is designed to
maintain the health, efficiency, and general wellbeing of workers and their
families, while economically the FLSA is designed to maintain the purchasing
power of the public, hence promoting the free flow of goods in interstate
commerce. This purchasing power (from the minimum-waged employee's
disposable income) does, in itself, contribute to sustaining a higher-level of
employment. Additionally, unfair competitive practices, gained from management's usage of substandard wages and long hours, are eliminated, hence
enhancing fair trade practices. The premium pay-rates for overtime are
designed as a penalty, to encourage management to hire additional employees,
rather than have present employees work overtime. (There is a breakeven
point, where it becomes less costly to hire additional employees at straight
time, than to pay overtime pay to present employees.) Thus, the overtime provisions of the FLSA are designed to reduce unemployment.

Is the FLSA, as it exists today, helping the economy? Unemployment
rates, during the past several years, have been exceedingly high: 6.5% and 6.7%
in 1982 and 1983, and 6.6% in early 1984, with nearly ten million people underemployed or unemployed as of April 1984.[1] To make matters worse, the rate of
inflation has also been exceedingly high, and the duration of unemployment
has increased from an average of 8.8 weeks in 1980, to an average of 15.3 weeks
in 1985. Given the hidden cost of such figures (it is estimated to cost $18,000
per year in social programs and lost revenue for every unemployed person in
the United States), I question whether FLSA in its present form is helping the

economy. Surely the entire blame for these economic problems cannot be placed at the doorstep of FLSA. But there are changes, to be discussed later, that would allow FLSA to have a more positive impact on these economic problems.

Is the FLSA, as it exists today, discouraging overtime employment? While the overall average weekly hours of work has decreased over the past decade, there is a marked difference between the work week in sectors of the economy covered by FLSA and sectors not covered. For the economy as a whole, 20% of all employees worked more than 40 hours a week in 1985, while in the uncovered sectors of service-producing industries and salaried employees, the number averaging more than 40 hours per week was 26% and 27.4%, respectively. Additionally, as of April 1985, only 11% of the workforce was receiving overtime pay, and over 90% of these were specifically covered by FLSA. The vast majority of workers who are working overtime and are not covered by FLSA are, therefore, not receiving overtime pay. This means that FLSA may be discouraging overtime for those it covers, but since so many are exempt (service, white collar, salaried, etc.), its overall effect is minimal.

Obviously, the original intent of FLSA, to promote full employment by discouraging overtime and to help the economy by establishing a minimum wage, has not been met. While, as stated earlier, it is too much to expect FLSA to achieve these goals in and of itself, there are changes to FLSA that if made, would increase its positive impact in those areas. One such amendment could establish new levels for the number of hours in a standard work week and for the overtime rate-of-pay.

During the past 15 years, several such amendments to the FLSA have been proposed. The Overtime Penalty Pay Act of 1964 (H.R. 9802) would have set an overtime pay rate of double the regular hourly rate in specific industries. The 1974 amendments to the FLSA (H.R. 12435) eliminated employees of hotels, motels, and restaurants from the overtime exemption and substituted a limited overtime exemption (by reducing the standard hours in a work week), to be phased in gradually. The Fair Labor Standards Amendments of 1975 (H.R. 10130) attempted to establish an overtime rate of two-and-one-half-times the regular hourly rate. In March 1978, Congressman Conyers introduced the Shorter Work Week Bill (H.R. 11784), which by 1982 would have shortened the work week to thirty-five hours, would have established an overtime rate of twice the regular hourly rate, and would have required employee consent for overtime work. (Although H.R. 11784 was defeated, Congressman Conyers introduced another such bill.)

In addition to the government's attempts to amend the FLSA, private organizations have also been interested in the hours and overtime standards. Leonard Woodcock and the UAW raised the issue of the FSLA's ineffectiveness about 12 years ago and expressed a desire to have it changed. Additionally, the AFLCIO has long been interested in a shorter work week and a higher overtime rate, and many union contracts already have an overtime rate of two- or two-and-a-half times the regular rate of pay, dependent upon the total number of hours worked, and whether the overtime is on a holiday or not. In 1984, about one-fourth of workers covered by a union contract were protected with graduated overtime provisions, i.e., the regular overtime rate was to be increased after a given number of overtime hours.[2]

The major argument against such amendments has been that such changes in overtime standards (a reduction in the work week or increase in overtime penalty) would only add to employer costs, inefficiencies, lost productivity, and disincentives to increase production. Employment may rise, but total hours worked would fall. Employers could either pay increased costs (due to either higher overtime pay or extra fringe benefits and training costs of hiring new employees), could cut back on production, or increase prices to maintain profit levels. Additionally, any amendments which would result in increased costs would have an inequitable impact on different industries, since the reasons for requiring overtime vary; many make the erroneous assumption that it is usually because of ineffective management. Overtime can be required for equipment breakdown, employee absenteeism, seasonal fluctuations, unpredictable demand for goods or services, strong pressures from current employees who want to work overtime, a lack of availability of skilled workers, or a lack of availability of workers willing to accept jobs of an uncertain duration. Hospitals experience both seasonal and unforeseeable demands for their services; rather than over-staff and add to the already high cost of medical care, it is more economical to pay overtime rates and have their regular staff work overtime or be on standby. Construction workers cannot easily change shifts in the middle of pouring concrete; a service technician on a repair call, located fifty miles away, cannot easily change shifts with another technician. Small business, with only one machine and one operator, cannot hire an additional tenth of a person to do the 10% surplus work, whereas big business could hire an extra person to perform the surplus work that its numerous workers could not complete in regular time. Cities, operating on fixed budgets, will not hire additional people to avoid overtime costs, rather, they will reduce services instead.[3] Thus, these industries would be exposed to increased costs, due to overtime pay and would cut down on production or service. Ultimately, the economy will be the loser.

In my opinion, each of these arguments against amending FLSA is legitimate in and of itself, but additionally, each is unique to a particular subset of the entire economy. While these problems will have to be worked out, they are nevertheless individualistic and should not overshadow the favorable effects of FLSA amendments on the economy as a whole.

Also to be remembered is that factors additional to the overtime penalty rate are considered by employers, when deciding whether to hire additional employees or to pay overtime premium pay. One such factor is the cost of fringe benefits. In 1938 fringe benefits amounted to five percent of the cost of total compensation, as compared to thirty-five percent today. These benefit payments (vacations; holidays; sick leave; life, accident, and health insurances; and retirement funds) are not considered when computing overtime pay; only the regular hourly rate is considered. Since fringe benefits are related only to the number of employees, and not to the number of hours the employees work, fringe benefits are fixed costs, regardless of the hours worked. Thus, overtime work actually decreases the costs-per-unit produced. As the cost of these benefits increases, the employer is no longer faced with a question of overtime pay for present employees versus new employees at straight time, but must also consider the additional cost of fringe benefits to these new employees. This factor, plus the increasing cost of hiring (advertising, interviewing, etc.) and training, has pushed the point higher where new employees will be hired, in terms of overtime hours.

Another consideration is that certain employers could substitute more equipment for employees, rather than pay the extra costs of overtime, or hiring and training new employees. Ultimately, this could lead to increased productivity and lower unit costs, but the immediate result would probably be increased unemployment and lower wages for those who are employed.

Thus, there are various arguments for retaining the present overtime provisions of the FLSA. As should be expected, there are equally numerous reasons in favor of changing the overtime provisions. Given the magnitude of the economic problem indicated by the unemployment statistics (discussed previously), *some* solution should be pursued.

One of the original purposes of the FLSA was to ". . .maintain the minimum standard of living necessary for the health, efficiency, and general well-being of workers." This is not being done today. The poverty guideline established by the U.S. Department of Labor in 1984 is almost 5% higher than the annual income of someone earning minimum wages, and the "lower budget necessary for decent living standard" set by the Labor Department is almost 80% higher.

Assuming the present provisions are not working, as seen by the data presented on unemployment, overtime hours, and minimum wages, I see no reason *not* to amend FLSA. There are several possibilities the author would suggest for such amendment(s). The standard work week could be reduced to 35 hours either immediately, or phased in over the next five years! This would create more jobs, including more full-tine, long-lasting jobs and would also satisfy a growing desire for more leisure time expressed by more and more workers. Another option is to establish a flexible work week, with automatic adjustments in the hours to reflect changes in the economy. That is, a shorter work week when the unemployment rate is up, and a longer work week when the unemployment rate is down. The "sliding" work week standard would become effective the first day of the second full month, following the date when the new unemployment rate is officially announced. Although there would be administrative problems with this changing work week (bookkeeping, etc.), experience could make these problems manageable.

Another amendment I would consider beneficial would increase the over-time penalty to double-time (or higher than the present time-and-a-half). This premium pay could be on a "straight" scale, i.e., be applied to all hours worked above the basic work week, or it could be on a "graduated" scale, i.e., becoming a higher penalty as the number of overtime hours increased. By increasing the overtime rate, new jobs would be created, as it would become more economical for employers to hire additional workers, at the regular rate, rather than to pay overtime premium pay. According to a Department of Labor study in late 1984, it was concluded after both theoretical and statistical work that an increase to doubletime would:

"...cause employment to increase between 2 and 4 percent, or by 320,000 to 640,000 workers, depending on whether industry added to the workforce, substituted capital for labor, or reduced their workforce."[4]

Another study, based upon an average of 35.6 million overtime hours for 13.2 million production workers in a single manufacturing week in September 1984 projected an equivalency of almost 900,000 forty-hour week jobs.[5]

Another badly-needed amendment would repeal some (or all) of the over-time exemptions from the FLSA. No matter how strong the law is for those covered, it will continue to fall short of its goal if the large percentage of workers now exempt, are not brought under its coverage. If I were to pick the most-needed amendment among those I have recommended, I would choose this repeal of exemptions, since without it the rest is merely window-dressing.

In summary then, there are many ways the overtime provisions of FLSA could be amended. Considering the high levels of unemployment and the number of hours of regularly worked overtime, it appears to me that such amendments are in order. While it has been shown to be impossible to create a new law or amend an old one to be perfectly fair to all parties, this should not stop us from trying. Those who criticized to amending FLSA in this article, seem to expect the amendment(s) to deal equitably with every conceivable individual case that may arise. Such unrealistic thinking must not be allowed to impede progress. The U.S. economy needs help today, if not yesterday, and one way to help is to enact the FLSA amendments proposed herein.

### Footnotes

[1]*Congressional Record – House of Representatives*, April 13, 1984, p. H2897.

[2]Statement of Abraham Weiss, Assistant Secretary of Labor for Policy, Evaluation, and Research, *et. al.*, Hearings before the *Subcommittee on Labor Standards of the Committee on Education and Labor, House of Representatives*, Ninety-fourth Congress, First Session, on H.R. 10130 (hereafter referred to as Hearings), November 6, 1984, p. 158.

[3]Prepared statement of Alan Beals, Executive Vice President, National League of Cities, *Hearings*, November 21, 1984, p. 211.

[4]*Congressional Record – House of Representatives*, p. cit., p. H2896. See also, Joyce Nussbaum and Donald Wise, *The Employment Impact of the Overtime Provisions of the FLSA*, submitted to USDL in response to RFP J-9-E-6-1015, December 14, 1984, pp. 8–9.

[5]Statement of Andrew J. Biemiller, on behalf of the AFLCIO, *Hearings*, November 6, 1984, p. 9.

# Comparable Worth Moves Into The Private Sector

*Kenneth A. Kovach*
*Peter E. Millspaugh*

Pay equity has been an issue of considerable discussion in the United States for decades. This discussion has led to such legislative and judicial initiatives as the Equal Pay Act of 1963, the Bennett Amendment to Title VII of the 1964 Civil Rights Act, and the Gunther and State of Washington court cases. Comparable worth is the most current area of pay equity to be addressed, yet major concerns have been expressed over the practicality of implementing this concept. The validity of such concerns is now being tested in the province of Ontario, Canada. For the first time in this hemisphere an aggressive comparable-worth law has been enacted which is applicable to both the public and private sectors. All Ontario employers are now attempting to achieve compliance. To say that proponents and opponents of comparable worth are watching the unfolding drama with intense interest would be a drastic understatement. The implications of the success or failure of this pioneering legislation are self-evident and enormous. Practical support for the validity of proponent or opponent arguments will emerge, and such support may well prove crucial in determining the future course of comparable worth in the U.S. and elsewhere.

## Overview

Simple economic justice dictates that wages in the workplace be the same for both men and women. Legislation in pursuit of this ideal was first content to strive for equal pay for equal, or substantially similar, work as it took form in the United States. In recent years however, strong advocates have urged that wage equity between the sexes not be confined just to similar jobs performed by both, but expanded to include jobs that are dissimilar but of comparable value. This extension of the pay equity concept has gathered a considerable following over the last decade-and-a-half in this country and become widely identified as the theory of "comparable worth."

An imposing literature has evolved over the years addressing the subject of comparable-worth pay equity from diverse perspectives. Although there have been applications of comparable-worth theory through legislation in the United States, these have been confined to state and local jurisdictions, and applicable to only the (government) public sector work places. There have been no instances where a political jurisdiction has imposed the application of

185

comparable-worth policies on its private-sector employers. Canada has likewise exhibited the same reluctance to move comparable-worth dictates into the private sector, until the province of Ontario stunned many observers by breaking ranks this year.

This article will explore the implications of this Canadian initiative by first sketching the evolution and applications of comparable-worth policy in the U.S. The pioneering Canadian law will then be carefully examined from the broader setting from which it emerged, to its final configuration and requirements. In conclusion, it will explore the broader implications of this type of legislation and offer some observations as to its applicability in the current U.S. setting.

## I. Comparable Worth Policy: The United States Setting

The importance society is attaching to pay equity and gender corresponds with the emergence of women as a factor in the labor force. The rise of the feminist movement and the increasing percentage of working women have been the two major factors driving the concern for wage comparability. Demographic changes reflected in the modern American work force, in particular, are instructive.

### A. The Demographic Underpinnings

The stereotypical family unit of a generation ago, with the male breadwinner, the female housewife and one-or-more children, applies to only 15% of U.S. families today.[1] While the vast majority of unmarried women have traditionally worked, at present in the U.S. nearly 50% of married women with children under two-years old are working, with 62% of all mothers working outside the home. These figures have doubled since 1973, and there is every indication that the trend will continue. It is projected that by 1995, over 80% of all mothers with children at home will be working.[2]

Part of this increase comes from women seeking self-fulfillment through careers—the feminist influence mentioned earlier. The rest is the result of economic necessity. From 1960 to 1973, family income increased every year, but the level achieved in 1973 has not been matched since, despite the rapid increase in dual-income families resulting from women entering the labor force.[3] One reason for this can be found by looking at sex-segregated labor markets that confine women to a limited number of low-paying jobs. For example, according to the last U.S. Census, women constitute 44% of all workers, but fill 81% of clerical, 97% of private household and 61% of other service occupations.[4] Other reasons include the average number of years of professional preparations (male 4.2, female 0.4) and average years of job seniority (male 12.6, female 2.4), both of which depress the wages of women and confine them to lower-paying jobs.

The earnings from jobs such as these, now being filled by an increasing percentage of married women, are not enough to offset the decrease in their husbands' real wages caused by inflation and the technologically forced shift from manufacturing jobs to lower paying service jobs. Thus, the decrease in real family income.

Proponents of comparable worth argue that one of the reasons these and other jobs, e.g., elementary and high school teachers, nurses, librarians, etc., are paid at their present low level, is because most of the positions are held by women. The same proponents contend that a fairly applied standard of comparable worth would raise the wages associated with these jobs and drastically alter many of the demographic patterns evident in today's work place.

### B. Legislative History

Congress first addressed the problem of gender pay equity through an amendment to the 1938 Fair Labor Standards Act (FLSA). In 1962 a bill was introduced to amend FLSA requiring equal pay for "comparable worth". First the House, and subsequently the Senate voted to narrow the concept to "equal work". This resulted in the passage of the Equal Pay Act (EPA) of 1963. Its provisions applied to those workers performing closely related jobs, not different jobs—even though they demanded the same degree of skill, effort and responsibility, and had the same working conditions. Exceptions were recognized to allow for merit and seniority systems along with the quality of the work product.

The following year Congress passed the Civil Rights Act. Under the language of Title VII, discrimination in employment decisions based on sex was outlawed. When concerns were raised about potential conflicts between the sex discrimination provisions of Title VII and the wage equality guarantees of the Equal Pay Act, Senator Wallace Bennett advanced an amendment designed to eliminate the perceived problem. Ultimately enacted, this amendment stated that an employer may differentiate on the basis of sex in determining pay under Title VII, if the differentiation is authorized by a fair reading of the Equal Pay Act of 1963. By limiting gender-based wage discrimination under Title VII to EPA. standards (equal work, not comparable), the Bennett amendment seemed to eliminate the statutory authority necessary to advance wage discrimination claims based on the theory of comparable worth.[5]

This question was later settled by the U.S. Supreme Court holding in *Gunther v. County of Washington*,[6] which ruled that claims of sex discrimination in compensation under Title VII were not necessarily limited to equal work situations. A claim of discriminatory pay, the High Court instructed, is not barred under Title VII, simply because the type of work associated with the jobs being compared is not identical.

Judicial sentiment for comparable worth as a viable legal doctrine was further tested in the celebrated case of *AFSCME v. State of Washington*.[7] Responding to a comparable-worth pay discrimination complaint, the State of Washington ordered a study to identify female-dominated job classifications that had salaries falling below male-dominated classifications of comparable skill and responsibility. This study, the first of its kind in the United States, found numerous such classifications. Breaking new ground, the District Court recognized the plaintiff's comparable-worth arguments and ruled in their favor. This decision was subsequently reversed by the Ninth Circuit Court of Appeals. A settlement between the parties prevented an opportunity for Supreme Court review, but this widely followed litigation symbolized the substantial moral sentiment, public opinion and pressure of group interest in promoting the comparable worth approach to pay equity.[8]

In 1984 Congress enacted the Pay Equity and Management Act reflecting the federal government's interest in the comparable-worth theory as it might be applied to the government work force. The law requires that outside experts conduct a study of pay and job classifications of federal employees to determine if gender-based wage discrimination is present. In 1987 the U.S. Federal Employee Compensation Equity Study Commission Act examined and attempted to promote equitable-pay practices within the federal work force. In search of ever-greater levels of sophistication, the Congress recently enacted the Federal Equitable Pay Practices Act of 1988 to determine the extent that wages are affected by gender alone, across the board, and the role this may play in the formation of wage differentials between male- and female-dominated occupations.

This flurry of federal activity has been matched by numerous state government actions as well. A recent survey indicated that some thirty-one states were formally examining their work forces for gender-based pay equity. Twenty states had specifically enacted legislation or adopted policies aggressively implementing comparable-worth standards in the state and civil service. Ten states simply enacted legal prohibition against unequal compensation rates for comparable jobs within their civil service ranks.[9]

Alongside the federal and state government activity must be placed that of the thousands of local government actions throughout the country. Despite a lack of data as to the precise extent, it is clear that comparable-worth pay policies are deeply penetrating the personnel systems of cities, countries and school districts around the nation today.[10] The comparable-worth approach to combat gender-based wage discrimination is clearly gaining acceptance in the public sector.

Despite considerable public-sector acceptance and experience to date, the merits of comparable worth as a matter of broad public policy remain highly controversial in the United States. While proponents argue for the concept based on its inherit fairness, its moral underpinnings and its impact on wage-based discrimination against women, opponents cite its lack of consideration of market forces, its impact on labor supply and demand, and the seemingly impossible task of consistent, objective and fair enforcement. These opponents contend that market forces such an inflation rates that dictate higher real-wage rates for those most recently hired in a particular job, the hazardous or unpleasant nature of certain tasks within a job or group of jobs, geographic location, location-specific inflation rates, and the level of competition for labor within a particular area all make implementation of comparable worth on a wide scale impractical.

Opponents further argue that even if these problems did not prevent implementation, they would cause major labor-force movements with no relation to supply and demand of labor. How then are employers to entice applicants to jobs not favored in a comparable-worth system? By paying more and thus upsetting the balance again? Finally, who is to administer and enforce such a system on a nationwide scale? Few in the private sector doubt what the answer will be, but even fewer look forward to government intervention to the degree seemingly required.

Although those opposed fiercely disagree, the proponents of a comparable-worth approach to pay equity contend that it is equally necessary and appropriate in the private sector, as in the public sector. For this and many other reasons, the recently enacted Ontario private-sector comparable-worth law will be followed closely by opponents and advocates of greater pay equity. Its implications for eventually moving an aggressive comparable-worth policy into the private sector in the United States need to be carefully examined.

## II. The Canadian Comparable-Worth Initiative

Canadian public policy concerning gender-based wage discrimination has undergone the same evolution as of the United States. Defined initially as comparisons between substantially similar jobs, the working definition of "equal pay" is gradually being expanded to jobs which may be dissimilar, but of comparable value. Unlike the United States, Canadian pay-equity legislation has not been confined only to the public sector.

## A. Equal-Pay Laws: Legislative Background

Equal-pay legislation in Canada first began to appear in the provinces and territories some four decades ago. Following the lead of Ontario in 1951,[11] subsequently enacted legislation in all provincial jurisdictions generally mandates that women be paid the same as men for equal or "substantially similar" work.[12]

At the national level, the principle of equal pay is addressed in careful detail in the Canadian Human Rights Act. Enacted in the mid–70's, evidence of the Canadian evolution toward a comparable-worth view of pay equity appears in the language of this statute. Under the title of "Equal Wages", the legislation clearly states that wage differentials between male and female employees are illegally discriminatory, if both are performing "work of equal value". This law and the provincial pay-equity laws throughout Canada are enforced by the Canadian Human Rights Commission, provincial departments of labor, or human rights agencies, separately or in combination.

Despite long-standing pay-equity provisions in Canadian law, survey data in the 1980's suggested that a substantial wage gap between men and women persisted. For example female average occupational earnings as a percentage of male average earnings was 59.4 percent, a full seven years after the Human Rights Act was passed, with a range across occupations of 46 to 68 percent.[13] Even comparisons between the same occupations within the same firm, reflected wage disparities between 10 to 20 percent.[14] Reasons advanced to explain the lack of sufficient progress under existing pay-equity law included the prevailing narrow interpretation of the laws and the extent of their enforcement. Despite the support for a comparable-worth approach to attaining pay equity on the part of a growing number of lawmakers and public policy advocates, existing laws were being interpreted to apply only to the same or similar jobs within the same firm. Enforcement was found to be lacking, because most laws were passive or essentially reactive in posture—merely declaring a general prohibition against gender-based wage discrimination. Cited also were impediments to meaningful litigation in the courts, such as the unavailability of class actions and a specific-intent burden-of-proof associated with enforcing some of the prevailing statutes.[15] It is largely the disappointing results experienced under the old regime that are fueling support for today's Canadian generation of aggressive, proactive pay-equity legislation utilizing comparable-worth standards.

## B. The Ontario Experiment: Pro-active Comparable-Worth Pay Equity

Before its daring new comparable-worth law took effect, Ontario's long-standing pay-equity statute carried the title "Equal Pay for Equal Work" and predictably set up a standard prohibition against gender-based wage discrimination between "substantially the same kind of work in the same establishment, the performance of which requires substantially the same skill, effort and responsibility, and which is performed under similar working conditions. . ."[16] Impatient with the marginal results this traditional approach had produced over the years, the government began work on pay-equity legislative reform in the fall of 1985.

Drawing on legislative ideas already emerging in Manitoba, Ontario first proceeded on the notion that two separate statutes would be necessary—one for the public sector and the other for the private sector. Through a lengthy two-year process that enlisted the participation of the Province's citizenry and organized interest groups, the legislative provisions applicable to both sectors were ultimately combined into a single law.

Secure in its determination and expertise to write legislation for its own employees, the provincial government concentrated on an approach best-suited to private-sector regulation. To stimulate public discussion on the proposition of extending an aggressive comparable-worth law to cover the province's private economy, the Ontario government issued a document entitled "Green Paper on Pay Equity."[17] A panel of distinguished citizens was then appointed which conducted public hearings on the proposition all across the province, gathering ideas and gauging public sentiment. At the same time, advisory groups from business organized labor were appointed to advise the premier and senior government officials at regular intervals the legislation was being developed.

The result was the enactment of the Pay Equity Act of 1987 by the Ontario Legislative Assembly that June, with its provisions enforced as of January 1, 1988. This precedent-setting law defines male and female job classes, establishes evaluative criteria, mandates equality of pay between classes of comparable worth in both the public and private sectors, and creates two permanent government agencies to insure its enforcement. A close look at each of the law's five major parts is instructive.

### (1) Part I: Definitions and Purpose

The act's singular purpose is "to redress systemic gender discrimination in compensation for work performed by employees in female jobs" (Sec. 4(1)). Discrimination in this form is identified by comparing each male and female job class in an organization, in terms of compensation for the work performed and its value. Female job classes are defined as those comprised of 60 percent-or-more female members, while male job classes are considered to be those with 70 percent-or-more male members (Sec. 1(1)).

The formulation employed to place a value on each designated job class specifies the applicable criterion. The criterion is described as "a composite of the skill, effort and responsibility normally required in the performance of the work and the conditions under which it is normally performed" (Sec. 5(1)). Nowhere in the law is it specified how the skill, effort and responsibility are to be evaluated. Thus far, most firms are using the point system of job evaluation to assess the level of each factor.

Once job class valuation has been completed, if the employer's workforce contains a trade union, only job classes contained within the bargaining unit may be compared. The same rule holds for comparisons of job classes established within that segment of the work force falling outside a bargaining unit (Sec. 6(4)).

The act specifically prohibits employers from reducing the compensation of any employee or position to meet the new pay-equity requirements (Sec. 9 (1)).

### (2) Part II. Implementation: Public-Sector and Large Private-Sector Employers

Where wage discrepancies appear, employers are required to prepare and post their pay-equity plans in the workplace. The employer with a segment of his employees within a bargaining unit and the remainder without, must prepare a separate plan for each (Sec. 14(1)). Employees not part of a bargaining unit have 90 days from posting to suggest changes in the employer's proposed plan. Whether these are incorporated or not is left to the discretion of the employer (Sec. 15(4)(5)).

The pay-equity plan and wage-adjustment posting deadlines under the new law are summarized in the table below.

**Pay-Equity Plan Requirements**[18]

| Location | No. of Employees | Mandatory Posting | Wage Adjustment |
|---|---|---|---|
| Public Sector | January 1, 1990 | January 1, 1990 | |
| Private Sector | | | |
| | 500 or more | January 1, 1990 | January 1, 1991 |
| | 100–499 | January 1, 1991 | January 1, 1992 |
| | 50–99* | January 1, 1992 | January 1, 1993 |
| | 10–49* | January 1, 1993 | January 1, 1994 |

(*Employers with 10- to-99 employees *may elect* to post a pay-equity plan.)

If an employer and the employees cannot agree on a plan, the Pay Equity Commission is to be notified (Sec. 15 (7)). A review officer is then assigned to investigate and effect a settlement. Failing a settlement, the review officer is empowered to choose the plan and order it placed into effect. Objection from either party to the review officer's disposition can be filed with the Commission within 30 days, in which case a tribunal (discussed below) shall make a final resolution of the matter (Secs. 16, 17).

### (3) Part III: Implementation: Small Private-Sector Employers

Formal pay equity plans for employers of more than nine but less than 100 employees are optional (Sec. 19). Should the employer choose to establish a plan, however, it would then be subjected to the same posting, amending, and formal objection requirements established for mandatory plans (Sec. 20).

### (4) Part IV: Enforcement

The creation of a formal Hearings Tribunal and a discussion of its powers are found in this section. Among the powers allocated to the Hearings Tribunal are the authority, when necessary, to order a review officer to prepare a pay-equity plan for an establishment (at the employer's and the bargaining agent's expense), to order reinstatement of an employee's job and previous pay level, to order back pay and wage adjustments, and to order revisions in an employer's pay equity plan (Sec. 25 (2)). Failure to comply with any provision of the act or any order issued by the Hearings Tribunal can result in fines of up to $2,000 in the case of individuals, and up to $25,000 in the case of firms or bargaining units.

### (5) Part V: Administration

This section describes the various institutional arrangements referred to briefly in the proceedings parts of the statute. For example, the creation and establishment of a "Pay-Equity Commission of Ontario" is to consist of two subagencies, the "Pay-Equity Hearing Tribunal" mentioned above, and the "Pay Equity Office" (Sec. 27 (1) (2)).

The Hearings Tribunal is similar in concept to the Industrial Tribunals introduced into British industrial relations in the mid 1960's. Pay-Equity Hearing Tribunals are to be comprised of a presiding officer and deputy officer, and include representatives from employers and employees in equal numbers (Sec. 28 (1)).

The Pay-Equity Office is conceived as a permanent provincial agency responsible for the ongoing enforcement of the provisions of the Act and the orders of the Hearings Tribunal (Sec. 33 (1)).

Finally, the pay-equity review officer, as the foot-soldier of the statute's implementation and enforcement programs, is granted unsettling powers by current United States standards. In pursuit of investigatory authority, the review officer is empowered to enter any premises at any time, request the production of relevant documents, remove those documents for purposes of making copies, and to interrogate persons (subject to their right to have counsel or another present) (Sec. 34(3)).

### C. Employer Experience To Date

The table on page 192 shows that the first group to comply does not have to take any posting or wage adjustment actions until January 1, 1990, so the best we can do for now is to look at early returns from those companies who are preparing to meet the laws' requirements.

The two large employers who are farther along the road to compliance than any others are Warner-Lambert, the Canadian arm of the Morris Plains, NJ, pharmaceutical company, and T. Eaton Company, the Toronto-based retailer. At Warner-Lambert an eight-factor point system was used to determine comparable jobs. The plan was posted for employees to see in May, and to date there has been no negative feedback. Donald Henley, Director of Employee Relations, attributes the ease with which the plan has advanced to the lack of labor organizations within the company. The company is pleasantly surprised at the amount of positive employee feedback from those whose jobs were not directly affected.

T. Eaton Company has 15,000 employees in 580 jobs within Ontario and in the past had used a different evaluation system at each of three organization levels. To comply with the new legislation the company went to a computer-scored version of the Weighted Job Questionnaire, modified specifically for T. Eaton. According to William F. Robinson, Compensation Manager, completion of this task has required four full-time employees, and the results will cost the company "quite a few million dollars annually" in equity adjustments. On the other hand, he notes benefits of increased internal communication including a monthly bulletin devoted solely to company actions relative to the new law, and an awareness of compensation inequities that had gone undetected in the past.

In at least one heavily unionized sector all major employers have come together in an attempt to achieve compliance. In the retail food industry where all employers deal with the United Food and Commercial Workers' Union, the industry has bargained as one with the union in an attempt to arrive at one overall plan. Here, again, the point system is being used, but major problems have arisen in reaching agreement about points assigned within each job factor for particular jobs. If this one situation is any indication of what lies ahead, large unionized firms or industries are going to have severe problems posting plans by the required January 1, 1990 date.

Wyatt Company, a Toronto-based consulting company, is presently working with over fifty firms on compliance with the new law. Sizes range from 200 to 20,000 employees and include many U.S. subsidiaries. According to Marc Lattoni, compensation consultant for Wyatt, while most of the larger employers have now formulated their plan, the majority will not post until the absolute deadline of January 1, 1990, for fear of being singled out. Collective wisdom seems to be that if your plan is posted at the same time as most others, less attention will be paid to yours, by either the general public or the Pay Equity Commission.

The major problem Wyatt clients are encountering is similar to that in the food industry—reaching agreement with bargaining agents over details of the plan. Those clients of Wyatt who are still struggling with formulation of their plan are those who have labor forces represented by automobile, steel and hotel workers' unions. To date the Pay Equity Commission has received over eighty formal complaints from unions under the Pay Equity Act, according to Nanette Weiner, the Commission Research Manager. Some employers are seriously considering letting the deadline for posting pass without complying. The rationale here is obvious, when one considers that the maximum fine is $25,000, while the difference between the plans proposed by the employer and the union is often several hundred thousand dollars. The lesson here for the U.S. is that if such legislation is enacted in this country, economic sanctions may not be enough, and if they are all that is available, the size of the fine should serve as a deterrent to even the largest employers.

## III. A Canadian Model For The American Workplace

As the Ontario Pay-Equity Act phases into effect over the next four years (1990–1994), attempts will be undertaken to gauge its success. With accumulated experience, the statute's impact on the political, social and economic life of the province will become more clear. In turn, this outcome will bear heavily on the influence this legislation can exert on lawmakers in the United States. For the present, there are certain particular features of the legislation that should be noted and monitored.

### A. Perspectives on the Ontario Law

The salient feature of this law distinguishes it from previous United States and Canada laws: its proactive imposition of comparable-worth wage scales on the private sector. Less obvious, but of equal importance, is its focus on jobs, as opposed to individual employees. The evaluations and comparisons called for by the statute pertain to job classes, not the workers themselves. Because the law represents a crusade against discriminatory wages paid to female-dominated job classes, it is only these jobs which can be affected. Therefore, the workers who stand to benefit are confined to those employed in female-dominated job classes found to be underpaid, in comparison with a comparable male-dominated class within the same establishment.

It is an intriguing irony that the structure of this approach to pay equity inevitably boosts the male worker minority, as well as female workers, in those female-dominated classes where wage adjustments will be required under the law. Disappointedly, the same structural limitations prevent the law from reaching those female employees who suffer from gender-based wage discrimination, but fall outside a female-dominated job class. Because of these design limitations, the present Ontario legislation can never be said to ensure fair compensation for all female employees, let alone employees of both genders.

Another obscure but important feature of the law pertains to the mechanics of evaluating job classes. Beyond the statutory requirement to take the criteria of skill, effort, responsibility and working conditions into consideration, the precise type of job evaluation scheme is left to the employer's discretion. This represents an area with potential for ongoing conflict between the

Pay Equity Commission and the provincial employers it must regulate. Its implementation could be extremely thorny and will bear watching.

Of far-reaching consequence is the statutory role envisioned for labor unions. In essence, implementation of the act, as it pertains to union members, is made largely a subject and function of collective bargaining. Presumably this allows critical aspects of how the law is to be applied to this segment of the work force, to be negotiated between unions and employers. Permitting key determinations of what constitutes a single "establishment" or "gender dominance" to be made through negotiation, seems to put the employee who is a union member on a footing different from that of a nonunion counterpart. In many respects, this feature of the new law would appear to benefit the unionized employee by virtue of the leverage which collective bargaining affords. One can argue that organized-labor lobbying may have come into play here. Were glaring discrepancies in the statute's application to begin appearing between the unionized and nonunionized employee, the credibility and full acceptance of the new law could be seriously impaired.

The final feature of this legislation which should not be overlooked pertains to the surprisingly broad categories of exempted wage discrepancies. Until some experience is gained, it is difficult to estimate the size of the hole that the exemption for wage differentials based on seniority, merit, temporary training, etc., will put in the overall legislative scheme. It is unlikely that employers will seek wholesale refuge in these exclusions, but the incentive to move in this direction is certainly present. Whether or not the exceptions ultimately overrun the rule, the swath they cut is certain to be wide.

## B. The Ontario Law's Adaptability to the United States

The adaptability of the Ontario legislative scheme to federal or local jurisdictions in the United States seems highly unlikely for the foreseeable future. Opposition to comparable-worth policies remains vocal and well organized among business, organizations and others. The aggressive scheme adopted by Ontario might be more palatable, here, if confined to the public sector where comparable-worth measures are gaining some degree of acceptability. Private-sector mandates such as these, however, would predictably encounter stiff opposition in this country.

Private-sector commercial interests opposed the Ontario legislation in its initial form. This caused Canadian lawmakers to accommodate a number of the business communities' concerns in the design and language of the legislation. Fully cognizant that moving comparable worth dictates into the private sector would raise problems unequal to the public sector's, the matter was studied intently.[19] The statutory accommodations to business interests ultimately adopted are particularly instructive to American policy analysts, since comparable-worth critics in the United States cite essentially the same objections.

The Ontario framers contemplated the concern that employers may be unable to afford the required wage adjustments, and that higher wages would lead to higher consumer prices and reduce much of the competitive advantage enjoyed by provincial employers. The lawmakers' response was to phase in pay-equity requirements starting with those sectors most easily able to make the adjustment, i.e., the public sector and large private-sector employers, followed by private firms of decreasing size. It was felt that the smaller firms could benefit with more time to adjust from the experiences of the larger firms preceding them. Also, private-sector employers were not placed under a calendar-date deadline for full compliance, as long as a minimum of 1 percent of the previous year's payroll was devoted to wage adjustments annually.

To offset concerns that the law would intervene in labor markets as it standardized wages across the entire province, the law limited wage comparisons geographically to single establishments, even though geographically dispersed establishments may share the same ownership. Wage comparisons were also limited to prohibit the matching of union with nonunion jobs, or the matching of job classes between different unions whenever possible. Wage control and standardization was further relaxed by allowing pay-equity plans and their implementation for unionized employees to be worked out through collective bargaining. Also, the statutory exemptions for established practices, e.g., seniority preferences and merit pay, can be viewed as an attempt to preserve certain wage-setting prerogatives important to the private sector.

## IV. Observations and Conclusions

A private-sector experiment with manditory comparable-worth standards has now been instituted in the Canadian province of Ontario. The neighboring province of Manitoba is preparing similar legislation. Drawn with elaborate care in an attempt to accommodate private-sector interests, the Ontario legislation still carries liabilities which would be considered unacceptable by contemporary U.S. standards. These shortcomings can be briefly summarized:

1.  The problems which have long plagued the comparable-worth theory of pay equity have not been overcome through this legislation. A meaningful and practical definition of "job worth" remains elusive, as does the basis for job class comparison with the requisite precision. The problems applying these amorphous concepts in the private sector

will only magnify as employer, employee and bargaining agent pursue advantage, while provincial review officers and hearing tribunals attempt to mediate and enforce.

2. The scale of intervention into labor markets and managerial operating prerogatives would be considered unnecessarily heavy-handed from a United States perspective. Only less-intrusive means could hope for acceptability.

3. The benefits sought are unlikely to outweigh the costs. The direct and indirect costs associated with employer compliance, sustaining an administrative provincial bureaucracy and market intervention generally would not likely be viewed as appropriate, achieving only marginal rate adjustments in a relatively small subsegment of the labor force.

It is certain that this controversial legislative experiment undertaken by our neighbors to the north will be closely followed, by both the advocates of comparable-worth pay-equity standards and its detractors. The prospects of similar laws rooting in the United States will inevitably hinge to a certain extent on the success or failure of the Ontario initiative presently underway. With a case study in process, perhaps the debate concerning the efficacy of comparable worth policy in the private sector can be joined once again. To be sure, the Canadian laboratory is, at best, a rough approximation of conditions in the United States. Much can be extrapolated from the Canadian effort, however, that will inform the debate in the future. All serious followers of comparable worth would be well-advised to become familiar with, and to follow the progress of, this new piece of legislation. It may well be the most important development to date in the area of comparable worth.

### Footnotes

[1]"Job Protection Guarantees for Workers'" *Congressional Quarterly*, June 14, 1986, p. 1361, and Samuelson, Robert J., "Uncle Sam in a Family Way", *Newsweek,* August 11, 1986, pg. 40.

[2]Giraldo, Z.I., *Public Policy and the Family: Wives and Mothers in the Labor Force* (Lexington Books, DC: Heath and Company, 1980), p. 31.

[3]Mann, Judy, "Families Need These Bills", *Washington Post*, July 3, 1987, p. 83.

[4]Patten, Thomas J., *Fair Pay* (San Francisco: Jossey-Bass, 1988), p. 31.

[5]Patten, *op. cit.,* p. 40–41.

[6]452 U.S. 161 (1981).

[7]578 F. Supp. 846 (W.D. Wash. 1983), 770 F. 2d 1401 (9th Cir. 1985).

[8]Hunter, F.C., *Equal Pay for Comparable Work: The Working Womens' Issue of the Eighties*, (New York: Praeger, 1986).

[9]Patten, *op. cit.*, pp. 74–81.

[10]Patten, *op. cit.*, pp. 97–102.

[11]*Ontario Female Employees Fair Remuneration Act*, 1951.

[12]Abella, R.S., "Employment Equity", 16 *Manitoba Law Journal* 187 (1987).

[13]Statistics Canada, unpublished data from *Survey of Consumer Finances*, 1983, cited in Abella, *op. cit.*, note 12, p. 186.

[14]Gunderson and Morley, "Work Patterns," in *Opportunity For Choice: A Goal For Women in Canada,* ed. A. Cook (Ottawa: Statistics Canada, 1988), p. 120.

[15]Abella, *op. cit.*, p. 189. See L. Nieman, *Wage Discrimination and Women Workers: The Move Toward Equal Pay for Equal Value in Canada*, Bureau Series A: Equity in the Workplace, No. 5 (Ottawa: Labour Canada, Women's Bureau, 1984).

[16]*Ontario Employment Standards Act*, 1981, Part IX.

[17]Ontario, *Green Paper on Pay Equity*, (Toronto: Queen's Printer, 1985).

[18]*Pay Equity Commission*, Pay Equity Implementation, Series 3: l, March, 1988.

[19]Discussed by the Assistant Deputy Minister of the Ontario Women's Directorate, in E.M. Todres, "With Deliberate Care: The Framing of Bill 154," 16 *Manitoba Law Journal* 202 (1987).

# State And Local Public-Employee
# Labor Relations

## Introduction

State and local public employees today constitute one of the fastest growing groups in the American labor movement. While unionization grew dramatically in the private sector during the late 1930's and early 1940's, much slower growth followed in the federal and local government sectors. The late 1970's and early 1980's were the period of the most rapid growth in the latter two sectors, primarily for the following reasons:

(1) The expanding demand for public service resulted in a dramatic increase in public employment, yet without a compatible rise in public income, thus increasing the already existing gap between public-sector and industrial wages.

(2) Public employees began to question their exclusion from the protections afforded private employees by the National Labor Relations Act.

(3) A younger, more militant influx of personnel sought to mobilize the public sector to realize the same benefits afforded public-sector employees in other countries and private-sector employees in this country.

(4) The traditional grants of prevailing wages extended to government-employed construction workers and others under the federal and state Davis-Bacon-type laws stirred the desire of noncovered public employees to achieve wages and working conditions matching those in the private sector.

(5) President Kennedy's Executive Order 10988 of 1962, granting limited collective bargaining rights to federal employees, was interpreted by state and local government employees as a mandate for protesting the historical denial of such rights on the state and local level.

(6) Rising civil disobedience in the nation, as evidenced by the civil rights movement, draft resistors' movement, etc., convinced militant public employees that protest versus "the establishment" and its laws was fruitful and could be a valued vehicle for bringing about desired change.

(7) The demonstrated success of initial illegal strikes became powerful proof that the *power* to strike was of far greater relevance than the *right* to strike. As long as some employees obtained improvements from the strike, others recognized it as a useful vehicle for their protest as well.[1]

Since the early 1960's, one objective identified by national unions has been the extension of union membership in the public service. To date, too little attention has been given by the citizen and elected representatives in our government to public-employee unionization. The complexity and magnitude, diversity and size of public employment has frustrated the citizen's understanding of labor relations in the public sector. One reason why it took so long for union action in the public sector to gain a foothold was the historic tendency of American citizens to believe that the government, as sovereign, could not negotiate with its own employees. These citizens also believed that the civil service system was equitable in its compensation system, projecting as part of its image to both the employee and the public the assurance of equal employment opportunity and merit promotion. The civil service concept also placed heavy emphasis on the individual and on the rights and benefits of the individual, and not on group action or decision. Additionally, there was a belief for many years that an incompatibility existed between collective bargaining and the civil service concept, this belief holding that standards of individual merit would clash with collective bargaining and membership practices of the union. It is my opinion that this belief has, and is continuing to change.

This new presence of labor organizations within the state and local public sector is going to mean considerable loss of legislative control over budgets, tax rates and other government programs and projects. Yet the fact remains that public employees, since the mid-1960's, have used labor organizations to realize an increasing degree of success in achieving their demands. Without legislation, some organized public employees (e.g., firemen and construction workers) have been able to achieve informal but highly effective bargaining conditions with public officials, and in many cases, legislation has just trailed along to give official approval to current practice.[2]

### Public-Employee Unions

Public-employee organizations are of several types:[3] craft unions, general or industrial unions, professional associations, and independent unions and associations. Some have a membership that includes employees in private industry—among these "mixed unions" are the Service Employees International Union (SEIU), the Laborers' International Union, the International Brotherhood of Teamsters, and 25 others.[4]

*The American Federation of State, County, and Municipal Employees* (AFSCME) is the fastest growing and most influential union in the municipal service, with approximately 750,000 dues-paying members and a representation that includes approximately 1.5 million workers. AFSCME evolved out of the Wisconsin State Administration Association in 1932 with a membership of less than 100. Under the leadership of its founder, Dr. Arnold Zander, it affiliated with the American Federation of Government Employees (AFGE) and extended AFGE's jurisdiction to include state, county and municipal employees. This affiliation was to be a brief one, however. AFSCME was granted its own charter by the AFL in 1936, and by 1950 it had a membership of 68,000. Organized into locals, usually grouped into larger district councils, AFSCME primarily operates on the municipal level, giving extensive autonomy to its locals. Membership includes 70 percent white, 30 percent black, 70 percent blue-collar, and 30 percent white-collar.

During the first decade of its existence, AFSCME stressed support of the merit system and civil-service legislation, relying heavily on lobbying to achieve its goals. But with the assumption of leadership by Jerry Wurf in 1964 (after a bitterly contested election), AFSCME questioned the adequacy of merit systems, proclaimed its right to strike, and escalated up both its political and collective bargaining roles. Within two years of Wurf's election, membership had risen by 50,000, and there was growing militancy among the organizations' members. In July 1966, AFSCME got an important collective bargaining law passed in Wisconsin which affirmed the right of public employees, except law enforcement officers, to strike, and in 1968 the union played an important role in the Memphis, Tennessee, sanitation workers' strike. Today AFSCME is the 2nd-largest union in the AFL-CIO. In 1971, Wurf was elected to a position on the AFL-CIO Executive Council, giving increased significance to AFSCME's growth and also recognition to the importance of public-employee unions.[5]

In my opinion, the most important *teacher unions* today are the American Federation of Teachers (AFT), the United Federation of Teachers (UFT), and the National Education Association (NEA).

Early teacher strikes were mainly over economic issues and were evidence of the great discontent among teachers over the way they had been treated for years by city school administrators and the Boards of Education. Among the early teacher unions were the Teachers' Union of New York City, founded in 1916 by a group of progressive teachers who believed that trade unionism was compatible with high professional standards. Teachers' associations dealt mainly with professional problems, but very little concern was given to the handling of complaints and grievances. The National Education Association was established in 1857 with membership open to any professional person engaged in service in an education enterprise. Superintendents, principals, and other supervisors, in addition to teachers, could be members, and their presence tended to push questions of salaries, pensions, and other matters affecting the teachers as employees into the background.[6]

During the 1920's, communists infiltrated certain sectors of the labor movement, and Local No. 5 of the Teachers' Union in New York City (affiliate of AFT) became dominated by the communists. The noncommunists within the local organization split and formed the Teachers' Guild in New York City, replacing the Teachers' Union as the affiliate to the AFT. This new guild immediately began merging with other teacher organizations and eventually formed the United Federation of Teachers (UFT) in 1960, the organization that was chosen to represent the New York City teachers in bargaining in 1961. Today UFT's interest is centered on such issues as teacher safety, pension rights, promotion, endorsements of local and state political candidates, higher wages, welfare and benefit packages, the length of workdays and lunch periods, the number of pupils assigned to different types of classes, and the conditions under which a teacher can transfer to another school.

The National Education Association has over 1 million members, 50 state affiliates, and approximately 8,000 local associations with public school teachers constituting over three-fourths of its membership. The American Federation of Teachers with over 200,000 members, is primarily a trade union for classroom teachers, excluding supervisory personnel from membership. AFT stresses the use of collective bargaining, including strikes, whereas NEA opposes these. This, and other basic philosophical differences between AFT and NEA, has led to keen competition between these two educational associations for members.

*The International Brotherhood of Teamsters* (IBT) is a very strong competitor of the AFSCME. IBT has long been engaged in public-employee organization as an independent industrial union, taking all classes of workers, including clerks, sanitation workers, laborers, correction officers, sheriff's deputies, policemen, and firemen, as well as school principals, nurses, and physicians. The Teamsters' size (2.2 million) and powerful image have helped them attract many state and local employees. IBT has organized approximately 75,000 public blue-collar employees into 170 separate locals—70 percent in towns, cities, or villages; 10 percent in special municipal authorities; and 6 percent in state-wide units.

*The Laborers' International Union* was established in 1903. Like the Teamsters, they organize all types and classes of workers but concentrate mostly on blue-collar workers and are also competitive with AFSCME for state and local members.

*The Service Employees' International Union* is an AFL-CIO affiliate which organizes both public- and private-sector workers. It has 600,000 members, approximately 160,000 of which are public employees—mostly maintenance, upkeep, cleaning, and servicing workers.

An example of the *independent associations* involved in public-sector organizing is the numerous Civil Service Employees Associations (CSEA) which exist in some 37 states, with memberships ranging from a few hundred in Florida to 170,000 in New York (where CSEA was founded in 1910). These associations stress their independence and claim they have freedom of action without interference or supervision from an international union. Most of these associations admit supervisory/management officials into membership and are regarded by the affiliated public-service labor unions as "company unions." Most of these types of state and local associations are now members of a loose confederation called the Assembly of Government Employees (AGE).

*Professional unions and associations* are also an important factor in the public sector. An example of this type of organization is the International Association of Fire Fighters (IAFF), which includes in its membership over 90 percent of the nation's uniformed firefighters.

Another example is *police labor organizations.* In recent years, we have witnessed a marked increase in police unionization through employee organizations or labor-union affiliations; police officers have organized to achieve economic improvements and resolve job-related problems. Police unions have concentrated on issues such as increased wages, shorter hours, uniform allowances, roll-call pay, premium pay for overtime, health and welfare plans, and other improvements in the terms and conditions of employment. Parity between police officers' and firefighters' wages has also become a principal issue in police bargaining. At present, the largest police unions are the Fraternal Order of Police, the International Brotherhood of Police Officers, and the International Conference of Police Associations, which serves as the Washington, DC, representative of local police organizations.[7]

## Union Security

Most state acts provide that the public employees have a right to join or not join a union. As a result, union security provisions that would require an employee to belong to a union (union shop, modified union shop, etc.) as a condition of employment are generally not permitted. During the past year, however, the U.S. Supreme Court gave agency shops in the public sector a boost when it upheld the right of government employee unions to require nonunion employees to pay a fee to defray the costs of union representation and contract enforcement. Negotiation of union or agency shops is now authorized in 15 states. Eight of these state laws apply to state and local employees—Alaska, Hawaii, Massachusetts, Minnesota, Montana, Oregon, Washington, and Wisconsin. The Connecticut and Rhode Island laws cover only state employees, and the Michigan and Vermont laws cover only local employees. A Kentucky law is limited to firefighters, while a California law applies only to school employees, and a Maine law applies only to university employees.[8]

To strengthen union security, public-employee unions seek contract provisions that are already generally accepted in the private sector, such as the dues checkoff, the union shop, maintenance of dues and membership, the agency shop, and exclusive bargaining rights. Municipalities have been the pacesetters on questions of union security. In 1974, 30 percent of AFSCME's agreements contained union security provisions, while four years later, the figure had risen to 40 percent. By 1985, AFSCME had negotiated approximately 1,100 agreements; 42 percent had union security provisions; 20 percent for a union shop or modified union shop; 8 percent for maintenance of membership; 8 percent for an agency shop; and 90 percent for exclusive recognition.

The most widespread and least controversial union security provision is the dues checkoff. In 1982, AFSCME reported that a checkoff of employees' dues had been authorized in 38 states and that more than 80 percent of AFSCME members paid their dues in this manner. Since this time, additional states and municipal jurisdictions have either legally authorized the checkoff or permitted it in practice. From 1982 to 1985, 16 states enacted statutes granting checkoff to recognized or certified employee organizations.

New York's Taylor Law granted the checkoff, but provided that it could be suspended for up to 18 months if unions struck in violation of the statute. The impact of this provision was apparent in the 1967 strike of the New York City UFT. The union resorted to a private computer service to bill teachers directly when the checkoff was suspended, and the estimated cost to the union for the first 8 months of operation was $500,000.

The checkoff has several advantages for public-employee organizations: (1) it insures a steady income on a year-round basis; (2) it provides for collection of dues from employees without pressure, coercion or resentment; (3) it eliminates the much larger expense of direct collection by the union itself; (4) it reduces the likelihood of membership withdrawal; and (5) union stewards are given more time for other more important union activities.

While the union shop is favored by most public-employee unions, the chief legal barrier to its implementation in public employment is the traditional concept of unrestricted employment in the public service sector. However, modified union shop agreements have been negotiated with municipal governments. Philadelphia's modified union shop agreement with AFSCME District Council No. 33 covers approximately 20,000 of the city's 30,000 employees. An AFSCME affiliate in Hartford, Connecticut, negotiated in 1984 for a union shop clause for labor and trades employees. Modified union shops exist in Lansing, Michigan; Paducah, Kentucky; and Vernon, Connecticut.

Because of the resistance, legal and political, to the union shop in the public sector, many unions have concentrated on the agency shop concept, in which a worker must pay either dues or a fee for union services, but need not join the union. The advantages of the agency shop to unions are many: it eliminates "free riders;" the union's financial position is strengthened, and; an overall increase in union security is gained. There is also an increased incentive for nonmembers to join the union, since they already are paying a fee and are thus likely to develop an interest in the organization's activities.

Opponents of the agency shop in the public sector say that it introduces new, nonmerit factors into the employment process.[9] Here again one hears the previously stated argument that public employees do not need the same protection and benefits characteristically accorded unions in the private sector. Whether one agrees or disagrees with this contention, the fact is that the agency shop is becoming a more prevalent form of security for state and local labor organizations.

## Collective Bargaining

Collective bargaining at the state and local level is at the same stage of development that collective bargaining was in the private sector in the late 1930's and the federal sector in the early 1960's. Like the private and federal sectors then, the state and local level is beset today with a growing militancy and a considerable uncertainty over the future. It is my opinion that the path travelled by state and local employees in this area will closely parallel that travelled by their private and federal counterparts previously. Many similar trends are already evident. Virtually all of the state statutes provide that public employees have the right to join unions and bargain collectively, yet some have no unfair labor practice provisions nor established administrative machinery to implement the rights granted such employees. The determination of the appropriate bargaining unit is made by the agency that administers the comprehensive state acts (in each state), in accordance with criteria set forth in the statute or in the rules and regulations set up by that administering agency. If one reviews the history of private and federal unions in this area, one will find that a similar state of affairs existed when those sectors were at a stage of development similar to state and local unions today.

The scope of bargaining in the public sector is not as broad as in the private sector. In the public sector, most state statutes provide that the parties negotiate in good faith "with respect to grievance procedures and conditions of employment," whereas under the NLRA, private employers and unions are required to bargain in good faith with respect to "wages, hours, and other terms and conditions of employment." Collective bargaining in the public sector has been recently expanded to include mandatory subjects (wages, hours, fringe benefits), voluntary subjects (joint employer-union recommendations to amend or change civil service or educational laws, promotional opportunities, and/or other personnel changes), and prohibited subjects (such as union shop provisions and members-only contracts providing benefits for only members of the union).

Virtually all of the state legislation concerning public employees establishes procedures to resolve collective bargaining disputes. The most prevalent provides for mediation, followed by fact-finding with nonbinding recommendations. This approach has been adopted by at least 12 states, including Connecticut, Michigan, New Jersey, New York, and Wisconsin. Additionally, despite the considerable resistance to compulsory arbitration for resolving disputes, an increasing number of states have enacted compulsory arbitration statutes especially for employees who provide essential services, e.g., police and firemen. Four states (Pennsylvania, Michigan, Rhode Island, and South Dakota) provide for compulsory arbitration of interest disputes (i.e., disputes over what the basic agreement should contain) for both firemen and policemen. Vermont and Wyoming have similar legislation covering only firemen.

There are now 20 states which meet the AFSCME's criteria of a "comprehensive broad scope law which mandates collective bargaining of wages, hours, and conditions of employment for state and local government workers." These are Alaska, Connecticut, Delaware, Florida, Hawaii, Iowa, Maine, Massachusetts, Minnesota, Montana, Nebraska, New Hampshire, New Jersey, New York, Oregon, Pennsylvania, Rhode Island, South Dakota, Vermont, and Wisconsin. Washington allows a limited form of collective bargaining for state employees. Michigan, Nevada and Washington have mandatory, comprehensive collective-bargaining laws for local employees. California, Kansas, and Michigan have mandatory meet-and-confer laws covering state and local government employees. In addition, many states have statutes which apply to certain employees, such as teachers or police.

There are presently two bills in Congress to require state and local governments to bargain collectively with their employees. One bill, H.R. 777, would extend the National Labor Relations Act to cover state and local governments. Another, H.R. 1488, would give state and local government employees collective-bargaining rights.[10] I expect no action on these bills in the near future, however.

## Strikes

The strike issue is probably the most controversial, urgent and misunderstood problem of labor relations in the public sector. Generally, strikes by public employees have been considered to be illegal by common law. At present, only four states (Alaska, Hawaii, Illinois, and Pennsylvania) allow strikes by public employees, while an additional four (Minnesota, Montana, Oregon, and Vermont) have granted a limited right to strike.

I raise the question as to whether it is sound public policy to guarantee workers the right to strike in the most vital sectors of private industry, yet deny that same right to all public employees, regardless of the importance of their function or the impact the stoppage might have on the public. Is it not possible that strikes by certain categories of state and local employees could be tolerated, while acceptable alternatives to a strike (similar to the Emergency Provisions of Taft-Hartley for the private sector or the Federal Service Impasse Panel for the federal sector) could be found for those employees not in these categories? I realize that if the states lift their ban on strikes by public employees, and no such alternative is provided, the public cannot be protected when such strikes interrupt services vital to the health, safety and welfare of the public. Thus, some neutral agency must be formed as the final authority when a strike threatens a sector whose services are continuously needed (policemen, prison guards, etc.). Under existing, all-encompassing legal bans, public employees have no realistic protection against an arbitrary employer who uses sovereign rights to implement personnel policies unilaterally or paternalistically. Anyone who would argue, as stated earlier, that their protection is the public-service system itself, with its stated assurance of an equitable reward system based on merit, is totally ignoring the facts of the last twenty years.

It is obvious from past experience that without the right to strike, these employees have no way to pressure officials to negotiate in good faith. Thus, strikes could and should be permitted for certain employees, e.g., those who perform a service that could be interrupted for a limited period of time and those performing functions with which the community could continue for an extended period of time without serious effects (not all public employees perform essential services).

Regardless of the prohibitions on striking, the number of strikes by public employees continues to increase every year. The new militancy of professional and other specialized workers, one of the most notable developments in local government labor relations, is the biggest single contributory factor. During the last few years, virtually every municipal service has suffered strikes. Public school teachers led the way with a variety of strikes, ranging from a one-teacher school in Maine to the massive statewide strike conducted by Florida teachers of the NEA and UFT. Sanitation, workers, with almost 200 recent strikes, have followed the educational workers lead. Other instances, too numerous to mention here, provide ample proof that strikes by state and local employees are here to stay.

## Conclusion

The basic question facing state and local public employee unions is whether or not labor relations in this sector should be patterned after those in the federal, or even the private sector. With each new state or municipal regulation, with each new "job action" by public employees, with each self-approved change in the bylaws of a public-employee union, this question is being answered. Indeed, present trends make the answer clear. Labor relations at the state and local level are being patterned after those of the federal sector, which in turn (with a 40- to 50-year time lag) are being patterned after those in the private sector. Any serious student of labor relations who carefully examines the historic (in the private) and present (in the federal, state, and local) trends and makes a rational comparison can arrive at with only one conclusion. All three groups are headed down the same path, although they are at different points along the way. The reader is urged to analyze any of the areas discussed in this paper—the right to organize strikes, dispute settlement, etc.—and see if this is not the case.

Whether such an occurrence is good or bad is a value judgment each individual must make for himself, but the fact that it is indeed the case cannot be denied.

**Table I. List of Public-Sector Unions/Associations**

AFGE    – American Federation of Government Employees

AFSCME – American Federation of State, County and Municipal Employees

AFT    – American Federation of Teachers

AGE    – Assembly of Government Employees

ANA    – American Nursing Association

CSEA    – Civil Service Employees' Association

FOP    – Fraternal Order of Police

IBPO    – International Brotherhood of Police Officers

IAFF    – International Association of Fire Fighters

IBT    – International Brotherhood of Teamsters

ICPA    – International Conference of Police Associations

IUOE    – International Union of Operating Engineers

LIU    – Laborers' International Union

NEA    – National Education Association

NFFE    – National Federation of Federal Employees

PBA    – Patrolmen's Benevolent Association

SCMWA – State, County and Municipal Workers of America

SEIU    – Service Employees' International Union

SSEU    – Social Services Employees' Union

TWU    – Transport Workers' Union

UAW    – United Auto Workers

UFA    – Uniformed Firefighters' Association

UFOA    – Uniformed Fire Officers' Association

UFT    – United Federation of Teachers

UPWA    – United Public Workers of America

**Table II. Full-Time State Employees
Who Belong to Employee Organizations***

| Rank by % of all full-time state employees | Members |
|---|---|
| 1. Hawaii | 25,379 |
| 2. Rhode Island | 13,569 |
| 3. Alaska | 9,661 |
| 4. Pennsylvania | 91,175 |
| 5. Maine | 11,151 |
| 6. Connecticut | 25,778 |
| 7. New York | 119,012 |
| 8. Vermont | 5,444 |
| 9. California | 114,134 |
| 10. Minnesota | 25,827 |
| 11. Oregon | 15,780 |
| 12. Michigan | 53,760 |
| 13. Montana | 7,063 |
| 14. Wisconsin | 23,336 |
| 15. New Jersey | 31,939 |
| 16. New Hampshire | 5,531 |
| 17. Massachusetts | 30,624 |
| 18. Delaware | 6,210 |
| 19. North Carolina | 52,691 |
| 20. Idaho | 5,864 |
| 21. Illinois | 44,585 |
| 22. Nevada | 3,841 |
| 23. Washington | 23,291 |
| 24. Maryland | 26,668 |
| 25. Ohio | 34,620 |
| 26. South Dakota | 3,830 |
| 27. Colorado | 14,413 |
| 28. Utah | 8,907 |
| 29. Wyoming | 2,532 |
| 30. Arizona | 9,746 |
| 31. Alabama | 16,506 |
| 32. Indiana | 17,202 |
| 33. Virginia | 23,508 |
| 34. South Carolina | 13,490 |
| 35. Iowa | 6,154 |
| 36. Texas | 32,784 |
| 37. Missouri | 11,563 |
| 38. Louisiana | 12,829 |
| 39. South Dakota | 2,085 |
| 40. New Mexico | 3,674 |

| Rank by % of all full-time state employees | Members |
|---|---|
| 41. Kansas | 5,010 |
| 42. Arkansas | 3,674 |
| 43. Nebraska | 2,729 |
| 44. Georgia | 7,151 |
| 45. Kentucky | 5,248 |
| 46. Tennessee | 5,199 |
| 47. Oklahoma | 1,663 |
| 48. West Virginia | 1,130 |
| 49. Mississippi | 940 |
| 50. Florida | 530 |

*Source: Bureau of the Census, U.S. Department of Commerce.

## Footnotes

[1]Zagoria, Sam, ed., *Public Workers and Public Unions*, (Englewood Cliffs, NJ: Prentice-Hall, Inc., 1972), pp. 101–102.

[2]Marx, Herbert L., Jr., ed., *Collective Bargaining for Public Employees*, H. W. Wilson Co., 1969, vol. 41, #5, pp. 1–23.

[3]See appendix, Table I, for list of public-sector unions/associations.

[4]*The Municipal Yearbook 1984*, The International City Management Association, 1984, p. 162.

[5]Billings, Richard N., and Greenya, John, *Power to the Public Worker*, (Washington – New York: FACT Research, Inc.), 1974, pp. 1–21.

[6]Taft, Philip, *United They Teach – The Story of the United Federation of Teachers*, (Los Angeles, CA: Nash Publishing, 1974), p. 26.

[7]*The Municipal Yearbook 1984*, op. cit., pp. 162–163.

[8]*State Government News*, The Council of State Governments, Washington, DC, October 1984, p. 6.

[9]Capozzola, John M. and Spero, Sterling D., *The Urban Community and Its Unionized Bureaucracies – Pressure Politics in Local Government Labor Relations*, (New York: Dunellen Publishing Co., Inc., 1973), pp. 150–157.

[10]*State Government News, op. cit.*, pp. 2, 6.

# Federal-Employee Unionism: An Overview

## ABSTRACT

An overview of the history, current status and trends in federal-employee unionism, and the laws relating to bargaining in the federal service are presented.

## Introduction

The field of public employment is today's new frontier in the realm of labor-management relations. *Business Week* has characterized the tremendous potential of this field as the real "growth stock" of the trade-union movement. But as recently as the 1950's, the subject of labor relations in public employment could not have meant less to more people, both in and out of government. It was a time in which public employees at all levels were excluded from the protection of our national and state labor relations laws. The reason for this is not clear. The United States Supreme Court and a New York court have ventured the following explanations: 1) public employees were so well taken care of by the governmental parent they served, that they did not need to band together to achieve better working conditions; and 2) collective bargaining was not shown to be as necessary in public employment as it was in private industry.

These explanations no longer hold true. The past few years have brought changes at a rapidly accelerating pace. Louder and more persistent employee demands, increased employee organization and better employee leadership, public awakening and governmental enlightenment, social contagion, and perhaps even political expediency have all played their part in fostering and shaping new relationships.[1]

Progress in the federal field has been marked by two separate phases. The first made fundamental policy and provided machinery for the enforcement of this policy, i.e., officially defining the rights of public employees and how those rights will be enjoyed. In the second phase, government assumed the direct role of employer; it applied its newly decorated policy to itself by attempting to establish and maintain what is, in essence, a collective-bargaining relationship between itself and its own employees.

## Legal Framework for Federal-Employee Unionism

In the late 1800's, the Post Office became the most heavily organized of all the government agencies, and with this growth came an increase in the activities in which the unions engaged, particularly the "lobbying" or petitioning of Congressional members on behalf of security and better working conditions for union members. The petitioning of Congress was necessary because the Pendleton Act, passed in 1883, gave Congress the right to regulate for public employees wages, hours, working conditions, and other terms of employment. This lobbying activity, which was to become the hallmark of public employee unionism for decades to come, was the cause of a series of "gag orders" issued by President Theodore Roosevelt in 1902 and made more restrictive by President Taft in 1909. These orders, which followed closely an order issued by Postmaster General Wilson in 1895 forbidding postal employees from visiting Washington for the purpose of influencing legislation, generally prohibited federal employees, under penalty of dismissal, from soliciting either by a group or individual methods, an increase in pay or influencing legislation on their behalf, save through the heads of their departments.[2]

It was through the culmination of a successful protest campaign against the restrictive and constitutionally-questionable provisions of these orders that the Lloyd-LaFollette Act was passed in 1912. In summary, that act simply gave: 1) federal employees the right to petition and to furnish information to Congress, and 2) postal employees the right to belong to employee organizations for the improvement of working conditions and the petitioning of Congress, provided such organizations did not assist in or impose upon their members an obligation to strike against the government.[3]

By implication, this latter right was interpreted by the workers as applying to federal employees, with the formation in 1917 of the National Federation of Federal Employees and in 1932 of the American Federation of Government Employees, two of the major federal unions existing today outside of the postal service.

In 1947 the second piece of important legislation affecting federal-employee relations was passed. The Taft-Hartley Act, although excluding the federal government as an employer from the provisions of the act (as did the Wagner Act of 1935), laid down a strong antistrike policy providing for mandatory loss of job and civil service status, as far as federal employees were concerned.

The 1950's were marked by frequent and sometimes bitter clashes between government and union leaders, particularly the postal unions and the Eisenhower Administration. In 1955 Public Law 330, was passed and superseded Section 305 of the Taft-Hartley Act. It made striking against the government a felony punishable by fine and imprisonment, and provided that anyone thus striking should not "accept" or "hold" any position in federal employment.

Also during this time, the American Federation of Labor repeatedly attempted to introduce a bill into Congress that would have provided for union recognition, consultation, binding arbitration, and union grievance handling for federal employees.

This bill never attained either administrative support or a congressional majority, but it did cause President Kennedy early in 1961 to appoint a Task Force on Employee-Management Relations in the Federal Service, chaired by Labor Secretary Arthur Goldberg and including Postmaster General Day, Civil Service Chairman Macy, Defense Secretary Robert McNamara, Budget Director Bell, and White House Counsel Theodore Sorensen. The task force report noted that although 3 percent of all federal employees belonged to national employee organizations, membership varied greatly among agencies, and there existed within the executive branch no general policy on employee-management relations. The result was wide variation among agencies in their dealings with employee organizations.

The main recommendations of the task force report submitted in November 1961 were incorporated into Executive Order 10988 issued by President Kennedy on January 7, 1962. This executive order, which required no congressional action, contained as its main provisions the following:

1. Federal employees were granted the right to form, join, and assist any employee organization or to refrain from such activity—no union- or closed-shop provisions permitted.

2. Three types of union recognition were established for the first time, based upon extent of employee membership within an appropriate unit: informal (less than 10 percent membership with the right to present petitions to be heard); formal (at least 10 percent membership, but less than 50 percent, with right to be consulted); and exclusive (at least 10 percent membership, and designated by the majority of employees in a unit as representative for all, with the right to bargain collectively).

3. Management officials were required to grant appropriate recognition; to meet and negotiate at reasonable times, and, if an agreement was reached, to execute a written agreement.

4. Exclusive unions had to represent everyone in the bargaining unit.

5. A strong management-rights clause was included, giving agency officials the right, without any negotiating requirement, to direct employees; to hire, fire, promote, suspend, assign, and demote employees; to relieve them from duty for lack of work; to determine methods, means, and personnel by which operations were to be

conducted, and; to take whatever action was necessary in emergency situations.

6. Privileges of the order were not to be extended to any organization that asserted the right to strike against the government, advocated its overthrow, or discriminated membership on racial or religious grounds.

7. Impasses of negotiable issues in the form written agreements, i.e., working conditions, promotion standards, apprenticeships, training, job classification, and safety, were to be settled by means short of arbitration.

8. Authorized establishment of a negotiated grievance procedure, with provisions for advisory arbitrations of grievances, as well as those relating to interpretations and application of agreements.

9. No unit for bargaining purposes could be established that included both managerial and supervisory, as well as rank-and-file employees, in the same units. Advisory arbitration for unit determinations and representation disputes was authorized.

10. The head of the government agency had to approve each local agreement.[4]

In May 1963, President Kennedy further supplemented E.O. 10988 with the issuance of a "Standards of Conduct for Employee Organizations" and a "Code of Fair Labor Practices." The standards called generally for the maintenance by employee organizations of certain democratic internal procedures, equal treatment of members, periodic elections, and due process. The code prohibited both management and labor from engaging in specified practices that tended to thwart free choice of individuals in the determination and selection of employee unions to which they might wish to belong, or to select as bargaining agent (similar to unfair labor practices of other federal labor laws). Significantly, it also prohibited employee organizations from calling or engaging in work stoppages, slowdowns, or related picketing engaged in as a substitute for such activities.

Also in 1963, the Comptroller General issued a ruling in response to a request from the administration that enabled the Civil Service Commission to issue regulations authorizing the voluntary withholding of dues of employee organizations under a checkoff arrangement, the administrative cost of which was to be defrayed by a small service charge.

Despite the acknowledged success of the executive order in promoting union membership and collective bargaining, employee organizations voiced criticism of it in five major areas. The first was the bargaining impasse. Critics suggested that there was a greater need to develop mediation and fact-finding procedures and also to expedite referrals to higher authority within a governmental agency to bring the parties to an agreement. The second problem area was the scope of negotiation. Some federal agencies had been against the use of mediation and advisory arbitration provisions to determine grievances and to deal with adverse actions by the agencies, an adverse action being an action in violation of the Code of Fair Labor Practices. The third problem area was agency review and delegation of authority. The unions complained that agency heads were overly restrictive in delegating sufficient local authority to permit meaningful negotiations. The fourth problem area was lack of binding arbitration of adverse actions. The unions also complained that the use of federal-agency hearing officers to determine alleged violations of fair labor practices was in itself unfair, for agencies would not be objective in evaluating their own compliance, and the tendency would be to approve the actions of supervisors. The fifth area was the scope of collective bargaining. Despite necessary limitations on issues subject to negotiations, there was far more room for bargaining than most agencies permitted.

Shortly after his inauguration in 1968, President Nixon appointed a study committee under the leadership of Civil Service Chairman Hampton to conduct an extensive review and evaluation of these union criticisms and the overall federal labor-relations program. This study determined that E.O. 10988 had produced some excellent results, but that several important changes were needed. These changes were made by President Nixon in October 1969 in Executive Order 11491. Major provisions included:

1. Establishing a Federal Labor Relations Council with the Secretary of Labor, an official of the Executive Office, and the Chairman of the Civil Service Commission responsible for administering the order, deciding major policy issues, prescribing regulations, and entertaining appeals.

2. Prohibiting supervisors from acting as union officers or representatives.

3. Establishing a Federal Service Impasse Panel of three members to assist in resolving, or to actually resolve, negotiation impasses.

4. Giving the Assistant Secretary of Labor for Labor-Management Relations the authority to decide "administrative" disputes and to order and supervise elections.

5. Establishing a required separate system for consultation with associations of supervisors.

6. Eliminating informal and formal recognition.

7. According exclusive recognition only on the basis of secret ballot elections having 51 percent of the vote obtained, and no minimum membership requirements.

8. Adding rules for settling disputes on negotiability issues.

9. Prohibiting union shop, agency shop, and maintenance of membership.

10. Permitting a single negotiated grievance system, eliminating advisory arbitration, and substituting binding arbitration on a cost-sharing basis.

11. Limiting agency headquarters' authority to disapprove locally negotiated agreements.

12. Authorizing full Federal Mediation and Conciliation Service services to assist parties.

13. Adding financial reporting and disclosure requirements for unions and transferring enforcement responsibility from agencies to the Assistant Secretary of Labor.

14. Making it an unfair labor practice for a labor organization to punish a member for his work performance, to condone a strike or prohibited picketing by failing to take "affirmative action" to stop or prevent it, or to refuse to consult or bargain as required.

15. Authorizing managerial and supervisory organizations to participate in voluntary dues withholding.

16. Continuing to exclude from bargaining wages, hours and terms of employment.

E.O. 11491 also contained a provision that required the establishment of a panel to study the effects of the order. The changes found by this panel to be needed were incorporated into E.O. 11616:

1. Professional employees were allowed to join regular employee unions.

2. Responsibility for enforcement in code and unfair labor practice cases was transferred from agency heads to the Secretary of Labor for Labor-Management Relations.

3. A grievance procedure was required to be included in each agreement.

4. The agency requirement to cover its expenses in check-off provisions was changed to a negotiable issue.[5]

These executive orders were, however, still inadequate to meet the demands for full-scale collective bargaining by postal employees, and a strike involving some 200,000 postal employees occurred in 1970. As a result of that strike, the executive branch engaged in direct collective bargaining with heads of the major postal organizations, and ultimately reached agreement on wage increases, wage progression schedules, fringe benefits, and endorsement of the Postal Reform Act to apply new bargaining procedures for postal employees. Congress confirmed the bargaining decisions reached, which included arbitration of contract terms as a substitute for the prohibited right to strike, and arbitration of interest disputes and grievances. This new postal law is based on private-sector principles set forth in the Wagner Act.

## The Unions Themselves

Contrary to popular knowledge, public-employee unionism has a very long and honorable tradition with the federal government, dating back to the early 1800's with craftsmen in the Navy shipyards, to the 1860's with workers in the Government Printing Office, and to the latter third of the nineteenth century with letter carriers in the Post Office Department. Historically, three major classifications of unions have existed in federal employment: 1) unions organizing solely in the post office, 2) unions composed primarily of employees in private employment, but also organizing blue-collar workers in federal employment, and 3) unions restricting their membership to federal employees but not those employed by the post office.

Beginning with the earliest postal union when the letter carriers in New York City organized in 1863, unions in the postal service have grown until today there are about a dozen, with the American Postal Workers' Union (membership 400,000) and the National Association of Letter Carriers (224,000 membership) as the two largest.

Blue-collar unions currently affiliated with the AFL-CIO Metal Trades Department have a long history of organization in federal employment, dating back to the 1830's in the Navy yards. These unions presently have the bulk of their membership in the Department of Defense, and Metal Trades Council representation was 58,629 in 1985. Blue-collar coverage had increased slightly in absolute numbers by 1985 to 410,716 (up 4,716 from 1984), or a 2 percent increase in percentage of representation in that segment of the work force.

The first of the unions that restricted their membership solely to federal employment—excluding postal employees—was the National Federation of Federal Employees. Jurisdiction over federal employees not covered by any craft unions was given to the NFFE in 1917 by the American Federation of Labor (AFL). In 1931, the AFL, at the instigation of craft unions having members in federal employment, went on record opposing the report of the U.S. Personnel Classification Board because the board had recommended the extension of the classification principles to all federal employees including the skilled crafts. NFFE, which strongly favored the classification principle for federal white-collar employees, left the AFL in protest over the fact that they were not consulted concerning AFL's position on this issue. To cover this jurisdiction, the American Federation of Government Employees (AFGE) was chartered by the AFL on August 18, 1932, with about two thousand former members of the original NFFE in thirty-nine lodges. For many years the NFFE was by far the largest of the two unions, but, partially as a result of its isolation, the NFFE has now dwindled in size and is presently the representative of 136,071 federal employees.[6]

By the mid–1960's the AFGE had grown into the largest of the unions representing federal-government workers, and today it represents over 670,000 federal employees. The AFGE's growth was encouraged by the jurisdiction allotted them in their charter by the AFL, which grants jurisdiction over all civilian employees of the United States government and the District of Columbia "excepting those over whom jurisdiction has been granted to other national or international unions by the AFL-CIO."

Along with wide jurisdiction for the AFGE came jurisdictional disputes with other AFL-CIO unions. The most significant involved the AFL-CIO's Metal Trades Department and the International Association of Machinists. These disputes arose, in large part, from the organizing techniques used by the unions. The AFGE was classified as an industrial union belonging to the AFL-CIO's Industrial Union Department. Organizing did not take place, however, on strictly industrial lines. Rather, a free form of organization developed where the union issued charters to virtually any unaffiliated group that showed a willingness to belong to the organization. In other words, craft or industrial locals were formed on the basis of the wishes of those applying for charters. The union, however, was industrial, in the sense that all workers within the general jurisdiction outlined above were accepted for membership, not just those in a particular craft.

In 1973 the AFL-CIO executive council recognized the growing importance of public-employee unionism by creating the public-employee department. The new two-million member department, which is equivalent to the AFL-CIO's industrial-union department, building and construction trades department, and eight similar bodies, is made up of 24 unions with public-employee membership. Its major roles are to serve as lobbying and collective-bargaining agent and to persuade people on government payrolls that unionization is the wave of the future.[7]

An area in which the AFGE differs most drastically from these AFL-CIO public-employee unions is strategy and tactics. It is generally believed that public-employee unions have two basic weapons at their disposal. These are passage of legislative acts improving the circumstances of employment and direct collective bargaining. The AFGE constitution emphasizes legislative action. Article II, Objects and Methods, Section 2 states that "the Federation shall strive to promote efficiency in the governmental service, and shall advance plans of improvement to be secured by legislative enactment through cooperation with governmental officials and other lawful means." Virtually all federal employees have their pay determined by congressional action. Similarly, Congress has jurisdiction over basic employee benefits such as annual and sick leave, compensation for injury insurance, and employer contributions to health and welfare plans. Until Congress relinquishes authority over these areas, the best way that unions representing federal employees can secure increased pay and improved benefits is to use legislative tactics.

Just as employee-management relations in private industry were revolutionized some forty years ago, employee-management relations in the public sector underwent drastic changes in the 1960's, changes that are continuing today. One such change is the tremendous growth in representation of federal employees by unions. Between the years 1983 and 1985, agreements were negotiated in 227 additional recognition units, an increase of 19 percent. Overall, 2,704 (75%) of all units are now covered by agreements. Employees covered by negotiated agreements are at a record level of 1,083,017, encompassing 90 percent of all employees under exclusive recognition. Of the entire nonpostal federal work force, 61 percent were covered by agreements as of November, 1985. A total of 1,200,336 (59%) nonpostal federal employees are represented by unions. When postal and nonpostal data are combined, the total coverage under exclusive recognition becomes 1,799,340, or 68 percent of total employment in 1985 (6, pp. 1-2) (See Tables 1, 2, and 3).

**Table 1**

**Total Federal Employees in Exclusive Units and
Covered by Agreement, 1974–1984**

| Year | Total Employees in Exclusive Units | | Employees Covered By Agreement | |
|------|-------|----|--------|----|
| | Total | % | Number | % |
| 1974 | 230,543 | 12 | 110,573 | 6 |
| 1975 | 319,724 | 16 | 241,850 | 12 |
| 1976 | 434,890 | 21 | 291,532 | 14 |
| 1977 | 629,915 | 29 | 423,052 | 20 |
| 1978 | 797,511 | 40 | 556,962 | 28 |
| 1979 | 842,843 | 42 | 559,415 | 28 |
| 1980 | 916,381 | 48 | 601,505 | 31 |
| 1981 | 1,038,288 | 53 | 707,067 | 36 |
| 1982 | 1,082,587 | 55 | 753,247 | 39 |
| 1983 | 1,086,361 | 56 | 837,410 | 43 |
| 1984 | 1,142,419 | 57 | 984,553 | 49 |

Source: Civil Service News, U.S. Civil Service Commission, Washington, D.C., 1985.

**Table 2**

**Exclusive Recognitions and Agreements by
Major Unions in Federal Sector, November 1984**
(Excluding Postal Workers)

| Union | Recognition Units | Employees Represented | Units Under Agreement | Employees Covered | Per Cent Covered |
|-------|-------|-------|-------|-------|-------|
| AFGE | 1,724 | 670,029 | 1,223 | 589,613 | 88 |
| NFFE | 690 | 136,071 | 521 | 116,465 | 86 |
| NTEU | 101 | 83,868 | 100 | 83,778 | 100 |
| NAGE | 333 | 77,878 | 236 | 72,134 | 93 |
| MTC | 51 | 58,629 | 49 | 58,560 | 100 |
| IAM | 96 | 32,859 | 90 | 39,362 | 98 |

Table 3

Growth in Exclusive Recognition,
By Major Units

| Union | Number of Units | | | Employees Represented | | |
|---|---|---|---|---|---|---|
| | 1984 | 1983 | Change | 1984 | 1983 | Change |
| AFGE[a] | 1,724 | 1,627 | + 6 | 670,029 | 650,038 | + 3 |
| NFFE | 690 | 672 | + 3 | 136,071 | 125,234 | + 9 |
| NTEU | 101 | 89 | + 13 | 83,868 | 65,417 | + 28 |
| NAGE | 333 | 328 | + 2 | 77,878 | 74,127 | + 5 |
| MTC | 51 | 48 | + 6 | 58,629 | 58,366 | — |
| IAM | 96 | 94 | + 2 | 32,859 | 30,166 | + 9 |

[a]Column definitions:   AFGE  – American Federation of Government Employees
NFFE  – National Federation of Federal Employees
NTEU  – National Treasury Employees' Union
NAGE  – National Association of Government Employees
MTC   – Metal Trades Council
IAM   – International Association of Machinists

Source: Civil Service News, U.S. Civil Service Commission, Washington, D.C., 1985.

Several conditions have led to the increased unionization of government employees. The substantial growth in public employment made inevitable the emergence of a public-employee group consciousness that led to group organization. When many employees are working at the same kind of job, they are bound to be drawn together when management disputes arise. Formal organization gave them a voice for expressing grievances and making demands.

Moreover, the growth of organized labor in the private sector has impacted on the public sector. Employee organizations in the public service are usually found in large cities and industrialized areas, where industrial unions have flourished. This affords public employees the opportunity to view first-hand the benefits of unionization for the individual employee in large organizations. In addition, the civil service system, originally conceived to protect public employees from the spoils system, has tended to create hostility toward public administration among some employees. Those who cannot advance under the merit principle of promotion seek other means of improving income and maintaining their self-respect, and employee organizations furnish both a method of challenging the rules of advancement under the merit system and a route toward self-satisfaction when advancement is stymied.

But perhaps the most specific reason for the growth of government unionism is the executive orders issued by Presidents Kennedy and Nixon. E.O. 10988 issued by President Kennedy in 1962 was as clear and unequivocal in its support of public unionism as the Wagner Act of 1935 had been in its support for unions and collective bargaining in the private sector. It declared that "the efficient administration of the government and the well-being of employees require that orderly and constructive relationships be maintained between employee organizations and management." E.O.'s 11491 and 11616 issued by President Nixon took this one step further by favorably responding to most of labor's criticisms regarding 10988.

## Activities of Federal Unions in the Last Fifteen Years

As 1970 began, a great deal of unrest among federal employee organizations arose in spite of numerous pay bills that dramatically improved federal wage scales: the adoption of the "comparability" pay principle into the Pay Comparability Act of 1970; passage of many additional employee benefits and the negotiation of hundreds of others in signed agreements, and; the establishment of a vigorous equal-employment-opportunity program. In addition, a great struggle was taking place over postal reform, which would eventually transform the postal service into a government corporation, with profound effects on direct negotiation between management and employee unions on an unrestricted range of items, including wages, hours and fringe benefits.

Moreover, an internal change was taking place within federal employee unions, for the mood of the rank and file, particularly the younger members, was growing more militant. The success of both the direct-action confrontations of the civil-rights movement and the spectacular success of local strikes that were taking place in city and state governments, especially since 1966, created strong pressures on federal-employee leaders, particularly in the large cities where the federal government's national wage scale was not competitive with municipal rates.

On March 18, 1970, postal service employees in the New York City area successfully carried out a week-long strike for higher wages. The strike affected over 200,000 postal workers and crippled postal operations in the entire northeastern area, making it the most widespread strike in government history. The executive branch chose not to invoke Public Law 330 against the strikers but, instead, entered into collective bargaining with the postal workers.[8] This strike was instrumental in hastening enactment of the Postal Reform Act, which gave to postal employees virtually every labor-relations benefit accorded workers in the private sector—except the right to strike.

During the next few years, a number of successful sick-outs and slowdowns took place among employees in the postal service and the Environmental Science Services Administration and among air traffic controllers. Although these activities are within the scope of the definitions of a strike under the Taft-Hartley Act, the government did not classify these activities as strikes.

In August of 1970, the historically-conservative AFGE followed the precedent set earlier by the postal service unions and deleted the no-strike clause from its constitution. The AFGE maintained that the deletion of the no-strike clause was not an assertion of the right to strike the government. The AFGE reaffirmed that its national policy was still to abide by the law. However, deletion of the no-strike clause was the first step taken toward strike action by the postal unions, and many feel that AFGE has consciously started down the same path.

In the face of continued insistence and demonstrations by public employees that the no-strike clause is unenforceable, the government seems to be forced to choose one of three alternatives: 1) to continue to assert sovereignty and the excuse of essential services in the face of "nonstrikes" by employees, and to continue to face the resulting embarrassment; 2) to allow strikes for nonessential but not for essential services, and; 3) to decentralize decision making to sanction an expansion of negotiable issues and broaden the scope of fact-finding and arbitration. No definite decision seems to have yet been reached as to the more acceptable of these to the federal government.

Another area in which public-employee unions have been active recently is that of political activity. The AFGE has been very forceful in lobbying Congress for the repeal of the Hatch Act, which restricts the activity of federal employees in political campaigns. Advocates of repeal claim that the act, which dates back to 1939, puts strictures on the freedom of federal employees and relegates them to the status of second-class citizens.[9]

In addition to lobbying, the AFGE ended the federal-employee unions' history of neutrality in presidential campaigns by organizing a coalition of thirteen federal unions to back Jimmy Carter. He promised in return that his government reorganization program would not become an anti-employee crusade and that federal workers would be paid fairly. The unions had bristled at President Ford's holddown of government salaries. To push Carter, the groups bought anti-Ford ads in a federal-employee newspaper, picketed the President in many states, and lent their staffs to AFL-CIO campaign efforts. Even rank-and-file civil servants, barred by law from partisan politics, were enlisted to help in nonpartisan voter-registration drives. But some locals refused to join the politicing, fearing that it was ethically wrong, even if legally permissible.[10]

A third area of recent activity by public-employee unions deals with the practice of federal agencies contracting with private firms to perform services and conduct programs previously assigned to federal employees. At their 1984 national convention, AFGE delegates almost unanimously rejected this contracting-out practice, attacking it on the basis of the performance of the contractors and the "pocketbook" aspects of the issue. They passed a recommendation for a continuing and concerted program to protect jobs held by the union's members and called on the nation's leadership to establish cooperative relations with other federal-employee unions for this purpose.[11]

In September 1984, Rep. Morris Udall and Rep. Christopher Dodd requested a General Accounting Office investigation of an administration plan to increase the contracting-out of federal services.[12] The AFGE predicted that this is the first move in a plan for the next Congress to improve and increase its oversight of federal government functions that are contracted-out to private industry. The union said it "opposes the juggling of cost-comparison figures in order to permit politically friendly private companies to take over traditional government work when government employees actually can do the work more efficiently and with more accountability to the public."[13] AFGE also objected to the arbitrary manpower ceilings placed on direct-hire federal employees to conceal the real size of the federal work force for political reasons, thereby forcing federal managers to contract-out work that could be done more cheaply and better by federal employees.

The newest area of public-union activity is the proposed organization of the military. This organization, which is just getting off the ground, gained a lot of angry support last spring with the Pentagon proposals to trim servicemen's pay raises, pensions, health insurance, and shopping discounts. The Fleet Reserve Association, which opposes the unions, warned Congress that, to its "shock and surprise" a "very large segment" of "senior" enlisted men recently surveyed favored by them a union. The Chairman of the Joint Chiefs of Staff complained that news articles highlighting plans for benefit cuts will assist at least three unions plotting military organizing drives. "The benefit cuts are the best damned recruiting devices we have," agreed the general counsel of the American Federation of Government Employees.[14]

### Summary

The advent of employee organizations and collective bargaining in the public sector is the most significant development from the industrial relations field in the last thirty years. In addition to the more obvious implications for employees, public officials, and the art of government, it may have important effects on the labor movement and on labor-management relations in the private sector.

Trade-union membership in the United States has not been keeping pace with the growth in the labor force, and union members as a percentage of the work force dropped from 25.7 percent in 1970 to 19.8 percent in 1985. This has been due largely to the relative employment decline in industries where unions have been strongest, and the failure of trade unions to appeal to the growing technical and white-collar segment of the labor force. The opening of public employment to trade unions may change this. As the fastest-growing industry, government could provide a source of enough new recruits to reverse the decline in trade-union membership. Government employees who join unions could also change the image of the labor movement to make it more acceptable to white-collar employees and technicians in private industry.

But whatever the effects of public unionism on these areas, the road ahead for federal unionism is not apt to provide smooth sailing. In the sense that public-employee unions are essentially political organizations, and they must be, given present legislation, they will interject into the daily routine of the public official substantial and sometimes startling changes. The basic conclusion must be reached, though, that no defensible reason exists for denying to federal employees this right to self-organize and collectively bargain over a wider range of issues than is presently permitted. The formation of employee organizations flows from deep-seated human needs. They will continue to be formed, and they will grow stronger. As legislation, with a certain time lag, reflects public opinion and human necessity, it will sanction this growth. It is only a matter of time.

### Footnotes

[1]D. H. Kruger, *Collective Bargaining in the Public Service*, (New York: Random House, 1969), pp. 10–11.

[2]L. Ulman, *Challenges to Collective Bargaining* (Englewood Cliffs, NJ: Prentice-Hall, Inc., 1967), p. 69.

[3]R. J. Murphy, *The Crisis in Public Employee Relations in the Decade of the Seventies*, The Bureau of National Affairs, Washington, 1970, pp. 1–2.

[4]S. Kaye, *International Manual on Collective Bargaining for Public Employees* (New York: Praeger Publishers, 1973), pp. 16–19.

[5]R. R. Nelson, "Collective Bargaining Agreements in the Federal Service," *Monthly Labor Review*, November 1972, pp. 51–53.

[6]*Civil Service News*, U.S. Civil Service Commission, Washington, D.C., February 18, 1985, p. 2.

[7]"Public Workers Test Their Clout," *Business Week*, November 16, 1974, p. 103.

[8]L. V. Imundo, "Strikes and the Strike Issue in Federal Government Labor-Management Relations," *Personnel Journal*, May 1973, p. 383.

[9]H. Flieger, "Second-Class Nonsense," *U.S. News and World Report*, September 2, 1975, p. 84.

[10]"Federal-Employee Unions Work for Carter," *The Wall Street Journal*, November 2, 1976, p. 1.

[11]H. R. Kemp, "AFGE Convention Issues," *Monthly Labor Review*, November 1984, pp. 51–52.

[12]S. Hernshaw, "Contract-Out Probe on Way," *Federal Times*, September 20, 1984, p. 1.

[13]"Contracting Retreat? Yes, AFGE Predicts," *Federal Times*, November 8, 1984, p. 3.

[14]"Military Benefit Cuts," *The Wall Street Journal*, November 10, 1984, p. 1.

# Federal-Sector Labor Relations As Seen
# Through The Executive Order System

The right of employees to bargain collectively has a long history in the United States. A part of this history has been the quest for collective bargaining by public employees, including those in the federal sector. It is only in recent history, however, that genuine progress has been made in bringing this part of the labor force into the American collective-bargaining process.

The problem with collective bargaining by federal employees first appeared back in the 1830's during the presidency of Andrew Jackson. Government employees belonged to the same craft unions as private employees and the government claimed no special status over there, resisting and yielding to union demands the same as any private firm. It was not until the late 1880's and 1890's, when the postal workers began to organize, that the government began to oppose labor activity in its federal sector. The first executive action taken against organized postal employee activity came in 1885 with an order by Postmaster General William L. Wilson which forbade any (postal) employee under "pain of removal" to visit Washington, whether on leave with or without pay, for the purpose of influencing legislation before Congress.[1] During the Theodore Roosevelt administration, union activity by federal employees was considered to be an interference with executive authority and a violation of the political neutrality of the civil service. In his famous "gag" order issued on January 25, 1902, Roosevelt forbade federal employees from "either directly or indirectly, individually or through association, soliciting any increase in pay or the influence of any other legislation except through the head of the department."[2]

This major barrier to federal employee unionism was removed on August 24, 1912, with the passage of the Lloyd-LaFollette Act which outlawed the presidential "gag" orders and gave postal workers the right to lobby, to organize, and to affiliate with outside organizations, yet did impose an obligation not to strike against the government. Following passage of this act, it became more practical for the postal workers to join Samuel Gomper's American Federation of Labor (AFL), which they did as soon as Lloyd-LaFollette had been ruled on by the courts. The act itself was not limited to postal employees, but gave all employees of the civil service the right to collectively or individually "petition Congress or any member thereof," a right which was not to be interfered with or denied. This piece of legislation, though not looked on with much favor by the executive branch, gave rise to the formation of a number of postal employee unions and remained the major piece of legislation dealing with federal labor-management relations until President Kennedy's Executive Order (E.O.) 10988 of 1962.

## The Executive Orders

In 1961 approximately 33 percent of all federal employees were unionized,[3] yet the federal government still had no effective labor-management relations policy.

Prior to the passage of E.O. 10988, there had been growing criticism of the government's lack of direction and cohesiveness between federal management and employee organizations. Since 1912 and the Lloyd-LaFollette Act, numerous employee organizations had sprung up, and the various government agencies dealing with them had each developed their own labor relations policy.

Shortly after his inauguration in January 1961, President Kennedy appointed a task force headed by the Secretary of Labor, Arthur J. Goldberg, to look into the question of labor-management relations in the federal system. The task force, which presented its report to the president in November 1961, concluded that "labor organizations were capable of contributing to the more effective conduct of the public business by insuring the positive participation of employees in the formulation and improvement of federal personnel policies and practices."[4] The task force also concluded that there were fundamental differences in employment conditions between the public and private sector, making it undesirable to pattern federal labor-management relations after those in private industry. While the task force agreed that important matters relating to federal employees fell within the jurisdiction of Congress, thus making it difficult to subject them to collective bargaining, it saw no difficulty between its recommendation concerning the desirability of labor organizations and the Civil Service merit system.

The recommendations made by the task force were as follows:

1. Federal employees should have the right to join or not to join *bona fide* employee organizations, and where there was sufficient desire to do so, the government should express a willingness to enter into such relationships.

2. All organizations not discriminating against individuals because of race, color, creed, sex, or national origin, who were free of corruption and who did not advocate strikes against the government or the overthrow of the government of the United States, should be recognized. Such organizations should be granted informal, formal, or exclusive recognition depending on the extent to which they represented a unit or activity within a government agency.

Informal recognition meant that the organization had a right to be heard in matters pertaining to its members, but placed an agency under no obligation to consult with that organization. This recognition was to be granted regardless of what recognition had been granted other organizations by that agency.

Formal recognition was to be given to an organization whose membership comprised 10 percent of the employees in a unit or activity and where no organization had been given exclusive recognition. In this case, the agency had to consult with the organization in matters pertaining to its members.

Exclusive recognition was to be given to organizations chosen by the majority of employees within a given unit. This status gave the organization the right to bargain collectively on behalf of its members. Collectively-bargained agreements could not conflict with established federal law, agency regulations, government personnel policies, or the authority of Congress.

3. The scope of consultation and negotiation was to depend on the form of recognition given the organization, and could concern working conditions and personnel policies within the limits of the law and in consonance with the principles of the merit system.

4. Impasses between federal agencies and employee organizations given exclusive recognition were to be settled by means other than arbitration, devised on an "agency-by-agency" basis.

5. All agreements with organizations granted exclusive or formal recognition were to be in writing and the effective dates kept within reasonable time limits.

6. Some of the "do's" and "don't's" recommended by the task force were:

a. Bulletin boards could and should be provided to the employee organizations.

b. Officially-approved or requested consultations with employee organizations should take place on official time.

c. An agency could require that negotiation with an employee organization granted exclusive recognition take place on employee's time.

d. No internal business of the employee organization could be conducted on official time.

e. Voluntary dues-withholding (checkoff) could be granted to an employee organization.

7. Employee organizations should have a recognized grievance procedure. Advisory arbitration which the agency did not have to abide with could be provided by agreement between an agency and an employee organization granted exclusive recognition.

8. Union shops and closed shops were declared "inappropriate" to the federal system.

9. Technical services required to implement the program were to be provided by the Department of Labor and the Civil Service Commission. The

program, when enacted into law, was to be administered by the Civil Service Commission.

These recommendations were accepted by President Kennedy and formed the basis for E.O. 10988. The above, of course, is a very general and broad description of what was contained in the order. The actual provisions of the order are numerous and much more specific. For instance, Section 6 paragraph (b) stated that while an employee organization granted exclusive recognition could negotiate with an agency on matters pertaining to employee's interests and working conditions, it could not negotiate on matters pertaining to "the mission of an agency, its budget, its organization and the assignment of its personnel, or the technology used for performing its work."

Section 13 paragraph (b) established a President's Temporary Committee on the Implementation of the Federal Employee-Management Relations Program, to consist of the Secretary of Labor, who was to be the Chairman, the Secretary of Defense, the Postmaster General and the Chairman of the Civil Service Commission. Section 16 stipulated that the order did not apply to such agencies as the CIA, FBI, National Security Agency and other intelligence and investigatory agencies.[5] The reason for this can be readily surmised.

While E.O. 10988 as originally adopted remained on the books only a short time (8 years), it nevertheless provided the first major guidelines and thus led to a considerable expansion of labor organizations within the federal system. During the period it was in effect, representation of employees in exclusive bargaining units expanded from two agencies with 29 units covering 19,000 employees, to 35 agencies (including the Post Office Department) within 2,305 units covering 1.4 million employees. This constituted 52 percent of the federal work force.[6]

On September 8, 1967, President Lyndon Johnson appointed a President's Review Committee on Federal Employee-Management Relations, known as the Johnson Review Committee. Its purpose was to review the program and determine its accomplishments, deficiencies, and needed modifications to insure "its continued vitality in the public interest." This committee was almost identical to the 1961 Kennedy Task Force. Again it was chaired by the Secretary of Labor, Willard Wirtz, and included John Macy, Chairman of the Civil Service Commission and Robert McNamara, Secretary of Defense. Although this committee did present to the President a completed review, with recommended changes, of the program in general and E.O. 10988 in particular, no action was taken on this report before President Johnson left office in January 1969.

When President Nixon took office, he appointed another study committee, with the same charge as its predecessor under President Johnson. As before, the committee included the Civil Service Commission's Robert Hampton, the Defense Department's Melvin Laird, Labor Secretary George Schultz, Postmaster General Winton Blount, and Budget Director Robert Mayo. This committee relied heavily on the study conducted by the Johnson committee and, in fact, adopted many of the recommendations that the Johnson committee had proposed. There were six major changes to the Kennedy order proposed by the Nixon committee which were accepted and incorporated into E.O. 10988 and reissued as E.O. 11491, signed October 29, 1969, to become effective January 1, 1970. The changes recommended were as follows:

1. The Kennedy order had given each agency head autonomy in the implementation of the order, while E.O. 11491 provided for one central authority to administer the order by the creation of the Federal Labor Relations Council (FLRC) (Section 4). This council is made up of the Chairman of the Civil Service Commission, who chairs the Council, the Secretary of Labor, and originally a member of the President's Executive Office to be appointed by the president. This third member, however, was later established as the Director of the Office of Management and Budget under the provisions of Executive Order 11616 of August, 1971. The functions of the council are to oversee the entire federal labor-management relations program, to interpret the order and rule on its provisions, to decide on policy issues, to hear appeals made on the decisions of the Assistant Secretary of Labor for Labor-Management Relations, to resolve unfair labor practices, to arbitrate grievances, and to make periodic reports to the president on the status of the program.

2. E.O. 11491 also provides for several third-party processes, differing from E.O. 10988; the latter stated that the head of each agency was to settle labor-management disputes. E.O. 11491 changed this and provided four basic third-party processes for settling disputes. The first gives the Assistant Secretary for Labor-Management Relations (Section 6) authority to decide on questions regarding the appropriateness of awarding a unit exclusive recognition. Empowered to supervise and certify all elections, the secretary can decide on unfair labor practice complaints, including violations of the standards of conduct for labor organizations. In cases involving the Labor Department, this authority is transferred to the chairman of the Civil Service Commission.

The second process is the provision that the Federal Mediation and Conciliation Service should extend its services to include the federal sector and provide the same mediation assistance it offers the private sector.

The third process is the creation of the Federal Service Impasse Panel (Section 5). This panel is an agency of the Federal Labor Relations Council, charged with providing additional assistance when all other efforts, including the services of the Federal Mediation and Conciliation Service, are unable to settle a dispute. The panel relies heavily on the technique of fact-finding and resultant recommendations.

The fourth process is binding arbitration. E.O. 10988 had provided that agencies did not have to abide by arbitration while the employee organizations did. Under E.O. 11491 the FLRC is empowered to make decisions on issues submitted for arbitration that are binding on **both** sides.

3. Another change to the labor-management relations program made by the Nixon order was to do away with two of the three forms of recognition provided for under E.O. 10988 (i.e., informal and formal) and limit recognition to exclusive units only (Sections 7 and 10). It also expanded the criteria for determining a unit's appropriateness to be given exclusive recognition to include not only "community of interest" but also that "it promote effective dealings and efficiency of agency operations" (Section 10). Another provision added was for national consultation rights (Section 9); i.e., agencies are required to give such a right to labor organizations when they represent a substantial number of employees in a given agency. This provision gives the organization the right to consult and make recommendations on personnel policies affecting its members. However, an agency is not obligated to follow through with such recommendations.

4. Under E.O. 10988 the status of supervisors was vague and confusing, as there was nothing in the order that really specified their role, other than the "rights of management" in Section 7 (2). E.O. 11491 clarified the status of supervisors in Section 2 (c), Section 10 (b (1)) and Section 24 (2). The former two define the terms "management official" and "supervisor" and prohibit exclusive recognition of units containing such personnel. The latter states that the order "did not preclude" granting exclusive recognition for units of management officials and supervisors represented by organizations which "historically and traditionally represented the management officials and supervisors in private industry." Otherwise, a unit which included such personnel could not be granted exclusive recognition (Section 10 (b (1)).

5. Another major change brought about by E.O. 11491 has to do with the negotiation of agreements. While the Kennedy order was rather vague on this subject, 11491 originally addressed the issue in seven separate sections (Sections 11–17, with 14 later revoked). It expanded the scope of negotiation to permit negotiations on shifts, overtime, and effects on the work force of

technological changes and provided more specific procedures for handling negotiable disputes. The FLRC was authorized to decide to what extent a proposal was negotiable or nonnegotiable, because it might be contrary to statute or regulations outside the agency or the order itself (Section 11). It also specified that review of an agency's approval of agreements, was limited to the agreement's conformity with the law, agency policies and regulations, and the regulations of authorities outside the agency. It further provided that an employee who represented a recognized labor organization could not do so on official time (Section 20).

6. Finally, one of the most significant changes to the Kennedy order was to specify what were to be considered unfair labor practices, both on the part of management and labor. This was spelled out in Section 19.

Briefly summarized these stated that management could not:

a. Interfere with employees' rights to join a union.
b. Encourage or discourage union membership by discriminating in regard to hiring, tenure, promotion, or other conditions of employment.
c. Discipline or discrimination against an employee who testified under the order.
d. Refuse to recognize an organization qualified for such recognition.
e. Refuse to consult, confer, or negotiate with a labor organization as required by the order.

On the other hand labor could not:

a. Interfere with an employee's right **not** to join a union.
b. Attempt to induce agency management to coerce an employee against exercising employee rights under the order.
c. Attempt to interfere in an employee's effort to discharge and responsibilities as an employee of the United States government.
d. Call or engage in a strike, stoppage or slowdown, or to picket any agency in a labor-management dispute, or fail to take appropriate action to prevent such activities.
e. Discriminate against an employee because of race, color, creed, sex, age, or national origin. This, as mentioned previously, was also stipulated in Executive Order 10988.
f. Refuse to consult, confer, or negotiate with an agency as required by the order.[7]

Thus E.O. 11491 was simply a reissuance of E.O. 10988 with the six changes detailed above. E.O. 11491 has itself undergone some major changes, but remains the basic document governing labor-management relations in the federal sector.

Changes to the order have dealt mainly with grievances and arbitration procedures. The first major change came on August 16, 1971, when President Nixon issued E.O. 11616, to become effective November 24, 1971. The most significant provision of this Order was the limit it placed on grievance procedures negotiated by exclusive unions. The only items suitable for inclusion in the grievance procedure were those dealing with interpretation and application of agreements. Employee grievances were taken out of collective bargaining and made grievable only under the agency stationary system that conformed with Civil Service standards. This meant that union and employee grievances were differentiated, the former to be administered by the negotiated machinery, the latter by the agency system.

The second major change came on February 4, 1975, with President Ford's signing of E.O. 11838. This order's main function was to broaden the scope of grievance negotiations. It simplified the language of Executive Order 11616 by simply granting (agencies and exclusive representatives) the power to negotiate grievances and arbitration procedures subject only to mandatory exclusions (Section 14).

Two other changes occurred during this period. E.O. 11636, dated December 17, 1971, removed the Foreign Service from the jurisdiction of 11491 and established a separate program for it, while Public Law 91–375 dated August 12, 1970, and passed as a result of the Postal Workers' strike in New York the year before, brought labor-management relations in the postal service under the provisions of the National Labor Relations Act.

## Conclusion

While many will disagree, federal labor-management relations, administered through the executive order system, are presently in an acceptable state. Certainly there is room for criticism of the system, and both management and labor, as well as the executive branch and the Congress, continue to seek ways to improve it. In fact, the United States House of Representatives' Subcommittee on Manpower and Civil Service held hearings in May, June, and July of 1984 to look into the status of federal labor-management relations with the aim of introducing legislation that would bring such relations more in line with the provisions of the National Labor Relations Act. These hearings produced no major revisions in the present Executive Order system, for, as stated by the Director of the Office of Personnel Management, testifing before the subcommittee, "there has been no compelling evidence that the proposals before this committee would provide a better or more balanced program."[8] This, to my way of thinking, represents tangible evidence that the part of the executive order system directed at federal labor relations is doing its job.

If one reflects on the fact that executive orders directed at federal labor relations have only come about in the last twenty years, and then looks at the state of labor relations in the private sector in the first twenty years after, say, the National Labor Relations Act, the situation in the federal sector is put into perspective. Problems of the type dealt with in the executive orders discussed above are complex ones that cannot be solved simply by the passage of a directive. The long, slow process of interpretation and administration is necessary before any resolution can be achieved. The federal sector is now in the middle of the process, and with each amended executive order, with each ruling by the FLRC, FSIP, or any other administrative agency, it will move closer to a clear definition of its own labor relations policy. Given the history of the private sector in this regard, it seems to me that, despite the standard criticism of some concerning the speed with which the federal government moves, progress is being made, and will continue to be made, as rapidly as can be expected given the complexity of the issues in this area.

### Footnotes

[1]Murray B. Nesbitt, *Labor Relations in.the Federal Government Service*, (Washington, DC, 1976), p. 6.

[2]*Ibid.*, p. 7.

[3]*Report of the Federal Labor Relations Council*, January 1, 1970 – December 31, 1976, (Washington, DC, 1977), p. 3.

[4]*Ibid.*, p. 4.

[5]Executive Order 10988: Employee-Management Cooperation in the Federal Service, (Washington, DC, 1962), p. 6.

[6]*Report of the Federal Labor Relations Council*, p. 9.

[7]Executive Order 11491: Labor-Management Relations in the Federal Service as Amended, (Washington, DC, 1969), p. 16.

[8]Federal Service Labor-Management Legislation, *Hearings: House of Representatives*, Ninety-Sixth Congress, May 21, 22, June 5, 12, 13, July 16, 25, 1984, (Washington, 1984), p. 18.

# Needed Changes In The Civil Service Reform Act
## To Improve Federal Sector Labor Relations

## Introduction

While unionization of federal employees can be traced as far back as the Philadelphia Navy Yard in the 1830's, it is only within the last generation that large numbers of federal employees have actually joined labor organizations. As a result, most government policies addressing federal labor relations are of recent origin.

Although the Lloyd-LaFollette Act of 1912 asserted the right of federal employees to unionize, it was not until a series of Executive Orders (E.O.'s) in the 1960's and early 1970's that a real sense of direction came to federal labor relations. President Kennedy's E.O. 10988 of 1962 and President Nixon's E.O.'s 11491 and 11616 were vital steps in the evolutionary process. Surely the biggest step in recent years has been the Civil Service Reform Act, signed by President Carter, effective January 11, 1979.

Title VII of the act cast into law certain provisions of the federal labor relations program previously covered under the E.O.'s, as well as adding significant new provisions. In general, these provisions have the dual intentions of assuring federal agencies a degree of management rights necessary to efficiently manage their internal operations, and to protect the basic employment rights of individual employees and their collective representatives.

Title VII also reaffirms the right of federal employees to organize or join labor organizations, and also emphasizes their right to refrain from any and all such activities. While stating that federal labor organizations are in the public interest, it cautions that the needs and conditions of government operations require restrictions on such organizations that are not found in the private sector: for example, it continues E.O. prohibitions against strikes, slowdowns, union security clauses, and most forms of picketing.

Seven years after its passage, most labor leaders hail the act as a kind of "emancipation proclamation," in that it freed federal employees and unions from what, in my opinion, was clearly management domination of the major dispute resolution aspects of labor relations (contract talks, grievance handling, impasses, etc.). On the other hand, these same labor leaders have, and still are, criticizing the narrowness of the scope of bargaining, relative to the private sector, the inability to even address wage and economic supplement issues, and the ban on union security clauses in federal labor contracts.

## The Intent of the Act

When signing the Civil Service Reform Act into law, President Carter stated that: "The goal of this legislation is to make executive branch labor relations more comparable to those of private business, while recognizing the special requirements of the federal government and the paramount public interest in the effective conduct of the public's business."[1] Seven years after the passage of this major piece of legislation, it is both important and instructive to discuss to what extent the two goals contained in the above quote have been realized, and to discuss needed changes for the future.

## Comparability to Private Business

As President Carter stated, one purpose of the act was to make federal-sector labor relations comparable to those of the private sector. I do not feel, however, that the act has done as much as could have been reasonably expected in this area, at the time of its passage. The main problem is that while it brought many of the trappings of private-sector labor relations to the executive branch, it did not bring all the substance. The mechanisms and processes have become more comparable, while the content and results have, to a certain extent, remained unchanged.

The main thrust of the act to achieve the desired "comparability" was to create a Federal Labor Relations Authority (FLRA)[2] to oversee federal labor relations, with a structure and procedures similar to the private sector's National Labor Relations Board (NLRB), and to give federal labor relations judicial review, a situation that has existed in the private sector since 1935.

In form, it appears these changes have gone a long way toward achieving the desired comparability. Decision making in labor matters has been moved outside management to the FLRA, certainly a more acceptable administrative procedure. In fact, however, little of substance has changed, because the act itself remains in alignment with the old E.O. program. The individual offices holding decision making authority have changed, yet, due to the extreme limitations of the act in the area of discretionary authority for the FLRA and its strict adherence to the policies and procedures of the earlier E.O. system, even individuals with the best of intentions and the newest of ideas are bringing forth the same results. Any serious student of federal-sector labor relations can look at the procedures of the FLRA's General Council and the decisions and orders of the authority itself, to see a continuation of the old E.O. system. I would argue that, to a certain degree, this is a result of President Reagan being in office for the majority of time since the act was signed. Under the act, FLRA members are appointed by the president and, as might well be expected,

President Reagan has appointed individuals with philosophies toward the management end of the labor-management continuum. This lack of philosophical differentiation between decision makers under the E.O. system and those under the CSRA explains part of the lack of movement toward comparability with the private sector. After all, only the most closed-minded labor supporter would argue that the private sector NLRB has not had its share of prolabor people. At some future point a president more sympathetic to labor's cause will appoint individuals with a prolabor stance to the FLRA, and then the comparability mentioned by President Carter in 1979 will begin to be realized to a greater degree.

As stated above, however, President Reagan's appointments to the authority are only part of the story. Anything near complete comparability can never be achieved under the act as presently written, due to its structural and procedural similarities to the old E.O. system. One need only take note of the fact that in the seven years since the act was passed, with its provisions for judicial review (similar to those in the private sector), the courts have upheld the FLRA in fully 92% of the cases closed. This figure is almost identical to results under the old E.O. system and is significantly higher than the private sector.

Hence, one proposed change in the CSRA would be (1) to rewrite the procedural and structural sections to make them similar to those in the private sector, as established by the National Labor Relations Act and its amendments, and the National Labor Relations Board, and to disregard completely (in these areas) the old executive order system. This would incorporate a degree of comparability and not relegate it to individual political appointees to accomplish.

Another reason comparability has not been achieved to a greater degree, is that no amount of activism by the FLRA, General Council, or even the courts, can overcome the fact that labor-management relations in the private sector are driven by economics, while in the federal sector such relations are subject to political considerations. As long as such economic issues as wages and economic supplements are decided in the federal sector on the basis of political considerations, it is fallacy to speak of comparability with the private sector in this area. I do not believe in subjecting these areas entirely to the collective-bargaining process in the federal sector, although that would be the surest way to insure comparability. The U.S. taxpayer does not need and cannot afford that much comparability! Instead, I propose that (2) a percentage increase for total compensation be presented to federal labor unions[3] who could then collectively bargain with management over the division of this increase across the various economic issues. While such a procedure will not change the present situation regarding comparability as to the level of total compensation, it will provide comparability, as far as process and content in the areas of wages and economic supplements—a major step forward.

A third and final proposed change in the comparability area concerns the nomination procedures tp confirm a General Council to the FLRA There are no estimates in the literature concerning the number of unfair labor practice charges that have not been filed because, at the time of their occurrence, there was no General Council to the FLRA, but I am sure the number is extremely significant. This is due to the CSRA requirement for Senate confirmation, a lengthy process in every case to date. A provision should be added to the CSRA (3) to permit the incumbent General Council to serve until a successor takes office, so as to eliminate the "gap" periods that presently exist, and also to reduce the backlog of cases.

## The Special Requirements of the Federal Government

The second stated purpose of the act was to recognize the special requirements of the federal government when addressing labor-management relations. The very fact that the federal labor relations program is governed by a law of its own and administered by a board of its own, attests to the fact that the federal government has special requirements in this area. The principle area of concern when speaking of the government's "special requirements" is that of dispute settlement. Obviously, the operations of the government cannot be interrupted by labor disputes, as they sometimes are in the private sector. Hence, mechanisms must be established to settle disputes before they reach the confrontation level. Here again, as in the previous section of this article, procedures in the CSRA are carried over from the E.O. system. To settle bargaining impasses, the CSRA uses the Federal Service Impasse Panel (F.S.I.P.), established under President Nixon's E.O. 11491 in 1970, and the special negotiability procedure of the FLRA In effect, the panel's decisions are subject to appeal to the FLRA The problem is that while the system yields good results, the procedure takes too long. Congress needs to amend the CSRA to (4) give the Impasse Panel total jurisdiction in bargaining disputes. Appeal to the FLRA at present is operating as a stay, which greatly increases the time between the Panel's decision and its resultant implementation. Elimination of the appeal to the FLRA would be more in keeping with the special requirements of the federal government, in that it would force final resolution of bargaining impasses at an earlier date, and hence, shorten the time when labor organizations at impasse would be forced to work without a contract, thus minimizing the temptation to disrupt the operations of the government.

### Serving the Public Interest

The final stated purpose of the act is to serve the paramount public interest in the effective conduct of the public business. While it is certainly beyond the scope of this article to attempt to evaluate the effectiveness of federal labor relations programs in terms of performance of employees and efficiency of operations, I do wish to examine internal measures of effectiveness, such as the use of negotiated grievance procedures and the size and level of bargaining units, in an attempt to see if the act is accomplishing its third and final purpose.

The grievance machinery established by the act is clearly more efficient and effective than that of the E.O.'s. Under the earlier system there was a time when local management officials were final arbitrators of grievances, and also a time when the independent arbitrator's decision was not binding on management! Any student of labor knows that these systems are both impractical, and that the second is a contradiction in terms—although E.O. 10988 called it "advisory arbitration". Such systems discouraged many individuals and labor organizations from both filing grievances, and, if filed, from spending the time and money necessary to carry through to the final step of arbitration. The CSRA grievance procedures lack the long delays of the E.O. procedures, arbitration is done by a neutral party, and it is legally binding on both sides. As a result, there were almost as many grievances arbitrated in the first three years of the act as had been the case under the E.O.'s for the previous seventeen years.[4] This is not to say, however, that the one recently employed in the federal sector cannot be improved. One problem is that Section 7121(c) of the act provides for exclusions from the grievance procedure, yet Section 7121(a)(1) mandates that negotiated grievance procedures leave decisions of arbitrability to the arbitrator. Unfortunately, there has developed over the last five years a very fine line between the exceptions of Section 7121(c) and many issues presented by aggrieved employees and ruled arbitrable under Section 7121(a)(1) by individual arbitrators. Case history indicates that this fine line is rapidly turning into a considerable gray area between subjects for arbitration review and those to be excluded.[5] The act should be amended to (5) clarify procedures for deciding questions of arbitratibility, either by leaving them exclusively up to the arbitrator under Section 7121(a)(1), or by expanding Section 7121(c) so as to come as close as possible to an all-inclusive list of excluded subjects with no provisions for interpretation by individual arbitrators.

Another problem with the present grievance procedure lies in the area of arbitration review. The scope of such review in the federal sector is significantly broader than that in the private sector, and includes considerations of relevant provisions of the CSRA itself, other existing laws such as the Fair Labor Standards Act, and regulations of appropriate authorities including policies contained in the Federal Personnel Manual and decisions by the FLRA To increase efficiency of grievance handling and to eliminate the present situation wherein many of the arbitrator frequently seeking guidance from the advocates involved in the grievance, I suggest that the act be amended to (6) narrow the scope of arbitration review, to include such traditional private-sector issues as interpretation of contract language, etc., and leave questions involving the CSRA and the Federal Personnel Manual to the Office of Personnel Management, the Fair Labor Standards Act to the Labor Department, and to let FLRA decisions be excluded from arbitration by adding them to Section 7121(c) of the CSRA

Thus, in the area of dispute resolution, the act has, indeed, made progress toward "the effective conduct of the public business". The addition of the two amendments discussed above would, in my opinion, further enhance the act in achieving this goal.

A second area in which the CSRA was fashioned so as to ensure effectiveness of operations relates to the configuration of bargaining units in federal agencies. It is clear that Congress, through the act, wished to encourage fewer and larger bargaining units, since administratively it is more efficient to negotiate one agreement covering a large unit than many agreements covering a number of smaller units. As a result, the number of bargaining units has dropped from over 3800, at the time the act was passed, to under 2,400 today, with the average size rising to over 500 employees. While in the private sector such a trend toward fewer and larger units might well lead to their increased strength and, as a result, be viewed as a threat by management, restrictions on federal unions regarding strikes, slowdowns, job actions, security clauses, and limits on bargainable subjects, serve to minimize this threat in the federal sector. As a result, this movement toward fewer and bigger units has, in fact, increased operational efficiency without the negative side effects experienced in the private sector. Preferring to leave well enough alone, I suggests no change in this section of the act.

## Conclusion

I have suggested six changes to the CSRA to improve federal sector labor relations:

1.  Rewrite the procedural and structural sections to make them comparable to those in the private sector, as established by the NLRA and NLRB, removing all vestiges in these areas of the old E.O. system.
2.  Present a percentage increase in total compensation to federal unions (to be determined under existing procedures outlined in the Pay Comparability Act of 1970) and allow them to bargain over its distribution among the various wage and economic supplement issues.
3.  Permit the incumbent General Council of the FLRA to serve until a successor takes office, so as to eliminate "gap" periods and reduce case backlogs.
4.  Give the FSIP total jurisdiction in bargaining disputes, by removing the lengthy appeal procedure to the FLRA
5.  Clarify procedures for settling questions or arbitrability, either by leaving them exclusively up to the arbitrator under Section 7121(a)(1), or by expanding the exclusions in Section 7121(c) so as to eliminate the need for judgments in this area by individual arbitrators.
6.  Narrow the scope of arbitration review, leaving questions presently decided by arbitrators to groups such as 0PM, FLRA, and the Labor Department where appropriate.

The act has been characterized by Scott Campbell, its prime mover, as "The first overhaul of the Federal Bureaucracy in almost a century".[6] I feel that, in the on balance, the act has been a very positive force in federal-sector labor relations. It is now seven years since its passage, however, and it is reasonable to expect that any piece of legislation this big, covering this many individuals, is going to need adjustments. Compared to amendments made to such laws as the FLSA and the NLRA, the changes proposed herein are not drastic—but are necessary. No upheaval of the system is needed, only some adjustments made with the benefit of some years hindsight and practice. I am convinced that the six changes proposed herein will go a long way toward helping the CSRA meet its stated goal of improving federal–sector labor relations.

### Footnotes

[1]Dickman, David Scott, "Something To Boast About", *The Bureaucrat*, Winter, 1982–1983, pg. 30.

[2]In fact, the act restructured the Federal Labor Relations Council, created by E.O. 11491 in January 1970.

[3]This figure is derived from specifications in the 1970 Pay Comparability Act, with the exception that the comparison with the private sector, and the resultant figure, be for total compensation (wages and economic supplements) and not, as is presently the case, simply wages.

[4]Editors Comments, "Putting Reform in Perspective", *The Bureaucrat*, Summer, 1983.

[5]Eickman, James, "Contrast Between Public and Private Sector Bargaining: Dispute Resolution Procedures", *Labor Law Journal*, August 1983, p. 484.

[6]Causey, Mike, "The Federal Diary", *The Washington Post*, January 12, 1979, p. B–2.

# Federal-Employee Unions: Blessing Or Curse?

The desirability of federal employees for labor unions is an issue which clearly divides public opinion. Many outside the federal service do not see the need for such organizations, espousing the theory that civil servants are to be tended by a benevolent public. Yet the drastic increase in the number of federal workers who have joined these unions over the past 10 years is clear evidence that those inside Uncle Sam's walls feel the need for such organizations.

No one argues with the assertion that one of the basic goals of unions is to increase the compensation their members receive for their work. As unions in the federal sector exert their increasing influence to push compensation rates higher, it stands to reason that careers in the federal service will attract an increasing number of applicants. With a larger pool to choose from, relative to the number of openings, higher qualifications can be demanded for entrance into the federal sector. The higher compensation, caused in part by union demands, will attract better-qualified individuals to the federal job market.

While it is true that the federal payroll will increase as a result of unions, the American public should not be upset. Typical resentment toward the size of the federal payroll is directed at its perceived waste. If the taxpayer gets a top-notch employee for the money, instead of the "do-nothing" bureaucrat believed to haunt the halls of government agencies, such resentment will fade. In the words of the old axiom, "you get what you pay for."

Some present public servants who entered when competition for such jobs was less severe, will in fact be overly compensated as a result of union-supported wage increases, but this is a short-term problem that will solve itself as these individuals leave the federal payroll. Their "free ride" is a small price to pay for the long-term overall improvement in personnel.

In addition to the increase in payroll size, another often-heard argument against federal-employee unions is that labor organizations use job security of their members as a cornerstone for their foundation. That is, many feel that unions cover their members with a blanket of job security so thick that it is nearly impossible for employers to increase efficiency by weeding out nonproductive or less-productive employees, once they are hired. While this argument has merit in the private sector, one must be careful to differentiate between private and federal employment. True, a private-sector employer whose labor force is newly unionized may notice this growing restriction on authority to replace, or even transfer, personnel. In the federal sector, however, such restrictions are already in place, to such an extent that it is hard to imagine what labor organizations could do to increase them. As evidence of this, one need only look at the 1979 Civil Service Reform Act. One of the most hotly debated provisions concerned easing the restrictions on appointment to, and removal from, upper-level federal service positions. This attempt to lessen such restrictions is clear evidence that they do, in fact, exist.

Also to be remembered is that the establishment of unions is usually accompanied by a greater specificity in requirements for appointment and promotion to certain jobs. In the federal sector this may well reduce the number of instances where political connections are a factor in personnel decisions, and, as such, would be a welcome change.

Thus while short-term factors like the increase in payroll size, the number of free riders, etc., may cause many to argue against the desirability of federal-employee unions, these factors are more than outweighed by the long-term results of these unions, like the improved caliber of federal employees and the decreased reliance on political patronage.

Federal-employee unions are, in the long run, a blessing.

# Cases

# Employer Dismissal Of A Union Official

During recent negotiations for the renewal of the contract between a federal agency and the union representing the agency's employees, some discontent developed on both sides because of different ploys used by both parties in attempting to gain an advantage at the beginning of the negotiations. One member of the union negotiating team, who was also a shop steward, appeared to interpret the "jockeying for position" by the management team as a personal affront to his intelligence and integrity, and was most boisterous in his criticism of management's "good faith" bargaining tactics.

On a day when the steward was working (because an impasse had been reached in the negotiations), he slipped on a wet spot in the men's restroom and slightly injured his wrist. The wet spot was caused by a leaky water pipe, and several attempts had been made in the recent past to repair it. The numerous unsuccessful attempts to repair the pipe had become a standing joke in the building and the hazardous condition was known to all, including the steward. The injury seemed to precipitate the steward's anger, and one day shortly after his accident the men's restroom was vandalized right before quitting time. A porcelain basin was pulled from the wall and broken, overhead fluorescent lights were smashed, and paper towels, toilet paper, and broken mirrors were strewn all over the floor.

Management was able to determine that five employees had been in the restroom at the time the vandalism occurred, but was unable to determine which of the five had actually taken part in the destruction. One of the five employees was the shop steward who had previously been injured in that same restroom. The employees were counseled individually, but while each admitted that the vandalism occurred while they were in the restroom, they all said they did not know who was responsible, because it was dark without the lights. Management told the employees that they had until the next day to reveal the offender. When no one came forward with any information, management gave three-day suspensions to all five of the employees.

The union filed a grievance, claiming that management's action was unjust, since none of the five were observed committing the acts of destruction in the restroom. It further argued that it was unfair to make five innocent people suffer simply because management was unable to uncover the real offender. The union also implied that management's action was highly suspect, in view of the fact that one of the five was the shop steward, a member of the union's negotiation team and most critical of management's negotiating strategy.

## Questions

1. Was management's mass discipline just? Was there a viable alternative?
2. What would be the consequences of not disciplining anyone, since the actual offender(s) could not be identified?
3. Did management violate the National Labor Relations Act in suspending the shop steward, when there was no real proof of his participation in the vandalism?

# Union Organizing: What Can And Cannot Be Done

A small suburban manufacturing plant employed 500 production personnel and 50 office personnel. Of the 50 office personnel, fifteen were management, and 35 were professionals or clerical support staff. Fifteen of the 35 nonmanagement employees were classified as secretaries and three of the 15 secretaries were differentiated as executive secretaries. Each of the three executive secretaries worked exclusively for one of the three company officers: the president, the vice-president of production, or the vice-president of finance. The secretary to the president was also his wife, and any confidential or sensitive company information, whether relating to personnel, finance, or production, etc., was processed by her and hand-carried directly to the appropriate department head in a "for eyes only," sealed folder.

The company distributed its product line through a network of manufacturer's representatives. Marketing, personnel, accounting, etc., were all middle-level management positions. Each section had a secretary that supported not only the manager, but also the manager's first-line supervisors, professional staff, and nontyping clerical support staff.

During the company's ten years of operation, there had been no attempts at, or talk of, unionization. The company officers were also the three major stockholders of the company and had operated under a paternalistic form of management that equated dissent with disloyalty. There was no formal system for voicing complaints; however, there was an informal discipline procedure. Usually an oral warning was issued and also documented in the employee's personnel folder. The succeeding steps included a written warning and, if necessary, discharge. Previous discharges had occurred for infraction of stated rules, noncompliance with established company procedural precedents, or for such nebulous reasons as not being suited for a particular type of work, or company disloyalty.

Recently, union representatives from a national industrial union had contacted key plant personnel several times and talked with them concerning the advantages of unionization. Management had become aware of these contacts through "old timers," who felt it their duty to warn management of the union interlopers. Through chance overhearing of a management discussion of the production employee/union situation, the executive secretary to the vice-president of production became aware of the union overtures to production personnel and began to promote the idea of unionization among the office clerical and professional staff.

Management, viewing unionization attempts as betrayal by their employees, was adamant in its opposition to recognition of any union. A bulletin was posted, stating that there were to be no union-organizing activities on company time, or the guilty employees would be discharged. Managers were instructed to conduct meetings with their subordinates, both office and plant personnel, warning them of the negative aspects of union membership and inferring possible reprisals for those employees who were so ungrateful to the company that they would entertain possible union membership. Each of the department secretaries, including those of the two vice-presidents, was called into their bosses' offices separately and warned that their participation in unionization efforts was, in the eyes of management, unforgiveable company disloyalty.

After the series of management-conducted meetings, during a lunch break in the employee's lounge, the production vice-president's secretary announced a union-organizing meeting for the office staff to be held that evening at a nearby motel. She further informed the other employees of information she had obtained from the union representatives as to employee rights to organize without management interference, including the fact that their jobs could not be taken away because of their union-organizing activities. During that afternoon, the vice-president of production again spoke with his secretary concerning her pro-union activities, reiterating his distaste for her lack of judgment, and warning her she was "skating on thin ice," since she had previously received a verbal warning for absenteeism and tardiness.

More than the required 30% of the production and office staff, including two of the three executive secretaries, signed cards requesting that a union election be conducted. The NLRB investigated to see if the proposed group of employees constituted an appropriate bargaining unit. The professional employees were polled separately and elected to be part of the unit with the production and clerical staff. The investigator met with management and reviewed working conditions, job descriptions, etc., in an effort to determine the appropriateness of the proposed unit. During one of the management/NLRB interviews one of the secretaries overheard the investigator being told that all of the executive secretaries had access to company confidential and sensitive material. The story of what she had overheard spread throughout the plant, so it came as no surprise to the employees when the NLRB determined the appropriate bargaining unit to be all production and office personnel, except the three executive secretaries. The NLRB stated that the three executive secretaries' commonality of interest lay with management, and not with their fellow clerical workers.

A union election was held and the approved bargaining unit became an official local of a national industrial union. Within a brief period of time after the election, the production vice-president's secretary was given a written warning for absenteeism and tardiness, and within the same month was discharged for "just cause." Her supervisor cited her poor-attendance record, which was, in fact, excessive, and disloyalty to the firm. The production and office personnel began to picket the company in support of the discharged secretary and threatened to walk out, if she were not returned to work immediately.

## Questions

1. Do the two secretaries have appeal rights for review of their exclusion from the bargaining unit?

2. Were the activities of management, i.e., meetings, bulletins, etc., within the framework of legal anti-union actions under the Taft-Hartley Act?

3. Does the secretary have appeal rights to the NLRB for unfair labor practices, even though she is not a member of the local union at the time she is fired?

4. Is picketing and striking by the local union, in support of the discharged secretary, legal?

# Notification Preceding Collective Bargaining

Employees of a federal agency have a union to represent them in negotiations with the agency's management, and a new contract is negotiated every two years. One of the provisions states the union has the right to be present at any meeting between two or more employees and a representative of management, when anything related to work (the working conditions, job performance standards, job assignments, proposed change of physical location of employees, times of break and lunch, etc.) is discussed. The union representative is to be notified forty-eight (48) hours in advance of a meeting to adjust the schedule and attend. The manner of the forty-eight hour notification is not specified in the contract.

Recently, a meeting between the manager of a branch of the agency and the bargaining unit employees of the branch was held, and the union steward was not present. The information passed to the employees was updated job-performance standards that were created solely by management, based upon past production levels that management considered outstanding, excellent, satisfactory, unsatisfactory, and cause for removal. The performance standards were for the various jobs within the branch and consisted of three (3) areas in which the employee would be appraised; quantity, quality, and manner of performance. The employees had no input to the standards, other than the sampling of their past performance. There was further discussion after the employees were told that they would be appraised by these new standards, because part of their task had been automated. Also, some reorganization within the branch had streamlined the operation, eliminating excess paperflow and establishing a review procedure which caught errors before they were input to the automated system. All of the above changes in the work environment had previously been approved in the union.

Two weeks after the meeting, the union filed an Unfair Labor Practice with the Federal Labor Relations Authority, charging that:

(1) The union did not receive proper and timely notice of the meeting between the bargaining unit employees and management.

(2) The union had not participated in the formulation of the job performance standards, nor was the union given the opportunity to review the standards before they were presented to the employees.

## Questions

1. Should the notification procedure be amended, to be more specific as to the manner of compliance (signed and receipted memo)?

2. What are the limits of the union's authority in developing procedures to be applied by management in establishing performance-appraisal systems?

3. Must the agency negotiate on a specific proposal for minimum performance standards?

4. Is the agency required to negotiate on union proposals for definitions of critical elements and standards?

5. Could the union's approval of the reorganization be construed as the point at which the union lost its opportunity for performance-appraisal input?

# Arbitration Of Grievances
## Regarding Employee Discharge

Howard Knoblock belongs to National Truck Workers (NTW), Local 42, and works for an assembly plant in Cleveland as a repairman. He has worked there for eight years and has been a competent worker. He works hard and is known as "one of the best repairmen in Q Department" according to Q Department's supervisor.

Howard was transferred to R Department in November of 1985. Steve Silberg has been supervisor of R Department for six years. For 8 months, Howard worked in R Department with no conflicts or problems. On April 1, 1986, however, when Howard was working his 11:00 p.m. to 7:00 a.m. shift, Steve approached him and asked, "Have you been drinking again?" Howard replied that he had not been drinking, nor did he ever drink on the job. Steve reprimanded him for doing sloppy work and warned that he should "never come in to work drunk again". The employees who were in the vicinity took notice of what was going on, and Steve told everybody to go back to work as he walked away, shaking his head. On April 5th, shortly after Howard arrived at work, Steve saw him drop a wrench. He immediately approached him and said, "Howard! I thought I told you a couple of days ago not to come to work when you've been drinking." Before Howard could reply, Steve said, "Look, buster, if you keep this up, I'm going to fire you." Other employees were looking on with interest as Steve was raising his voice. Howard's reaction was very cool and calm. He quietly explained that he had not been drinking and the dropping of the wrench was only a harmless accident. Steve returned to his office after warning Howard to be more careful in the future.

The following night, April 6th, about an hour after Howard began his shift, he slipped on some oil and fell on the floor, cutting his knee and tearing his pants. Steve happened to see his fall and ran to him yelling, "Dammit, Howard, I warned you about coming here drunk. Don't lie to me this time, because I saw you going into the Silver Slipper Bar earlier this evening while I was driving to the post office." Steve was extremely angry and loud and had not even inquired if Howard was injured in his fall. Some of Howard's coworkers had rushed over to aid him while Howard blurted to Steve, "You S.O.B., I told you I don't come to work drunk, and if you don't stop harassing me about it, I'm going to punch your lights out." As Howard finished saying this, he started getting up off the floor. Howard's fellow employees thought he was getting up to hit Steve and attempted to restrain him. Steve's immediate reaction was to flinch and raise his fist. Howard, thinking Steve was going to strike him because of his threat, hit him and bloodied his nose. Howard immediately apologized, and Steve left the scene cussing, holding his nose, while headed to the infirmary. Howard tended to his cut knee and returned to his work at hand. When Steve returned from the infirmary and found Howard working at his job as if nothing had happened, he approached him in a very business-like fashion and told him he was fired. He did this by reciting a specific section of the contract agreement that deals with discharge in general, as if he had just memorized it (i.e., management retains the right to discharge employees for lack of work, fighting, drinking, or other just causes). He told Howard he could come in the next day to get his wages, written notice of discharge, and personal belongings, but "to get the hell out of" his sight, because he no longer worked at the plant. Howard said, "Okay, chump," as he dropped his tools and walked out.

The next day, he met with his shop steward and filed a written grievance statement within the strict rules set forth in the grievance procedure of the contract. He then went in to get his personal belongings, received his written notice of discharge and wages, and left the plant with a smile on his face, whistling, as he walked off the premises.

There was a usual conference and investigation of facts, as provided for in the first step of the grievance procedure, but there was no agreement. Management's stand was strong, as was the union's. It was obvious after the third step of the grievance procedure that arbitration was inevitable. At this juncture, the facts accumulated through investigation by both sides had become somewhat complex.

Management's argument was based on the following facts:

(1) Management could prove that Howard had been in the Silver Slipper the evening of April 6th, and had been drinking while there. In fact, management could prove that he was a regular customer, according to one of the employees there.

(2) Howard was known to be an excellent fighter and seemed to be proud of his reputation. Also, it was discovered that Howard was fired from a previous job 8 years ago for fighting with a fellow employee.

(3) Evidence was presented against Howard's character concerning his drinking habits. Howard was arrested two times during the past three years for being drunk in public: July 4, 1984, and January 1, 1986.

(4) Howard did receive written notice on the morning of April 7th that "according to the contract agreement, he was being discharged for fighting." Management argues that Steve, the supervisor, did not give written notice with an outline of the specific charges at the time he fired Howard, because he thought it was obvious, and he was in a great deal of pain with the broken nose.

The union representatives argued that the following issues could not be overlooked in arriving at a fair and just decision:

(1) When Steve discharged Howard, he only quoted the discharge clause *verbatim*, and never specifically stated which specific reason he was being fired for, nor did he receive written notice until mid-day the following day, although he was in the office at 8:00 a.m. to obtain this notice before taking his complaint to the shop steward.

(2) The union argued that the earlier reprimands on Howard were not warranted, and were a direct attack on him because of some of Steve's personal problems involving drinking. The investigation revealed that Steve's wife has a serious drinking problem and only one week prior to Steve's first attack on Howard, she was involved in a serious car accident resulting from her drinking to a point of intoxication.

(3) Howard only defended himself by hitting Steve, because it appeared as if Steve were going to strike him first. Witnesses could only testify to the fact that both men were angry and were threatening one another, but had also said that it appeared as though the supervisor was going to strike Howard, upon hearing his threat.

(4) The union argued that the Silver Slipper is a restaurant where Howard frequently eats meals and occasionally drinks beer with his meals, and has never been considered a rowdy drinker while there, nor has he ever instigated fighting in the bar.

### Questions

1. In placing one's self in the position of an arbitrator, how much emphasis and/or weight can be placed on the extenuating circumstances surrounding the incidents in question?

2. Does the arbitrator have to make a decision based strictly on the simple facts—i.e., (a) Howard did, in fact, strike his supervisor; (b) management did, in fact, fail to comply with the discharge procedures to give written notice setting forth the cause of discharge at the time Howard was instructed to leave the plant—or should the arbitrator, to arrive at a "just" decision, include all the circumstantial issues? In other words, will the final decision here be made strictly on "technical" input, or can it take into consideration secondary circumstantial evidence which obviously deals with personalities and timing of events?

# Management Persuasion
## Of Potential Union Members

A large textile corporation in the southeastern portion of the United States had an opening for the position of machine operator. The company had thirty machine operators already on their staff.

The company had in recent months been hearing rumors that the machine operators wanted to form a union, because of inadequate pay for the job they performed.

Mr. Hall, the president of the textile company, was informed of this rumor and quickly put out the word to his staff supervisors to try and squash this intention. He also stated to his personnel director, Mr. Jones, that the vacant position should be filled by an applicant with no prior record of union membership.

Mr. Jones had tried to recruit a candidate who would comply with Mr. Hall's request, but after weeks the only candidate to possess all other qualifications had prior union affiliation. Mr. Jones was very upset about this, since he had a candidate who was suitable, except for the union history.

Mr. Jones, in his worried state, went to Mr. Hall and mentioned the circumstances. Mr. Hall flatly refused to even consider hiring an individual with union affiliation, even if it meant hiring one with less experience.

Mr. Jones continued to advertise for several more weeks without success. Mr. Swigart (the earlier candidate with prior union experience) noticed that the company was still in need of help and called Mr. Jones to ask why he had not been awarded the position. Mr. Swigart knew that he had all the qualifications, and that because of the unique requirements, not too many candidates would be recruited. Mr. Jones told Mr. Swigart over the phone that he wanted to talk to him about the possibility of hiring him for the job; however, he wanted to clear up some matters first.

Mr. Swigart came in the next day, and Mr. Jones proceeded to say that he could have the job, on the condition that he would not try to organize or bring in a union. Mr. Jones said that the company was anti-union and that they wanted no new employees with prior union background. Mr. Swigart readily agreed to the terms, since he had just moved into town and needed a job. Mr. Jones also stated that he would pay him a higher wage than any of his counterparts, if he would refrain from any union activities.

Mr. Jones was very happy that Mr. Swigart readily agreed to his terms and thought that because of this, Mr. Hall would agree with what he had done. Since Mr. Hall was out of town temporarily, Mr. Jones went ahead and hired Mr. Swigart at the higher pay rate.

Several months later, Mr. Hall happened to be going over the payroll computer print-out sheet when he came across the machine operator's payroll and noticed a discrepancy in the operator's pay rates. He immediately called the finance department and asked what was going on. Mr. Hall was told that Mr. Jones had sanctioned the pay rate for Mr. Swigart. Mr. Hall immediately called in Mr. Jones and asked him why he had done this without prior approval. Mr. Jones stated the circumstances surrounding the higher wage offer and said that his scheme was working well. Mr. Hall, still not very happy with the whole situation, called the finance department and told them that, as of now, Mr. Swigart would earn the same wage as the other machine operators.

When Mr. Swigart learned of this, he requested a meeting with Mr. Hall. Mr. Hall refused, and instructed the foreman to start writing Mr. Swigart up for any and everything he could think of. As a result of this, Mr. Swigart resigned.

## Questions

1. Has an unfair labor practice been committed? If so, what, and by whom?
2. Should Mr. Swigart be reinstated?
3. Was the situation regarding Mr. Swigart's original pay rate legal?

# Unfair Labor Practices

Tom Jackson has worked on the autoblock assembly line at the Mt. Gilead, Pennsylvania, plant of the American Metal Manufacturing Company for 13 years. During this time he has been quite active in union activity, doing things such as helping to organize workers, doing investigative work into health and safety standards, and talking with other workers about problems they are having and urging them to file grievances.

The investigation of health and safety standards by Jackson resulted in charges being brought against the American Metal Manufacturing Company for violation of the 1970 Occupational Safety and Health Act. He testified before members of the agency regarding violations of the standards, some of which included improper ventilation, lighting, operation of equipment, and excessive heat in the welding department. His testimony was largely responsible for American Manufacturing being assessed a stiff penalty and a warning of future consequences, if conditions were not improved.

Shortly after Jackson's testimony, he was told he was being promoted to assistant foreman on the day run. He was promoted, even though there was someone in his department who had greater seniority than he did. His major responsibility was to take over for the foreman during his lunch period and on his days off, and to help distribute work orders and keep track of employee mistakes. He had a few other small duties, but had to confirm everything with the foreman, and in all activities was under the foreman's control.

Now that Jackson had become an assistant foreman, he was put on salary instead of getting an hourly wage, and was also told that he would have to drop his union membership because, according to Taft-Hartley, supervisors and could not belong to a union.

This action on the part of management thoroughly enraged Jackson, as he felt that, while the promotion was more prestigous, the job offer was simply a method management had used to get him out of the union. He felt that they had done this because of his recent testimony on safety matters and his continuous union activities over the years. Jackson went to the union and told them of his predicament and asked them to file an unfair labor practice suit with the National Labor Relations Board. The union agreed to file and represent Jackson.

Each side presented arguments before the NLRB.

Management based their arguments on:

(1) The position of assistant foreman was created to take over when the foreman was absent.

(2) Tom Jackson was the person with the most seniority.

(3) Since Jackson's job was now that of a foreman, according to Taft-Hartley, he had to give up his membership in the union.

(4) Jackson became a salaried employee and, under the Fair Labor Standards Act, no longer entitled to overtime.

The union and Jackson countered these points by stating:

1. While the job of assistant foreman was needed, the duties being performed by Jackson did not contain any actual responsibility, because he needed to check out everything with his foreman. Since he was not, in actuality, a foreman, he was entitled to overtime.

2. Jackson was promoted, over a more-senior employee, to get him out of the union.

3. The above constituted an unfair labor practice under the Wagner Act, because they were discriminating to discourage membership in a labor organization.

The case went to the NLRB and is on the docket to be heard next week.

## Questions

1. Did management discriminate against Jackson?

2. Were the responsibilities of the job sufficient to make Jackson a part of management? If so, did this exclude him from coverage of FLSA?

3. Did he need to relinquish his membership in a union under Taft-Hartley, as management contended?

# Transition And Turnover Problems Caused
## By Technological Advances

A large firm manufacturing stereophonic equipment and specializing in amplifiers has been a leading regional distributor for over 25 years. Its expansion has been due to continuously-increasing profits over the years; however, in the past several years it has incurred a substantial reduction in sales and profits as a result of increased competition from foreign markets.

In an attempt to increase efficiency and sales, the main office called in consultants to advise on updating equipment. Based on their recommendations, new equipment was purchased, and subsequently several hundred employees had to be laid off. The new automatic machinery was to increase production and decrease staff by requiring a higher level of skills. Management felt if the new machinery had to remain idle during the training period for the present staff, it would cause further delay in production, and that the process of training some employees and gradually reducing the staff would be too costly and too slow. Since the older employees were unfamiliar with the new machinery, it was advised that an outsider be hired to oversee the training. A supervisor from a competitive company was offered an attractive salary to which he agreed, and when he came, he brought his own staff of operators. The new staff caused a further decrease in older employees and created conflicts between them and the new people. Many departments had a difficult time maintaining morale in light of the changes that were taking place.

After several months the new staff and new machinery were working smoothly, but expenditures were still higher than the consultants had predicted. Suddenly, one day the main terminal broke down and production had to be halted until the parts arrived. If something was not done immediately, production would fall behind schedule, resulting in financial losses to the company. The only alternative was to return to the old machinery, even though it was slower and might not meet contract deadlines.

A problem developed, because the new skilled employees were unfamiliar with the old machinery, and there were not enough of the older employees remaining, to do the job. Pressed for time, the remaining older employees were asked to work nights and the following weekend.

## Questions

1. Should management have dismissed the old system and staff, before the new machinery had all the bugs out and the new staff had proven efficient?
2. How could the old system have been utilized to prevent production slow-down and company loss?

3. How could the impact of the machinery transition on the employees have been minimized?

# Unfair Labor Practices During
# Union-Organizing Attempts

John R. Snelt and Sons was a nonunion shoe factory and had had this status since its inception in 1947. Lately, numerous supervisors had been reporting to their managers that talk of joining a union by the employees had been overheard. Needless to say, the owners were upset and a little puzzled as to why the employees would want a union. Mr. Snelt, Sr., felt he had always paid competitive wages, provided good benefits, and had been open to employee suggestions. He knew the business had changed dramatically since 1947, but did not feel these changes would warrant the need for a union.

Joe Snelt commented to his father that, for the past five years, they had hired new employees, and that the few employees left from the beginning were now a minority. He implied that these newly hired employees were the instigators of the union.

Mr. Snelt decided that he, his managers and also his supervisors should gather as much information as possible to see if they would be able to change their employees' minds about needing union status.

A few of the supervisors decided they would get to the heart of the problem, and did so immediately. They proceeded to ask the employees under them what they thought of all this union talk, and if they were going to join.

As the weeks went on, it seemed to Mr. Snelt that the union talk was getting very serious. Supervisors were reporting that union literature was being passed out in the parking lot areas and that authorization cards were being distributed.

As the talk became more and more serious and more of the employees seemed to be signing authorization cards, the same group of supervisors decided to visit some of the homes of their friends who were employees to discuss the pros and cons of union membership.

These employees reported to the other employees that management said many of them would be losing jobs if the union came in, and that they would have to start from scratch for their fringe benefits. However, they also told them if the union did not come in, management had made promises of raises and would try to promote a few more employees.

When the organizers heard what was going on, they claimed unfair labor practices and petitioned the NLRB, claiming that the union should be recognized even without an election.

Mr. Snelt, of course, disagreed and demanded an election.

## Questions

1. Did the union have grounds for their unfair labor practices charges? If so, what were they?
2. Could the company have claimed the union violated and hampered management rights? If so, how?
3. Was it possible to have a union represent this group without an election?

# Seniority vs. Ability In Layoff Determination

Lancor Tool and Maintenance Company had a history of promotion from within, based on longevity with the company. Employees were hired as apprentice workers and were promoted to better jobs as they learned skills and had more experience with the company. The more-established workers with the company were eager to get a job driving a company truck of their own and answering trouble calls to surrounding areas, when these calls came into the Lancor Company. This traveling repair service was considered more desirable work, than staying on the premises of the Lancor Company to accept and repair equipment from off-the-street customers. Recently the company became concerned with the fact that the more senior workers could not repair the new, more-sophisticated equipment as well as the younger, newer workers. Complaints were coming into Lancor concerning problems in the field. The older workers could not repair the equipment on-the-spot and were forced to bring it back to the inhouse service department of Lancor, so that the younger workers could complete the job.

The company finally negotiated an agreement with the union to permit it to use ability and skill tests in the selection of new repair crews. The older workers were no longer able to bid on the more-desirable jobs. For the first time, Lancor was able to go outside the organization and hire young students just out of trade school. These students learned quickly and had the knowledge and understanding to work on the new equipment. After a while the older repairmen who had come into their jobs prior to being screened, were shifted to less-desirable jobs.

The problem facing the Lancor Tool and Maintenance Company was one of declining business forcing a cutback in the size of the repair department. Since layoffs were based on seniority, nearly all of the relatively new, and more able, younger employees, would be laid off, if the present decline continued. Lancor feared the loss of their young, skilled workers would further erode their business, and that eventually competitors would begin making inroads.

## Question

1. What alternative courses of action were available to Lancor? What were the implementation problems and possible implications of each?

## Favored Employees, Discrimination And
## Unfair Labor Practices

About two weeks following the end of a strike of the registered nurses at St. Luke's Hospital, the hospital administrator sent a note of appreciation to the registered nurses who continued to work during the strike, and to the extra RN's who were transferred from St. Mary's to help cover the shifts of the striking nurses. In a letter of appreciation, the RN's were praised for their hard work, long working hours, and for "overcoming hardships and personal sacrifice in a definite gesture of dedication to duty as a professional." The letter indicated that nurses should rightly be concerned with taking care of the sick and walking wounded, rather than striking for higher wages.

The chief nurse gave all the nurses who worked more than one shift during the strike, compensatory time or a day off. In addition, the LPN's were given time off with pay for their efforts in assisting with patient treatment during the strike, because without their services, the hospital would not have been able to fulfill all their goals, according to management.

The union filed an unfair labor practice charge with the National Labor Relations Board, alleging that the hospital had infringed upon their right to strike, and showed partial treatment in the working conditions afforded their peer employees. The union also alleged that they should have been consulted before other nurses were granted time off or a change in working schedule made.

### Questions

1. Under the Wagner Act, had management interfered with a portion of "collective bargaining" or violated any rights of nonunion members?
2. Was management discriminating against the union members?
3. Could the NLRB have forced the hospital staff to grant days off with pay to all RN's, including the nurses on strike?

# Just Cause For Separation

Mary Johnson had just graduated from the University of Florida with a Bachelor of Science in Business Administration. She moved to Miami immediately after graduation and looked for a job in retail management. She had worked as an Assistant Manager for a boutique in Gainesville for four years while she attended college, and felt she was now qualified to be a manager.

Mary was hired as manager of a fashionable boutique in Miami Beach. The boutique was part of a Florida-based chain and had a reputation for its high-fashion merchandise and expensive accessories. Mary had the duties of a regular manager, as well as the responsibility for all hiring and firing of personnel. Although Mary had a degree in business administration, she had majored in management and had taken only one basic personnel course. At the time she accepted the position as manager, she felt she would have no trouble handling the personnel responsibilities.

The chain of boutiques that Mary worked for was owned by a husband and wife who visited the stores approximately once a month. On their first visit since the hiring of Mary, they were quite pleased with the shape of the store. Sales figures were good and the store was making good profits under Mary's management. A problem came up, however, when reviewing the new employees that Mary had hired. It seemed that two of the young women hired did not fit the "image" that the owners wanted for their sales personnel. Their merchandise was high-fashion and expensive, and the salespeople needed "a special look." In other words, the two employees in question were just not *attractive* enough. Mary was called into the back room and was told that she had to fire the two employees. Mary was upset over the situation, but had no choice in the matter. Either she fired the two young women, or the owners would do it, and replace Mary, as well.

Mary made up some story to tell the employees about having to cut back the staff, and informed them that they had the least seniority and consequently they would have to be the first ones dismissed. A month later, the two employees found out from friends still working at the boutique the *real* reason they were fired. They considered filing suit against the boutique for wrongful dismissal.

## Questions

1. Under the law, if any, could the girls have claimed discrimination?
2. Were the two girls entitled to unemployment compensation?
3. Would the real reason the girls were fired have been considered just cause for purposes of unemployment compensation?

4. If Mary had refused to fire the girls, could she have legally been fired by the owners?

5. If Mary had been fired, could she have received unemployment compensation?

# Factors To Be Considered During
# A Reduction-In-Force

As of July 1, 1986, Company X will be changing from a cost-reimbursement environment to a grant environment, with a resultant budget cut of approximately fifty percent and a fixed source of revenue. As a result of this change, personnel in one division must be reduced from 12 FTE's (full-time equivalent positions) to 7 FTE's. The questions become:

1) Who to retain and/or terminate, and
2) What parameters to develop to implement this action?

The positions involved in this personnel action can be divided into two main activities, each requiring specialized knowledge and expertise. One aspect of the job requires medical judgment and background, while the remaining job element requires a specialized technical ability. In the original hiring situations, managers preferred employees with medical knowledge and felt that on-the-job training (OJT) could compensate for a lack of technical ability. At that time, both job elements were performed by a single employee. As the years progressed, it became apparent that OJT was not sufficient and that hiring practices should recognize this deficiency. Therefore, the positions were filled accordingly, with 9 of the 12 positions having credentialed medical abilities divided into 2 levels of competency, and 3 of the 12 having credentialed technical abilities. With the new grant system, medical personnel will comprise 4.5 FTE's and technical personnel will comprise 2.5 FTE's.

### Personnel

Ms. A (Black) has been working in the company for three years, has a high-level medical certification and performs her job well. Ms. B (White) has been working in the company for two years, has a high-level medical certification and her performance is above average. Ms. C (Other) has been working at the company for six months, has a language problem, poor work habits and a high-level medical certification. Ms. D (White) has been employed for 11 months, is technically certified, and performs well, but has some problems in following supervisory directions. She is somewhat outspoken and headstrong. Ms. E (White) has been employed for seven months, has a high-level medical certification, and is an outstanding employee, but has indicated she is only interested in part-time work in the future. Ms. F (Black) has been working in the company for four years, has a low-level medical certification, has noticeable deficiencies

279

in certain medical areas, but is well liked and has developed a very good rapport in her work environment, which is extremely critical in this position. She performs above average in many areas, but cannot perform adequately in all areas, because of her limited knowledge. Ms. G (Black) has been with the company longer than any other employee. She has a low-level medical certification, and it has been noted by a number of people that her medical deficiencies limit the scope of her performance. She also recognizes her limitations, and is attending school to eliminate this problem. Ms. H (White), I (Black), and J (Black) all have high-level medical certificates, have been with the company approximately the same length of time (two years), and perform very well in the work environment. Ms. K (White) has been with the company for two months, has certified technical ability, is a quick learner, and has proven that she is flexible and an enthusiastic worker. Ms. L (White) has also been with the company two months, has certified technical ability and is a good worker, but somewhat less enthusiastic and vivacious than Ms. K. The technical skills of Ms. K and Ms. L are equal.

## Questions

Management has suggested that high-level medical certification become a requirement for those employees hired to use medical judgment. As the decision maker in this case:

(1) Who would you retain, and why?
(2) Who would you terminate, and why?

Make sure that the solution addresses the following issues:

(1) Job performance,
(2) Race and/or ethnic group, and
(3) Longevity.

# Distribution Of Union Literature On
# Company Property

John Smith had been warned by his supervisor that if he were late one more time, he would be fired. The day after his last warning, John came to work at 7:45, 45 minutes late. At 7:46, he was fired. He was told that his final pay would be ready around noontime. As a rule, discharged employees were allowed to remain on the premises until receiving their final paycheck.

After staying in the lunchroom for a half hour, Smith left the plant. Shortly afterward, he returned to the lunchroom with an NLRB pamphlet and some union literature. During the morning coffee break, as the former employee was discussing the NLRB pamphlet with other employees, he was interrupted by a supervisor. The supervisor said that it was illegal to have the literature on company property. The supervisor threatened to have Smith arrested if he did not leave the plant and take the material with him.

## Questions

1. Was the employee within his rights to distribute the NLRB pamphlet, or handing out union literature on company property?
2. What difference does the fact that Smith is no longer an employee make, in the answers to Question 1?

# Equal Work Or Sex Discrimination?

On Fort Confused (an Army installation in the Midwest) there was a requirement to have a single guard on duty at the Post motor pool after normal duty hours. Because the guard was to be alone, the Post Commander decided that only males would be assigned to this guard duty. She also stipulated that the females who would normally be assigned to pull guard duty, would be assigned other additional duties, such as clean-up details, in a proportion that would equal out the time both males and females would have to spend on extra duty.

Other than the fact that they would be alone, there were no requirements on this guard duty that could not be handled equally well by either a male or a female. There was no policy stating that females could not pull guard duty alone, and, in fact, other installations did utilize females as guards.

Although there were both males and females satisfied with this particular policy, there was also a contingent of males and females who felt it was discriminatory. In other words, there were personnel of both sexes who felt that the other was being favored. The Post Commander was informed by members of her command that one or both groups were about to file a discrimination case with the Post Equal Opportunity Office.

## Questions

1. Although the Post Commander might feel her policy was both morally right and equally fair to both sexes, was there still a legitimate case for discrimination by either side?
2. What rights, if any, did those personnel, who wanted to see the policy remain as written, have in this case?

# Employee Discharges Preceding Union Representation Votes

A midwestern department chain-store called Plus Value was opening another unit in its chain. A reason for the location selected for the new store was that management knew the unions were not strong in that particular area. Some of Plus Value's stores were union and some were not, and the management badly wanted the new store to be nonunion.

Management undertook a massive recruitment campaign through advertising in the area newspapers. After testing and interviewing of all the applicants, people were hired as sales clerks, cashiers, and loading-dock clerks. As the company knew, the threat of the retail clerks' union organizing the workers was ever-present. Upon opening, Plus Value hired about 40 people to handle the big crowds at the store's grand opening. About 30 of the 40 employees were originally hired as permanent help; the other ten were temporary.

Approximately two weeks after the store had opened and the ten temporary employees were released, the union came to the store and started to encourage the employees to organize. Eventually, the union claimed it had at least a 30% quota to call for a union election. The management, having only 30 employees, had a good idea who most of the pro-union employees were, and they also knew there were probably 12–15 employees who were against the union. Overall, the management knew it would be a close vote, in any case.

About a week before the election, a disciplinary incident occurred between the assistant manager of the store and one of the men on the loading dock. They had an agitated verbal exchange, which climaxed in a shoving match. The cause of the fight was not clearly known, but the dock clerk was known to be very verbal about his pro-union views. The dock employee was dismissed. In protest, two of his friends, who also were dock employees and were on the scene of the fight, quit their jobs also. They said their friend's dismissal was not just, and he did not deserve to be fired. The management took all this at face value, and did not discourage the other two from quitting, because they knew they were also pro-union.

The management was faced with three loading dock vacancies and three less-pro-union employees. Immediately, the management realized the advantage they had gained in the union vote. Therefore, without hesitation, Plus Value hired three replacements from the pool of the ten temporary employees who were previously released. These three happened to be anti-union.

Finally, when the vote for the union did come, the union only came up with 42% of the vote. The union was very upset about the outcome and claimed that

Plus Value had staged the incident with the dock employee, and did not act in good faith while dealing with the union issue.

## Questions

1. Did the union have a legal issue in questioning the firing of the pro-union employee?
2. Did Plus Value legally manipulate the vote of the union election?
3. Could the union have brought charges against Plus Value for using unfair selection practices in hiring the three new anti-union employees? If so, could the seven other temporary employees *not* hired, sue Plus Value for discriminatory practices?

# Administration Of Discharge Authority

Mr. West has been employed in the shipping department of the Zargo Company for 17 years. Through his years of employment with Zargo, Mr. West has become familiar with all the company rules, including the rule stating that employees are terminated when found guilty of crimes.

Mr. West committed a crime of moral turpitude, which resulting in a jail sentence of two to three years in prison. His sentence was subsequently modified and he was placed on probation for three years while being ordered to obtain psychotherapy.

While under indictment, Mr. West was continued as an employee by Zargo, but was discharged when he pleaded guilty to the morals charge, in exchange for the modified sentence.

Zargo's company policy with respect to employees under indictment for crime was that the employee was innocent until proven guilty, but when found guilty, the employee would be immediately discharged. This rule of employee conduct had been in effect by Zargo for years, and had been administered uniformly.

Zargo's position was that modification of the sentence handed down by the court did not change Mr. West's guilt. Zargo felt that Mr. West's crime of moral turpitude was a crime against society, and his guilt and conduct did not deserve consideration for employment with the organization.

As an aside, Mr. West's son petitioned Zargo to grant his father a leave of absence, rather than discharge him from the company in consideration of the sentence modification. Zargo stated that its policy did not allow for leaves of absence.

## Questions

1. Did Zargo unjustly discharge Mr. West?
2. Was Mr. West suffering "double jeopardy" (punished both by the courts and Zargo for the same offense)?
3. What were some possible implications of Mr. West's discharge being overturned?
4. What were some possible alternative solutions to this problem?

# Implicit Company Policies And Discharge

Alice, Betty, and Carol are three of fifteen employees of a private-school cafeteria in a large eastern city. All the employees are Black. Alice is American-born and has worked at the cafeteria for five years. Betty and Carol were born in the West Indies and have been at the cafeteria for one year.

Betty and Carol were observed taking leftover food home one afternoon. Taking leftover food home was not an unusual occurrence in this kitchen, but the pressure to hold down costs had caused management to decide to try to stop it. As a result, Betty and Carol were fired for stealing.

Betty sued for reinstatement, claiming discrimination against her because she was foreign-born. She did not deny taking the leftover food, but claimed that Alice had been observed doing the same thing, and had not been fired. Management countered that while Alice may have been observed taking food home before the decision to crack down, no discrimination was intended. Betty and Carol were simply the first ones caught after the decision had been made.

## Questions

1. How would you expect the local Fair Employment Practices Commission to rule?
2. Should Carol, who did not sue, be entitled to whatever relief, if any, Betty receives?
3. What can management do to avoid being sued again without assenting to stealing?

# Plant Closings Due To Union Demands

The ABC Electrical Company had been in business for more than 25 years. It was owned by two brothers and was located in the State of Maryland. The company was not unionized, and until last year union organizing activities had never occurred. The owners were against unions and tried to be very fair with their employees to keep unions out. Last year, when some union organizing activity occurred, the owners brought all of their workers together and made it known that it would be up to each individual to decide if a union were desirable. During this assembly, management also announced increases in their vacation and retirement programs for the employees. Within a week after this assembly, union-organizing activities had diminished. However, the following year union activities occurred again. Management, once again, assembled their employees and informed them of their preference for a nonunion environment. During this meeting, no increases of any type were offered to the employees. Two months later a union was voted into the company. As a result of the union being voted in, all employees were given two weeks' notice that the company was being shut down. Three months after the shutdown, the brothers opened up a new electrical company in the State of Maryland, about 30 miles from their old business location.

## Questions

1. Did the company have the legal right to close and reopen the business in this manner?
2. Could the employees take court action, under the premise that the company was trying to restrain employees from joining a union?
3. Did the employees have any legal rights regarding a position in the new company?
4. Was what the brothers did during the first union-organizing drive legal?

# Union Influence On Construction Company Hiring Practices

Brown Bros. Construction Company operates in the suburban areas just south of a large, northern industrial city. The city proper has a 55% nonwhite population; however, the bulk of Brown Bros. construction work involves large housing subdivisions in predominantly-white communities.

The company has been in existence since 1948. In 1953, the electricians employed by Brown Bros. elected to be represented by Local #444 of the Brotherhood of Electrical Workers, which has its headquarters in the largest of the suburban communities that surround the city. Local #444 has remained the bargaining unit for electricians employed by Brown Bros. up to the present. Brown Bros. is an all-union construction company; therefore, all of its electricians must belong to Local #444.

Aside from Local #444, there is another union local, Local #432 of the Brotherhood of Electrical Workers that represents electrical workers who live within the city limits. Because of different structures of the two electrician labor markets represented by the two locals, there is a corresponding difference between the labor pools of Local #444 and Local #432, as indicated below.

**Analysis of Electricians within**
**A 50-Mile Radius of Brown Bros. Headquarters**

|  | White | | Nonwhite | | Total |
| --- | --- | --- | --- | --- | --- |
|  | No. | (%) | No. | (%) | No. |
| Local #432 | 267 | (58) | 193 | (42) | 460 |
| Local #444 | 420 | (92) | 35 | (08) | 455 |
| Nonunion Electricians | 165 | (72) | 65 | (28) | 230 |
| Entire Labor Market | 852 | (74) | 293 | (26) | 1145 |

The electricians employed by Brown Bros. are distributed as follows:

| White | | Nonwhite | | Total |
| --- | --- | --- | --- | --- |
| No. | (%) | No. | (%) | No. |
| 15 | (88) | 2 | (12) | 17 |

The economic conditions are such that industries in the area employing electricians have fewer jobs open than there are unemployed electricians in the labor market.

293

The Local #444—Brown Bros. contract calls for employment priority to be given to personnel furnished by the local's hiring hall. Among the members of Local #444, the unemployment rate has averaged 10% over the past 12-month period.

Brown Bros. recently won a federal contract to renovate a local defense ammunitions plant. The company president is apprehensive about Brown Bros. compliance with Title VII of the 1964 Civil Rights Act as interpreted by the Office of Federal Contract Compliance.

### Questions

1. To attain a more favorable racial balance, can Brown Bros. hire only nonwhite members of Local #444 as jobs in the company become available?
2. Can the union legally refer only nonwhite applicants to Brown Bros.?
3. Is Brown Bros. in violation of Federal Fair Employment Practices?
4. What influences can be brought to bear on the Brotherhood of Electrical Workers to establish a more equitable distribution of nonwhite workers in the two locals?

# Fired-Before-Quitting: The Implications For Unemployment Compensation

Chuck Nolson has been working with a merchandise-liquidating company for 16 months. His job responsibilities included unloading tractor trailors full of merchandise, operating a fork lift, organizing the merchandise in the warehouse, loading the company's trucks with various merchandise, driving the trucks to the different outlet stores, and assisting with the unloading and return to the warehouse. In other words, Chuck did everything from sweeping up the warehouse to cleaning up after the warehouse cat. Because merchandise was bought on a sporadic basis, his working hours were also sporadic: 12 hours one day, six hours the next, etc. His wages were a nickel above minimum wage.

Chuck disliked his job, but more than that, strongly disliked his boss, the warehouse supervisor. He felt the supervisor took advantage of his easy-going nature and constantly assigned him the unpleasant tasks. He had already enrolled for the upcoming fall semester at a local college and planned on quitting his job two weeks prior to this, to take a vacation. Because of his animosity toward his supervisor, he was not going to inform him of his departure until the end of his final working day. Unfortunately, a few days prior to this, it slipped out in conversation with some fellow workers and made its way back to the supervisor.

The supervisor became irate, realizing in two days he would be understaffed. When he asked Chuck why he did not notify him, Chuck shrugged it off and replied "I forgot." The supervisor, not one to take things lightly, fired Chuck on the spot. Chuck felt since he was fired for no just cause, he was entitled to collect unemployment compensation.

## Questions

1. According to the law, is Chuck entitled to unemployment compensation?
2. If he is entitled to unemployment compensation, will it continue throughout a given benefit period, even though Chuck will be in college and not seeking employment?
3. Was Chuck's behavior sufficient grounds for firing?

# Selection Of Union Members For Supervisory Positions — A Conflict Of Interest

Wagner Auto Parts is in the business of producing and selling quality automobile parts for American-made cars. It started as a family business over 50 years ago and is still run by the son of the original owner. Its central management and research headquarters is located in St. Louis, and its two manufacturing plants are located in Detroit and Newark. All of the laborers within the plants are unionized. One of the unwritten rules between management and the union concerns seniority. It is well understood that promotions within the plants are based on seniority.

When it came time for a new foreman to be hired, the production worker who had the best combination of merit and seniority was typically hired to fill the vacancy. This method proved to be less and less effective. The foreman invariably remained a member of the union, most often becoming one of the officers as a result of his new status and position within the management of the company. It usually seemed that the major priority of new foremen was to work for the goals of the union and the workers, rather than those of the company as a whole.

Two weeks ago, a foreman position in the Newark plant became available. The union members within the plant immediately began to speculate which among them would be selected, and had their candidate pretty well chosen, when management announced their plans to hire someone from outside the plant. By the time the new foreman showed up for work the next day, members of the union had already held a meeting and decided to strike. They demanded that a clause be written into their contract, guaranteeing that all foremen would be chosen from within their membership. Management attempts to compromise with the union failed, and three days later the workers in the Detroit plant went on a sympathy strike.

## Questions

1. Did the union members have a right to demand that the foremen be chosen from within their membership?
2. Did management have the right to choose the man they felt would best fill the job, regardless of whether or not he was a union member?
3. What were some of the possible implications of the strike?
4. Discuss possible alternative solutions to this problem.

# Resistance To Safety Management

Mr. White has been recently appointed safety director of Atlas Steel, Inc. A union represents approximately 1,000 production and maintenance employees at the plant in Detroit, Michigan. As the safety director, Mr. White is very concerned over the high accident rate the company has been experiencing for the past several years. To help solve the problem, a better program of machine guarding and plant maintenance was initiated. This program did reduce the severity of the accidents; however, work injuries continued to occur just as frequently.

Mr. White decided to analyze all of the work injuries that had occurred over the past year. He found that in a majority of instances, the injuries were due to (1) failure to follow safety rules, (2) incorrect use of machines and hand tools, and (3) sloppy cleaning of work areas. Furthermore, Mr. White looked into some research studies that proved employee attitudes, emotions, and knowledge greatly influence accident rates on the job.

Due to the above information, Mr. White concluded that a plant-wide employee education program needed to be initiated. However, the problem of accidents was accentuated by the high rate of employee turnover, due to Atlas' wage level being somewhat lower than the rates paid by other companies in the area. Many quit and took better jobs, especially since Atlas had periodic layoffs.

Mr. White has now obtained the support of top management to try and solve or improve the accident problem. To educate employees in safety, Mr. White decided to have each foreman hold a safety meeting with his workers at least once a month, but found that the foremen vehemently objected to the added burden, claiming the extra time needed for the meeting would slow down production (which will make them look bad).

## Questions

1. How should Mr. White have handled the foremen who refused to conduct the safety meetings?
2. How should Mr. White have accomplished the objective of teaching the employees safety education, if (a) the foremen agreed to conduct the meetings, and (b) if the foremen did not agree to conduct the meetings—i.e., what methods and channels should be employed in each instance?

# Problems Associated With A Change
## In The Basic Work Week

In the autumn of 1973, President Nixon issued his "energy conservation" mandate (e.g., 55 mph, etc.). In keeping with the edict to be a good American citizen and staunch Republican, Jack Armstrong, President of Pinetree Plastics, Inc., initiated a new work schedule. Instead of a 5-day, 40-hour work week, he was going to have a 3-day, 13 1/2-hour work day. Industrial engineers and management consultants assured him that it would be 50% more economical and 25% more efficient.

Pinetree employs 2,500 nonmanagement people from a town of 8,900, and many were upset with the new schedule. If they quit, they could not find jobs anywhere else — the town's other major employer, the Chrysler parts plant, was already furloughing people. Armstrong felt he was being very fair and equitable: anyone and everyone who could not meet the guidelines would be dismissed.

The employees, who were not unionized, selected a group to approach Armstrong with their grievance. He agreed to establish a day-care center for parents whose children had no place or person to stay with before and after school. Their other requests were rejected. They were:

1. Time-and-a-half for over 8 hours worked in a day. (Armstrong said he could not afford to pay any more, since he would probably have to let people go anyway—also, the employees were free to get second or "nighttime" jobs now.)

2. The establishment of a seniority system, in case workers had to be let go. (Armstrong said it would impair the firm's efficiency—selected cuts in less-crucial departments would be more economical to the firm.)

3. The employees' request to help determine which three days and which 13 1/2 hours would be worked. (Armstrong felt it was his prerogative.)

4. Cost-of-living wage increases. (Armstrong: "too inflationary in these uncertain times!")

The employees were even more upset after this meeting with Armstrong. They brooded over their alternatives:

1. They could ask for a vote to unionize and let the union air their grievances.

2. They could stage a full or partial "wildcat" strike. (But Armstrong had hinted that if this happened, he would lock them all out and then slowly and selectively hire them back later.)

3.  They could seek a court injunction to enjoin Armstrong from starting and using these "unfair labor practices."

## Questions

1.  What course of action should the employees take? Why?
2.  Would unionization really help the employees in an economic climate such as this?
3.  Are there any other viable alternatives?

# Abuses Of Compensatory Time

The Sperry Univac Corporation sells, rents, and services electronic data-processing equipment and employs a large staff of servicepeople to keep its customers' equipment in order. The 30 servicepeople who work out of the St. Paul district office (which covers most of the Midwest) all live in the St. Paul area and are often required to travel to customers in distant locations; usually they travel by air. A given trouble call may take several hours, or even days of work.

A problem has arisen from the fact that, when an assignment is completed, the technicians fly back to St. Paul and often arrive home late in the evening or even after midnight. Under these circumstances, management has always allowed the employees to take a few hours extra sleep and not report to the office the first thing the next morning. Recently there have been signs that the employees have begun to abuse this privilege. A few have developed the habit of taking the entire morning off after every out-of-town trip, even if they arrive back at their home by 5:00 the previous evening.

Management has considered imposing a hard-and-fast rule that all servicepeople must report for work at 9:00 a.m., regardless of what time they arrived the night before. But in some cases, this would impose an obvious hardship, and it might encourage the employees to spread their work out, so that instead of finishing their job in the afternoon and returning home late, they would slow down and work through the next morning, returning home in the afternoon.

Above all, management is anxious not to disturb the employees' high morale and interest in their work. These people are paid a salary, receive liberal fringe benefits, and are treated almost like members of the management.

## Question

1. What action should management take to handle this problem?

# Forming A Union

Mary is a nurse at County Hospital. Although she loves her work and is considered one of the best nurses at County, Mary is dissatisfied with working conditions, pay and benefits. Talking with other nurses, she comes to the conclusion that a union would be the answer to nurses' grievances with County Hospital.

One of the most important issues facing the nurses concerns the staffing situation. More nurses are needed to handle the workload, but the hospital administration says the budget will not allow the hiring of more nurses. Another item of contention is the differential pay scale for nurses on the day, evening and night shifts. Evenings and nights get ten percent more than day, but the nurses want a further differential between the evening and night shift, since the night shift is the hardest of the three. Along the lines of pay, the nurses would also like an across-the-board pay raise. One other major subject is the lack of any benefits for the part-time nurses. They get no life insurance, medical, dental, nor credit-union benefits, even though these part-timers often work as much as the full-timers due to the staffing problems.

To get a nurses' union started, Mary and a few friends had flyers printed up calling for an organizational meeting. However, these flyers were intercepted by the hospital administration, and Mary was verbally reprimanded by her head nurse. Mary found that on her next monthly schedule, she was shifted from days to evenings, two weeks prior to normal shift rotation, and she did not get her requested days off. Suspecting harassment for her union attempt, Mary confronted her head nurse and was told that if she desisted with union organizing, she would find her schedule a bit more to her liking. She was also told that if she continued trying to organize the nurses, she might find herself out of work.

## Questions

1. Can the hospital administration harrass and threaten to fire her for trying to organize a nursing union?
2. Is the hospital acting legally in not providing benefits for the part-time nurses?

# About The Author

Dr. Kenneth A. Kovach is a Full Professor in the School of Business at George Mason University, where he has been voted Outstanding Faculty Member and received the Distinguished Faculty Award. He specializes in Human Resource Management/Labor Relations research and has published five books, over fifty articles, and over two hundred cases on these topics. Additionally, he is a consultant to numerous local and national firms, including the U.S. Department of Defense, American Red Cross, and the American Council on Education.